HOW THINGS WORK

DISCOVER SECRETS AND SCIENCE BEHIND TRICK CANDLES, 3-D PRINTERS, PENGUIN PROPULSION, AND EVERYTHING IN BETWEEN

T. J. RESLER

NATIONAL GEOGRAPHIC
WASHINGTON, D.C.

LOOK, YOU NEED TO KNOW THREE THINGS ABOUT THIS BOOK.

ONE:

It's for kids who aren't afraid to think. You know the type: the ones who always have questions. The kids who stop to watch how a crane hoists a beam to the top of a new building, the ones who want to tear open a cool gadget and figure out what its parts do, the ones who can watch a fish swish, swish, swish through the water for hours. They're the kids who want to know *how* something works and *why*. They want answers today, not tomorrow, not "when you get older." If you're one of those thinkers, read on. If not, maybe you'd like to go watch some paint dry. (Which might just spark the question: *How* does paint actually dry?)

TWO:

This book tells secrets. Think you can handle that? It reveals why trick candles light back up, how bridges can span crazy distances with nothing under them, and how some cars can zoom around without drivers. It uncovers how scientists borrow secrets from nature to make their inventions better. It exposes the truth behind some of the coolest things we have. Many were accidental discoveries. Yeah, this book tells you that kind of stuff—the inside scoop.

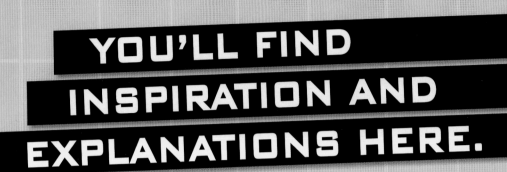

YOU'LL FIND INSPIRATION AND EXPLANATIONS HERE.

THREE:

This book is infectious. You'll read about inventors, scientists, engineers, and architects who dreamed big and didn't stop—not when they were told to quit daydreaming, not when they were told something was impossible, not even when they failed. Their stories are contagious. They'll feed your inner dreamer. You might find yourself imagining ways to strap on personal jet packs to zoom over traffic, or swim underwater with penguins, or invent sculptures that suck the pollution out of the air. Crazy? That's what those other inventors were told.

If you want to dream on, if you want to feed your brain, take a look inside. You'll find inspiration and explanations here. You'll meet real-life inventors, designers, and scientists who work to make things better, whether it's robots, the environment, or squirt guns. You'll read "Tales From the Lab," the stories behind how things were invented, like microscopes that fold into your pocket or shelters that you make out of shipping pallets.

And you'll definitely get answers. You'll learn all about *how* things work and *why*. You'll see the inner workings of cool gizmos and gadgets, like 3-D printers, cameras, and microscopes—without having to crack open your own. You'll learn how scientists are using nature's secrets to stop infections, create more energy, and make super-strong adhesives. You'll satisfy your curiosity about weird and wacky inventions, and you'll find out why skyscrapers are getting taller and tunnels getting longer. You'll relax with the knowledge that a lot of inventions, like the machine that swipes a credit card or the voice inside a smartphone, work to make life easier.

If you need a quick answer about how something works, you'll find it on the "Just the Facts" page. If you want to dive in deeper, check out the "Tell Me More!" section.

Get inspired, and find out what you can do. We'll get you started with "Try This!" challenges that let you become a scientist, engineer, or architect. Then dream on. Create, invent, and explore. You're a thinker, after all.

WHAT'S INSIDE

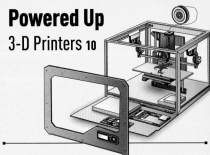
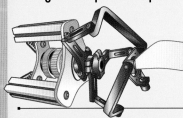

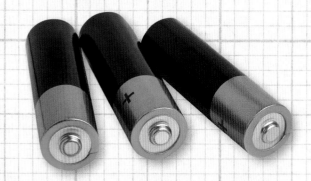

CHAPTER 1

GIZMOS & GADGETS

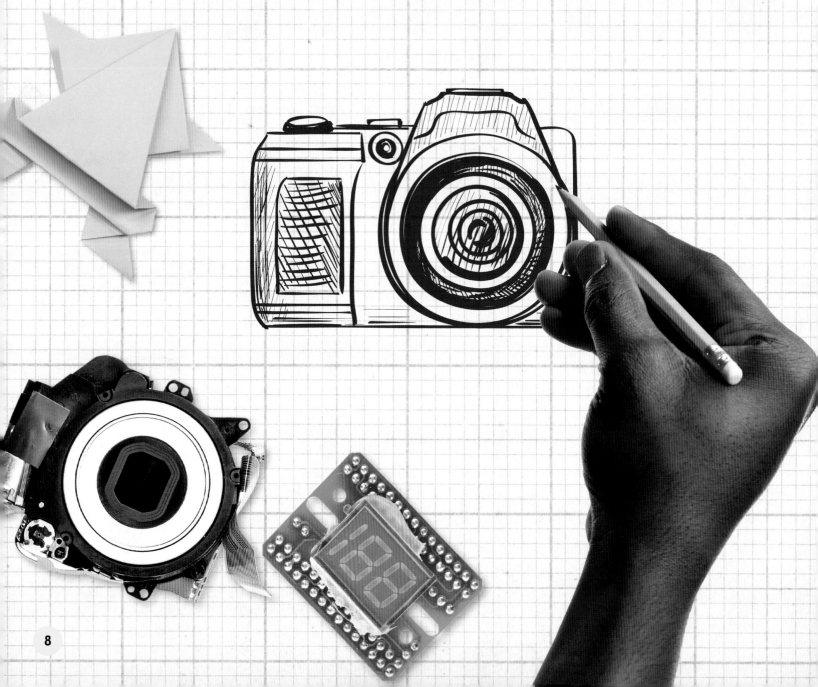

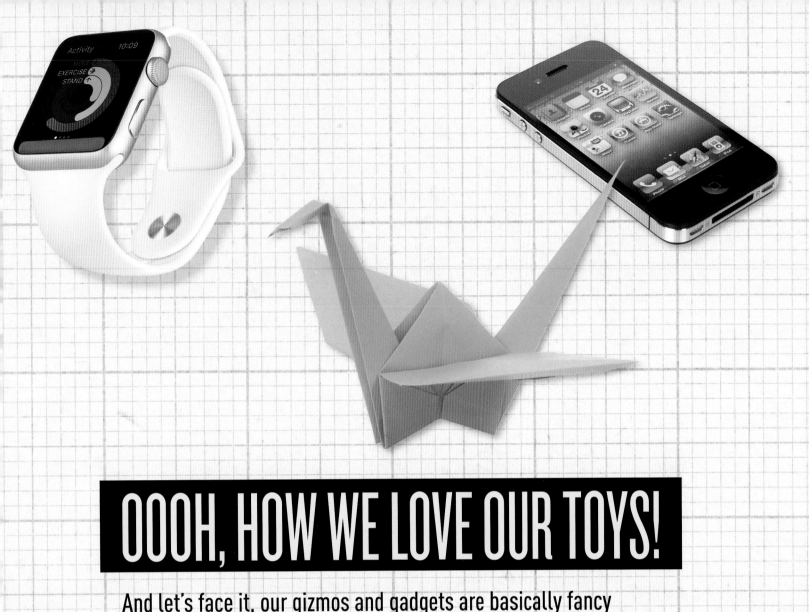

OOOH, HOW WE LOVE OUR TOYS!

And let's face it, our gizmos and gadgets are basically fancy toys—whether they are ingenious mechanical tools or novel electronic devices. Sure, we can point out a bajillion ways they save us time, make it easier to do things, or help us be better people. Of course, they do. We couldn't live without them. But when it comes down to it, we love our gizmos and gadgets because they're just plain awesome.

POWERED UP

How do 3-D PRINTERS work?

The Inside Scoop

Bored with your toys? Whip up a new batch without even leaving home. It's possible, if you own a 3-D printer. These amazing gadgets can create models of dinosaur bones, artificial limbs, even cars and houses. Yeah, real ones. So, toys? Easy-peasy. Find out what goes into printing three-dimensional objects.

How do the printers "know" what to build ?

What is the print made of ?

Where do you get the designs ?

JUST THE FACTS

Layer Up

A 3-D printer looks like an overgrown sibling to the inkjet printer you may have in your house. And it works in a remarkably similar way: It has a nozzle that moves back and forth, putting layer on top of layer of material to create its "print." Each layer is fused, or joined, to the layer below it. 3-D printers often build with a type of plastic, but they can also use other materials, including rubber, paper, ceramics, glass, metal, and even food! Depending on how complex the design is, printing can take several minutes, hours, or even days.

Addition, Not Subtraction

Creating a 3-D object by building it up one layer at a time is an "additive" process—and it's not the way most things are made. Instead, a lot of things are assembled, put together by joining individual parts. Many other objects are made by cutting materials into a desired shape. That way of making things is called "subtractive" manufacturing.

MIT scientist Skylar Tibbits, a National Geographic Emerging Explorer, is taking 3-D printing to the next dimension: **"4-D PRINTING."** He prints materials that are programmed to build themselves or transform from one shape to another on their own.

BEFORE

AFTER

A NEW BEAK was 3-D printed for an injured bald eagle.

FUN FACT — LOCAL MOTORS, AN ARIZONA-BASED CARMAKER, IS WORKING TO **3-D PRINT** CUSTOM **ELECTRIC CARS.** IT PRINTED ITS FIRST VEHICLE, THE STRATI, IN 44 HOURS AT A TECHNOLOGY SHOW IN 2015.

BUILDING  UP

A 3-D printer builds a toy by adding layer upon layer of material.

A Minnesota man, Andrey Rudenko, built a large 3-D printer and used it in 2014 to print a 12-foot (3.6-m)-tall **CASTLE** out of cement. It was a test run for 3-D printing houses.

The building material—often a type of plastic—comes out of an extruder nozzle, which moves to form the toy's shape.

The toy is built up, layer by layer.

FUN FACT

ARTIST JONTY HURWITZ 3-D PRINTED SOME OF THE SMALLEST SCULPTURES **EVER MADE.** THE NANOSCULPTURES WERE SO SMALL THEY COULD FIT ON AN ANT'S HEAD—SO SMALL THAT **HE LOST THEM.**

WANT TO KNOW MORE?

DETAILS, DETAILS

Have you ever seen a blueprint of a building? It's an architectural drawing with all the details of a building's design, so that builders know exactly how to put it together. When you're using a 3-D printer, you first use a computer program to make a virtual blueprint of the object you want to print. This blueprint exists only inside your computer. It's a digital model created with a special computer-aided design or modeling program. After you have the design you want, the program figures out how each layer needs to be made, so it's the exact size and shape you want. When you press "print," the computer program sends the layer-by-layer instructions to the 3-D printer. Then the fun begins.

OH, THE POSSIBILITIES!

Where does the design come from? Your imagination! The design can be anything you dream up—as long as you know how to use the computer programs to model it. If you don't know where to start, you can use a 3-D scanner to make a 3-D digital copy of something. You can either print an exact copy or work your own magic on the design. If you're not really into computer programming—or feeling a bit lazy—no worries. You also can buy and download ready-made 3-D designs. Three-dimensional printing has options for everyone.

Myth vs. FACT

MYTH: You can 3-D print a human body part.

FACT: Shhh, don't tell Dr. Frankenstein ... but, yes, doctors and researchers are figuring out how to print human flesh and bones. The benefits of using 3-D printing to help people are enormous. Like our fingerprints, we're all unique. Being able to 3-D print an exact match for an injured person is a doctor's dream come true. Doctors already have 3-D printed made-to-order bones to reconstruct severely damaged fingers, hips, and skulls. The new bones are made with a special material that encourages surrounding tissues to grow and attach to them. Other researchers have figured out how to use printing materials that include living cells, which a 3-D printer can build layer by layer into living tissue. The 3-D-printed tissue can be used to test the safety of medicines. Now research doctors are 3-D printing living tissues and organs large and strong enough for humans.

Some researchers used a 3-D printer to combine living and electronic parts to make a functioning ear. It has a soft ear-shaped frame, living cells that will grow cartilage (the firm, flexible tissue in our nose, ears, and joints), and silver nanoparticles too small to see but that work like an antenna. When implanted in a living being, 3-D-printed materials grow blood vessels and cartilage. It's already worked in animals. Researchers hope it won't be long before 3-D-printed organs and tissues help humans. Thankfully, though, we're still a long way from 3-D printing Frankenstein's monster. Or are we?

FUN FACTS

As if 3-D printing weren't cool enough ... An engineer designed a 3-D printer to **print pizza** and other foods for astronauts on a long trip.

MASTER BUILDER

Each type of 3-D printer works a little differently, depending on its size and what it can make. Take a look at how a popular, home-size 3-D printer stacks layer after layer of plastic to make an awesome toy.

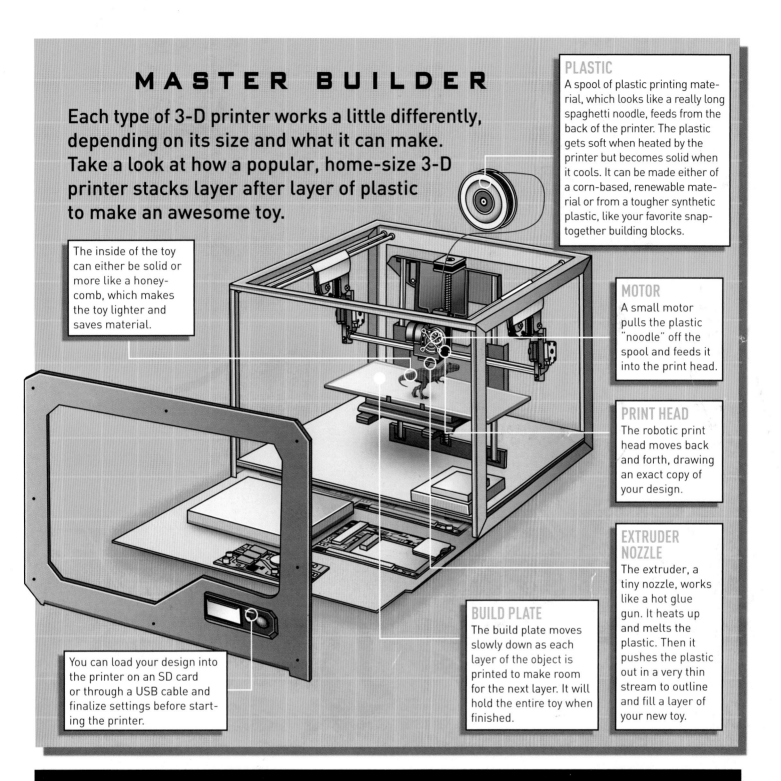

PLASTIC
A spool of plastic printing material, which looks like a really long spaghetti noodle, feeds from the back of the printer. The plastic gets soft when heated by the printer but becomes solid when it cools. It can be made either of a corn-based, renewable material or from a tougher synthetic plastic, like your favorite snap-together building blocks.

The inside of the toy can either be solid or more like a honeycomb, which makes the toy lighter and saves material.

MOTOR
A small motor pulls the plastic "noodle" off the spool and feeds it into the print head.

PRINT HEAD
The robotic print head moves back and forth, drawing an exact copy of your design.

EXTRUDER NOZZLE
The extruder, a tiny nozzle, works like a hot glue gun. It heats up and melts the plastic. Then it pushes the plastic out in a very thin stream to outline and fill a layer of your new toy.

BUILD PLATE
The build plate moves slowly down as each layer of the object is printed to make room for the next layer. It will hold the entire toy when finished.

You can load your design into the printer on an SD card or through a USB cable and finalize settings before starting the printer.

TRY THIS!

Here's a quick—and delicious—way to learn more about additive and subtractive ways of making things. Get a tube or two of cake decorating frosting. Don't eat it! You're going to use it to make a very small, shallow bowl. On a plate or large piece of wax paper, squirt out a blob of frosting. Go on, squeeze hard! Dig out a hole in the middle and scrape away the outsides until the blob is bowl-shaped. That's a traditional, subtractive way of making things. Now you're going to act like a 3-D printer and use an additive approach to making your bowl. On a clean area of the plate or wax paper, use your tube of frosting to slowly draw a small circle. Fill in the circle with more frosting. When you're finished, draw another circle—just the outline of the circle—right on top of it. Keep adding layers on top of the outside circle until it stands up a bit. Just go round and round with the tube of frosting. You just "3-D printed" a bowl! OK, it's not sturdy enough to use as a real bowl. But we bet you can figure out something else to do with it.* Yum.

* But don't eat it. If you want some frosting, get a clean glob from the tube!

SCOPE IT OUT

How do TELESCOPES and MICROSCOPES help us see?

The Inside Scoop

Our eyes are amazing. They let us see a rainbow of colors and objects big and small. We use them to read books close to us and to gaze out at sunsets on the horizon. But sometimes we want to see even farther—or to get a better view of something really, really small. When our eyes can't do it alone, some amazing gadgets can help us out. Come see how telescopes and microscopes expand our vision.

Why are telescopes so long?

How do you load something on a microscope?

How strong are these instruments?

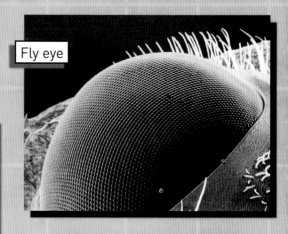

Fly eye

Worlds Beyond

Telescopes help you see far away. They can bring the stars, planets, and distant galaxies into view. Microscopes do the opposite. They help you look at things way too small for eyes to see: the tiny cells inside a plant's leaf, the eyes of a fly, the germs crawling around on your skin. (Gross!) Those things may be worlds apart, but the way most telescopes and microscopes work is very similar. They both gather rays of light to focus an image and magnify it, making it large enough for you to see. Most microscopes do this with lenses, which are curved pieces of glass. Telescopes use either lenses or mirrors.

Lens Power

When they both use lenses, telescopes and microscopes work in similar—but opposite—ways. Telescopes look at faraway objects, so they need to gather as much light as possible. That takes a big lens. Big lenses need room to focus the image, so telescopes have long tubes to hold them. Microscopes only need to gather light from a thin, nearby specimen. They use smaller lenses that can focus an image in a short distance, so they don't need long tubes. The specimen is not only close, it's also well lit. Most microscopes have their own light sources and systems for focusing light on a small spot. Both gadgets have lenses in their eyepieces that magnify the images.

SAMPLE SANDWICH
To view something with a microscope, you need a specimen, a sample of what you want to study, on a slide. A slide is actually a few pieces sandwiched together: the rectangular glass slide, the specimen in the middle, and a thin cover slip.

SPACE PROBES

From their humble beginnings **four centuries ago,** telescopes have evolved into amazing instruments. Here are some highlights of telescope history.

1609
Italian scientist Galileo Galilei builds a working telescope with a 1.5-inch (3.8-cm) lens fitted inside a wooden tube and launches the modern field of astronomy. He soon discovers craters on Earth's moon, sunspots, and Jupiter's largest moons.

1789
Sir William Herschel, a British orchestra director and astronomer who discovered Uranus, builds the first giant reflector telescope, a massive 40 feet (12 m) long.

1608
Hans Lippershey, a German-Dutch lens maker, works on an instrument to see faraway things as if they were nearby.

1670
Polish astronomer Johannes Hevelius develops a 150-foot (45-m)-long refracting telescope. It hangs on ropes from a pole and swings in the slightest breeze.

1672
Laurent Cassegrain, a French priest, develops a telescope that uses mirrors.

1729
British lawyer and inventor Chester Moore Hall uses two types of glass together, creating a lens that improves a telescope's performance. It's a huge leap for refracting telescopes.

1845
The "Leviathan of Parsonstown," built in Ireland by William Parsons, the third earl of Rosse, has a six-foot (1.8-m)-wide mirror and is the largest telescope for years. Rosse is the first person to see the spiral arms of a galaxy.

EXPLORER  AIDS

Telescopes and microscopes help you explore worlds that you can't see with your unaided eyes.

The telescope is a long tube with a large lens at the end.

REFRACTING TELESCOPE

Telescopes are designed to gather light so we can see objects far away. This telescope uses lenses, but others use mirrors.

MICROSCOPE

Most microscopes light up specimens mounted on slides and use lenses to magnify the image enough for you to see.

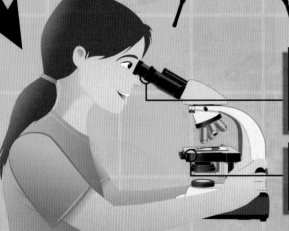

You get a close view of your specimen by looking through an eyepiece that contains a lens.

A movable platform, called the stage, holds the specimen slide under another lens.

Seeing The Past

Have you heard of the "speed of light"? When we see something, we're actually seeing the light that travels from it to our eyes. Nothing goes faster than light—it covers 186,000 miles (300,000 km) in a single second!—but it still takes time to reach us. The farther light has to travel, the longer it takes. It takes light from the sun eight minutes to travel to Earth. And when we see something really far off in space through a telescope, we're seeing light that has been traveling for years—even decades or centuries. The light we see today from something really, really deep in space may have started its journey back when dinosaurs roamed our planet! We're seeing history! Distances in the universe are so vast that scientists measure them in "light-years," the distance light travels in one year. A light-year is approximately 5.88 trillion miles (9.5 trillion km). Yeah, that's 5,880,000,000,000 miles. Wow.

1990
The space shuttle *Discovery* boosts the Hubble Space Telescope into orbit, where it records information about our universe in amazing detail.

2022
The Great Magellan Telescope, set to be the largest optical telescope yet, is supposed to see first light. Astronomers hope the telescope, which will be built in Chile, will look deeper into space and farther back in time than any other.

1897
American astronomer Alvan Clark builds the 40-inch (1-m)-wide telescope at the Yerkes Observatory, the largest refracting telescope ever, in Wisconsin. Astronomers fear that putting any bigger lenses in telescopes would make them collapse under their own weight, so they decide large telescopes should have mirrors.

1949
The Hale Telescope, at the Palomar Observatory in California, sees first light with its 200-inch (5.1-m) mirror, making it the largest optical telescope until 1993. It helps astronomers discover quasars—extremely bright objects far, far away—and the first direct evidence of stars in distant galaxies.

2005
The twin-mirrored Large Binocular Telescope, designed to deliver images ten times sharper than Hubble's, begins to operate in Arizona.

2010
The Gran Telescopio Canarias, built on top of a volcanic peak in Spain's Canary Islands, sets a new record as the world's largest optical telescope.

WANT TO KNOW MORE?

TELL ME MORE

BENDING AND BOUNCING

Many telescopes use lenses to bring things into view. In fact, they usually use multiple lenses. In a refracting telescope—one that uses lenses to bend, or refract, light—one lens focuses the light rays into an image and another magnifies that image. But that's not the only way to stargaze. Some telescopes, called reflecting telescopes, use mirrors instead of lenses. Light entering the tube bounces off a big mirror at the far end and back up to a smaller mirror. That secondary mirror bounces it into the lens in your eyepiece.

MULTIPLICATION MADE EASY

Microscopes usually pack several lenses into their tubes, so we call them compound microscopes. Both the objective lens (nearest the object) and the eyepiece's lens may actually be made of several different lenses that work together. There's a big advantage to this complicated arrangement. A strong magnifying glass, which uses only one lens, may enlarge an image five to ten times its size. A compound microscope can magnify it 100 times. Professional scientific microscopes can do even better, magnifying objects 1,000 times or more.

GOING TEENSY-TINY

Sometimes we want to see something smaller than light allows. Superpowerful microscopes, called electron microscopes, don't use lenses that bend light. They use a stream of electrons—the charged particles circling the outer regions of atoms. (Atoms are the tiny bits that make up everything.) Electron microscopes use coil-shaped electromagnets to bend the electron beams, letting us see things that are smaller than light itself. Mind. Blown.

● The **Hubble Space Telescope** had slightly blurry "vision" when it first launched. The outer edge of its main mirror was too flat, resulting in fuzzy images. In 1993, scientists added five pairs of **corrective mirrors** to the telescope to fix the problem. Yes, it's kind of like the Hubble wears **glasses.**

● Though German-Dutch lens maker Hans Lippershey gets credit for inventing the telescope in 1608, legend has it that a **group of kids** playing in a spectacle maker's shop really invented the device three years earlier.

● A lens gets its name from the Latin word for **"lentil"** because of the similarity in their shapes.

FUN FACTS

MOON BEAM BENDER

Check out how a refracting telescope—one that uses lenses—brings you a close-up view of the moon.

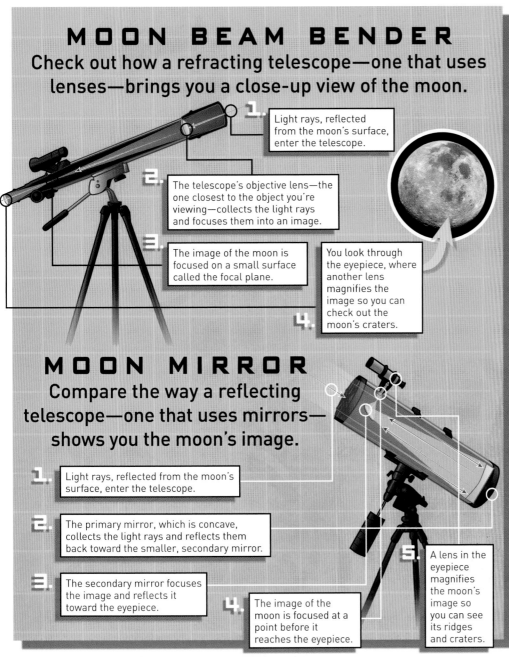

1. Light rays, reflected from the moon's surface, enter the telescope.

2. The telescope's objective lens—the one closest to the object you're viewing—collects the light rays and focuses them into an image.

3. The image of the moon is focused on a small surface called the focal plane.

4. You look through the eyepiece, where another lens magnifies the image so you can check out the moon's craters.

MOON MIRROR

Compare the way a reflecting telescope—one that uses mirrors—shows you the moon's image.

1. Light rays, reflected from the moon's surface, enter the telescope.

2. The primary mirror, which is concave, collects the light rays and reflects them back toward the smaller, secondary mirror.

3. The secondary mirror focuses the image and reflects it toward the eyepiece.

4. The image of the moon is focused at a point before it reaches the eyepiece.

5. A lens in the eyepiece magnifies the moon's image so you can see its ridges and craters.

MICRO REVEALER

A compound microscope uses a series of lenses to give you a close-up view of a plant cell.

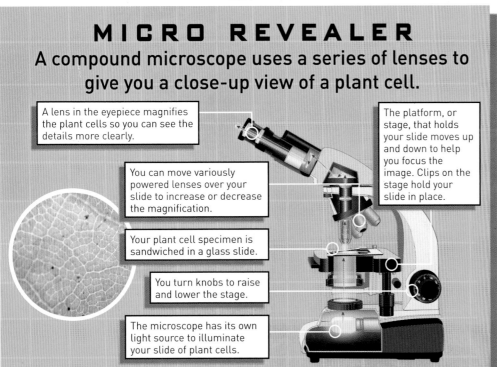

A lens in the eyepiece magnifies the plant cells so you can see the details more clearly.

You can move variously powered lenses over your slide to increase or decrease the magnification.

The platform, or stage, that holds your slide moves up and down to help you focus the image. Clips on the stage hold your slide in place.

Your plant cell specimen is sandwiched in a glass slide.

You turn knobs to raise and lower the stage.

The microscope has its own light source to illuminate your slide of plant cells.

Why are lenses different shapes? It's not so they can fit in gadgets of different sizes. It's so they can bend light in different ways. A lens is a curved piece of glass (or sometimes, plastic). When light rays hit a lens, they bend. Which way they bend depends on the shape of the lens. If you've ever looked through a magnifying glass, you've used a convex lens. A convex lens is shaped like a lentil, with a thicker middle and thinner edges. When light rays enter a convex lens, they bend in toward the middle, or converge. (A convex lens is also called a converging lens.) It's like the light rays are pulled into the center of the lens. That's how a convex lens focuses light rays into an image. A concave lens works the opposite way. It's shaped with a thin middle and thicker edges—like the middle is caved in. A concave lens makes light rays spread out, or diverge. (A concave lens is also called—you guessed it—a diverging lens.) Projectors use concave lenses to spread an image over a large screen or wall.

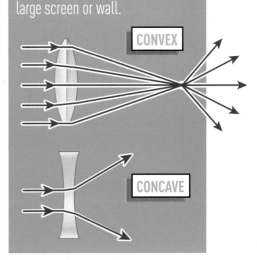

CONVEX

CONCAVE

ORIGAMI-INSPIRED:
DESIGNING A MICROSCOPE FOR THE MASSES

If you think origami is only for making birds and flowers, think again.

Manu Prakash, a biophysicist at Stanford University, has designed a microscope that you put together by folding pieces of paper, just like origami. And, no, it's not a model or toy. It's a real, powerful microscope

> ❝MANU SAW A NEED FOR A CHEAP, PORTABLE, RUGGED MICROSCOPE.❞

you can carry around in your pocket and whip out to examine all sorts of tiny, creepy, and fascinating stuff.

The microscope, which he calls a Foldscope, is printed on a colorful sheet of paper. A tiny lens, battery, and electrical circuits are pressed into the paper. You punch out a few pieces, fold them up, and, presto, you have a working microscope. Just like in a science lab!

Wait, scratch that. Not like in a science lab. Not at all. That's the whole point.

Manu saw a need for a cheap, portable, rugged microscope that doctors—and kids—could carry with them and use wherever they wanted.

Too often, people in developing countries wait for months for important medical tests because it's too hard to get a sample of their blood under a microscope. The problem, Manu says, is most microscopes are designed for scientists doing research in a laboratory. It's tough to take them into remote areas where people need the tests.

"They're heavy, bulky, really hard to maintain, and cost a lot of money," he says.

A couple of his students traveled through India and Thailand and saw lots of donated microscopes in labs. They weren't used. Some were broken. Some had fungus growing on the lenses. Others worked, but no one knew how to use them.

The Foldscope can solve that problem.

It's flat and easy to carry, costs less than a dollar to make, and is simple to use. It can be put together in about 15 minutes. And did we mention it's durable?

"I can turn it on and throw it on the floor and really try to stomp on it," Manu says. "And they last, even though they are designed from a very flexible material, like paper."

They even last if they get wet. Manu found that out by accident when he left one in his pocket. It still worked after going through the laundry.

PRACTICE MAKES PERFECT

The Foldscope isn't the first microscope Manu made—or, at least, tried to make.

When he was a kid growing up in India, Manu and his brother loved tinkering and experimenting with things. They built radios, did a lot of chemistry experiments, and made their own fireworks. (Yikes.)

One day, Manu decided to make a microscope, and he thought his brother's glasses might help him. "I had never seen a microscope before, but it was clear to me that it needed lenses," he recalls. "So, I stole his glasses and took the lenses out."

That microscope didn't work—probably a good thing for his brother's eyesight—but it fed his lifelong fascination with using scientific instruments to learn more about the world.

He wants other kids to have that opportunity, too. He has a vision of every kid in the world carrying around a microscope.

As a step in that direction, 50,000 Foldscopes were sent to kids in 130 countries so they could share their experiments with each other. "If the instrument is exactly the same, an experiment done by a kid in Alaska can be copied by one in Nigeria and repeated by somebody in Mongolia," he says. "This idea of observation-driven science is very critical. At an early age, that's what defines science."

He encourages kids to look at anything and every-thing under a microscope. Seeing one thing is likely to spark interest in another. "The idea is open-ended curiosity," he says.

Manu says he spends a lot of time being curious. It inspires him to see things in a new way.

Like seeing a microscope in the folds of origami.

ON SOME MORNINGS, MANU TREATS HIMSELF TO A LATTE, A COFFEE DRINK WITH STEAMED MILK AND A **LAYER OF FOAM** ON THE TOP. ONE DAY, HE WAS SO CURIOUS ABOUT HIS TASTY DRINK THAT HE SPOONED OFF SOME OF THE FOAM, WHIPPED OUT HIS **FOLDSCOPE,** AND STUDIED IT.

IN 2014, MANU PRAKASH WAS INVITED TO DEMONSTRATE HIS FOLDSCOPE AT THE WHITE HOUSE'S FIRST EVER **MAKER FAIRE.**

MANU GREW UP IN **RAMPUR,** IN THE NORTHERN PART OF INDIA. HE MOVED TO THE UNITED STATES TO GO TO **GRADUATE SCHOOL** AT THE MASSACHUSETTS INSTITUTE OF TECHNOLOGY **(MIT).**

Make It BETTER!

Manu Prakash's research group at Stanford University wants to make it easy for everyone to do science. That was part of the inspiration for the Foldscope: putting a microscope in the hands of everyone who needed one or could use one to discover more about their world.

The lab also invented another pocket-size scientific instrument: a mini chemistry set in a box. Inspired by a music box, the gadget is worked by a hand crank and punch cards. Like the Foldscope, it's a lot of fun. But you can also use it for doing serious science, like a chemical analysis of water quality to make sure it's clean enough to drink.

Those are two fun, but important, scientific tools. But scientists need different tools to solve other problems. If you worked in Manu's lab, what kind of instrument would you try to make available to everyone? How would you take an expensive, high-tech gadget and make it affordable and portable? Get curious and creative, and brainstorm some ideas for a pocket-size scientific instrument.

CONSTANT CONTACT

How do CELL PHONES keep us connected?

The Inside Scoop

It's more than a communication device. A cell phone is a computer in your pocket. Small, lightweight, and portable, the handy gadget lets you snap selfies, play games, surf the Web, and text your bestie. And it even makes phone calls! Those are some kind of smarts. Read on to find out how it works.

How do calls get from one phone to another?

How does roaming work?

What do the towers do?

JUST THE FACTS

Smoke Signals

If you look at the high-tech electronic gadget in your hand, the last thing you'd think of is smoke signals. But using a cell phone is a bit like that old form of long-distance communication. Your text message or phone call doesn't go straight from your phone to your bestie's. It goes to a high place that relays it along. Of course, there's no guy waving a blanket over a fire there. Instead, it's a nearby cell tower, a tall structure connected to a base station, packed with antennas and electronic gizmos that receive, process, and send electrical signals. But your message is coded—just not on clouds of smoke—and carried through the air. Your phone beams it to the nearest cell tower, which passes it along to the tower closest to your bestie. That tower delivers your message to your bestie's phone.

People have used **SMOKE SIGNALS** to communicate with each other for centuries. Native Americans passed along messages to neighbors using smoky fires on raised hills. Australian Aboriginals, ancient Chinese, and others also have used such communication. Even the Boy Scouts learn how to send up three puffs of smoke as a call for help.

Touching Base

Each cell tower stands on a patch of ground. That patch is—you guessed it—the cell, and it's usually hexagonal in shape. A communications network is an invisible patchwork of these cells. The cells do two important things: First, their huge, high-powered antennas carry along your message, so you don't need a beast of a phone with ginormous antennas and batteries (which would defeat the whole purpose of a mobile phone, right?). Second, they let the network handle more calls at the same time. Each call rides on a radio wave of a certain frequency. By having multiple cells, the network can use that same frequency in each little area, so more calls can be made at the same time.

BRICKS TO BRAINS

From **massive** to **modern,** mobile phones have come a long way.

1984
The first cell phone, the Motorola DynaTac 8000x, hits the market. Nicknamed the "brick phone" because of its size, it sells for $3,995 (about $9,500 in today's terms) and weighs just under two pounds (0.9 kg).

1989
The Motorola MicroTAC becomes the first "clamshell" phone, with a mouthpiece that folds over the keypad. It's the smallest and lightest phone available at the time and sells for more than $2,500 (about $4,800 in today's terms). Its plastic antenna looks cool but doesn't actually do anything.

1992
The first mass-produced, handheld digital phone, the Nokia 1011, becomes wildly popular. This early phone is candy bar–shaped and sells for about $400 (about $675 in today's terms).

1993
The IBM Simon is the first phone with a touch screen and "smart" features, like a calculator, address book, email, and games. It costs about $900 (about $1,400 in today's terms) and works in only about 15 states in the United States.

1996
The Motorola StarTAC, the first true flip phone, goes on to sell more than 60 million units at $1,000 each (about $1,500 in today's terms). And, no, it's not just a coincidence that its name sounds like a certain science-fiction show.

NETWORKING

Your cell phone regularly sends and receives signals to and from nearby towers, so the network always knows which phone is closest to which tower. If you're on the move, the signal is passed from cell to cell, so you don't miss a call or text. That's called roaming.

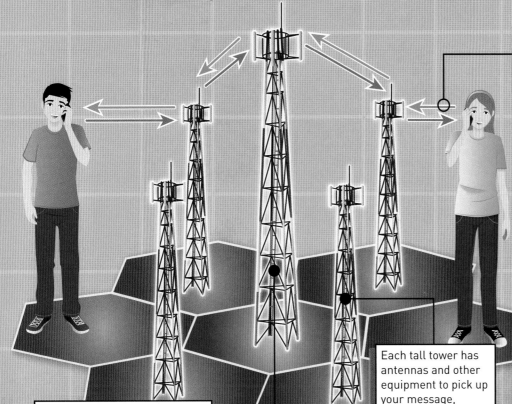

Your cell phone beams a message through the air on radio waves to the nearest cell tower.

The network is a patchwork of cells, each with its own tower that sends and receives signals.

Each tall tower has antennas and other equipment to pick up your message, process it, and send it to a tower closest to your bestie.

Smartphones of the future may not look anything like what we have today. Several companies are developing **FLEXIBLE SCREENS** that can fold or roll up into much smaller devices or even be worn like jewelry.

1998
The Nokia 5110/5190, available in a rainbow of colors, puts mobile phones in the hands of millions of people around the world. It can send short texts and includes a popular game called Snake. It costs less than $200 (about $293 in today's terms).

2000
The Ericsson R380, the first device marketed as a smartphone, breaks ground with its small, lightweight design and capabilities. It sells for $700 (about $960 in today's terms).

2004
The Motorola RAZR's thin, beautiful design makes a fashion statement in the mobile phone world. It sells initially for $500, after a rebate (about $640 in today's terms).

2006
The Blackberry Pearl, which makes e-mailing so easy that people jokingly call it an addiction, sells for about $170 (about $204 in today's terms).

2007
The Apple iPhone, featuring a touch screen, debuts at $500 (about $570 in today's terms). It's a powerful pocket computer, which brings smartphones into the mainstream.

What's Next?

? ? ?
? ? ?

Only time will tell.

TELL ME MORE

MAKING WAVES

When you talk on a cell phone, your friend hears your exact words. But that's not how they travel through the air. Your phone converts your voice into an electrical signal, which travels on radio waves to the nearest cell tower. The tower and its base station coordinate all the radio waves traveling through that cell. They route your message onward to your friend's phone, which converts it back to sound. That's a lot of distance to cover, but the radio waves travel at the speed of light. Your friend doesn't miss a word.

● **Long, long** ago, in the dark ages before cell phones (like when your parents were young), **everyone** used **land-line** phones to call their best friends. Yes, call. No texting—it **didn't exist.**

● A single smart-phone today has more **computer power than all of NASA did back** in 1969, when Apollo 11 landed two humans on the moon.

● The first phone to play MP3 **music** in the U.S. was the 2001 **Samsung** Uproar, but it could only play tunes for about **an hour.**

FUN FACTS

STAYING IN TOUCH

Your cell phone works to convert your conversation
into electrical signals that can travel
through the cellular network to your friend's phone.

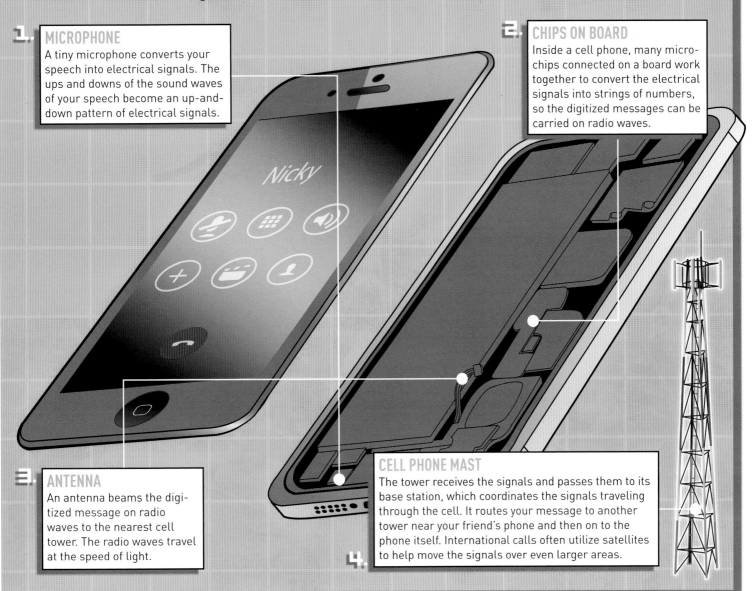

1. MICROPHONE

A tiny microphone converts your speech into electrical signals. The ups and downs of the sound waves of your speech become an up-and-down pattern of electrical signals.

2. CHIPS ON BOARD

Inside a cell phone, many micro-chips connected on a board work together to convert the electrical signals into strings of numbers, so the digitized messages can be carried on radio waves.

3. ANTENNA

An antenna beams the digitized message on radio waves to the nearest cell tower. The radio waves travel at the speed of light.

4. CELL PHONE MAST

The tower receives the signals and passes them to its base station, which coordinates the signals traveling through the cell. It routes your message to another tower near your friend's phone and then on to the phone itself. International calls often utilize satellites to help move the signals over even larger areas.

The REAL DEAL

Captain Kirk's handheld communicator, seen in the 1960s science-fiction television show *Star Trek*, inspired the invention of the first personal cell phone. That first gadget, the hefty "brick phone" didn't look anything like Kirk's sleek device, but the flip phones of the mid-1990s clearly did. Today's smartphones are even sleeker. But can they do what their sci-fi counterparts could do? The answer is a definite yes ... and no. They do many of the same things: letting us talk to each other and even helping us to find out where someone is (a relatively new trick for smartphones). But in many ways, smartphones are far more advanced than *Star Trek*'s communicator. They send texts and e-mail, play music and videos, and snap pictures. Voice recognition programs let you tell them what to do, so you don't have to punch in phone numbers or type out messages. So smartphones win, right? Well, not so fast. Remember that smartphones can only send signals a few dozen miles. They rely on cell towers to send messages farther across networks. *Star Trek*'s communicator didn't need any of that. It allowed *Enterprise* crew members to contact any starship or starbase in a similar orbit and sometimes even farther away—without relying on satellites to relay the signals. Most amazingly, they never seemed to run out of battery power or need a charge. Now that's science *fiction*!

PICTURE PERFECT

How do CAMERAS capture your favorite snaps?

The Inside Scoop

Cameras come in a bajillion shapes and sizes: simple boxes, phone cameras, disposable models, and fancy single-lens reflex cameras with lots of buttons and dials. No matter how they look, they are amazing gadgets. They help us make art, hold on to our favorite memories, and impress our friends. But how do they do it? Get ready to see cameras in a new light.

How does the picture get inside the camera **?**

What do all the knobs and buttons do **?**

How do you get the picture out **?**

JUST THE FACTS

Lighthearted

Cameras work their magic by capturing light. The light bounces off your subject and enters your camera through a special hole, called an aperture, and the camera's lens. The lens, usually curved glass, brings all the light rays together and focuses them into a small image of what you're seeing. (It'd be pretty hard to fit a life-size image inside a little camera.) When you snap your picture, the camera opens its shutter, a curtainlike mechanism that lets the light hit a special material that saves the image. The aperture's size and the shutter's speed can be changed to let in the right amount of light and, depending on the camera, let you make some cool effects.

A Moment in Time

When you press the shutter button, your camera captures a permanent record of what it "sees" at that precise moment. But what is this "special material" that saves the image? It depends on the kind of camera. A digital camera has a special light-detecting sensor. It captures the incoming light rays and turns them into electrical signals, which are stored on a memory card or the hard drive inside your camera or smartphone. A traditional film camera is different. It captures images on a light-sensitive film, which you've loaded into the camera. The film is a special plastic that's coated with chemicals that react to light. You can show off your digital images right away, but you have to develop film before you can print your awesome photographs.

This photo was taken with a slow shutter speed to capture the moving light being "painted" into flowers.

An incredibly **POWERFUL CAMERA,** to be mounted on the Large Synoptic Survey Telescope in Chile, will see more widely and deeply into space than any earlier telescope.

FUN FACT

"PHOTOGRAPHY" MEANS "DRAWING WITH LIGHT." SIR JOHN HERSCHEL ENCOURAGED THE USE OF THE TERM IN 1839 BY COMBINING TWO **GREEK WORDS:** *PHŌTOS*, A FORM OF THE WORD *PHŌS* (LIGHT), AND *GRAPHEIN* (DRAWING).

ARTIST'S  TOOLS

Part of the fun of photography is using the cameras. Both digital and film cameras can help you express your art.

Researchers in Germany, in 2011, made a microcamera the **SIZE OF A COARSE GRAIN OF SALT.** Measuring .0015 square inch (1 sq mm) the incredibly tiny camera was designed to be used in medical scopes that help in surgeries and examinations. And you thought your cell phone camera was small!

Digital cameras record images by converting light into electrical signals. The cameras usually have displays that let you see your pictures instantly.

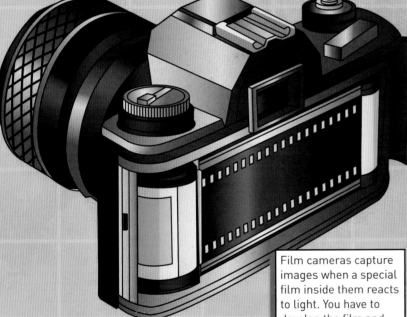

Film cameras capture images when a special film inside them reacts to light. You have to develop the film and print the pictures to see what you captured.

FUN FACT

PIGEON PHOTOGRAPHERS? WHY NOT?! IN THE EARLY 1900s, GERMAN INVENTOR JULIUS NEUBRONNER STRAPPED LIGHTWEIGHT **MINIATURE** CAMERAS TO HIS PET PIGEONS AND SENT THEM OFF TO TAKE AERIAL PHOTOGRAPHS.

WANT TO **KNOW MORE?**

TELL ME MORE

CIRCUITS VERSUS SILVER

It's a little hard to picture what an image made of electrical signals looks like. But if you've ever closely examined a picture on a television screen (don't do it for a long time!), you probably saw lots of tiny dots. Those are pixels, the stuff of digital images. When light hits a digital camera's sensor, the image is turned into millions of pixels. When they're stored on a memory card, the pixels get coded as data, which contain measurements of their color and brightness.

BLING

A traditional film camera also records a picture in lots of little dots. But they're not pixels. They're grains of silver, and they come from the light-sensitive film. The film is a thin sheet of plastic with a special coating that contains silver crystals. When the light hits them, the crystals react in different ways, creating the image on the film. As the film is processed, more chemical reactions develop the image and make it permanent. But it doesn't look exactly like what you photographed. The developed film is a negative, a reverse image. Bright skies appear dark, tires look white. Freaky. You have to print the film to get everything straightened out.

How Things Worked

Looking at a modern camera, you'd never suspect its roots go back to the fifth and fourth centuries B.C. Ancient Greek and Chinese thinkers passed light through a small hole to project an image into a darkened room. That's a "camera obscura." In the 1600s, artists used them to trace images. Admirers oohed and aahed over how realistic the paintings turned out.

But understanding how light works wasn't enough to make photographs. It also took a knowledge of chemistry. People long knew that things changed color when left out in sunlight, but they weren't sure if it was because of the heat, light, or air. In 1727, Johann Heinrich Schulze, a German professor, figured it out—by accident. He left out some chemicals and the light coming through a window made light-and-dark patterns in them.

It took a century for someone to successfully combine Schulze's discovery with a camera obscura. A French amateur inventor, Joseph Nicéphore Niépce, produced the first successful permanent photograph, a view out his window. It took two days to expose!

He later worked with Louis Daguerre, who found a quicker way to develop pictures on photographic plates. Making "daguerreotypes" became a craze. Meanwhile, English scientist William Henry Fox Talbot developed "photogenic drawing," producing a negative on light-sensitive paper. It was a desperate act. He couldn't draw well enough to record his scientific observations.

Scientists and artists improved the photographic process, and it became popular for making portraits and documenting important events, like the U.S. Civil War. But it was hard work. Photographers had to haul around large boxes mounted on tripods.

In 1871, Richard Leach Maddox, an English physician, figured out how to coat special plates with light-sensitive silver crystals. American inventor George Eastman adapted the idea to make flexible rolls of film and introduced his popular Kodak camera in 1888. Soon, shutterbugs everywhere were taking snapshots with small, handheld cameras.

TRY THIS!

There's a secret why some pictures look better to us than others. It's geometry. When you put your subject right smack dab in the center of your picture, it can be a bit boring. Instead, try composing your pictures using the "rule of thirds." Imagine two parallel lines (like railroad tracks) running across the camera screen in each direction and dividing the view into nine equal sections. Put whatever you want to emphasize along a line or at the intersection of two lines. If you want to get even more sophisticated, slide the imaginary railroad tracks a little closer together, leaving the outside grid sections a tiny bit bigger than the ones in the middle row and column. That's called a "phi grid," and it's based on a special mathematical relationship called the "golden ratio." (The golden ratio can also create a spiral, like those found in nature, but the grid may be easier to use.) Frame your shot with the most important part of your subject in one of the corner boxes, close to where the lines intersect. Pictures composed using the golden ratio look perfectly balanced. Yes, even a selfie.

SMILE CATCHERS
A traditional single-lens reflex camera, or SLR, shoots film.

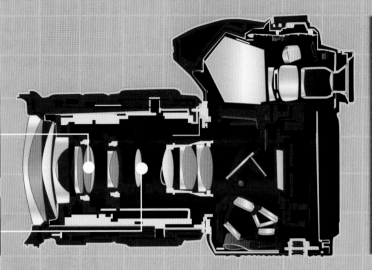

Light rays enter your camera through the lens. (The light rays that bounced off whatever you're photographing.) The LENS focuses the light toward the back of the camera. A camera "lens" isn't only one piece of glass. It's several lenses packaged together. A single lens would project the image back, but parts of the image might be a little messed up. Some colors might be off, and the edges of the image might look weird. The other lenses help correct all that.

The APERTURE, a hole with overlapping metal blades that change its size, can get bigger or smaller, depending on how much light your camera needs.

FILM, which comes in long, rolled-up strips, moves through your camera. When you push the shutter button, one frame of film gets exposed to light. The film then advances so an unexposed part of the film is ready for your next shot. You insert the film into your camera and take it out after it's all exposed. A roll of film usually holds 24 or 36 images.

A digital single-lens reflex, or DSLR, records images electronically.

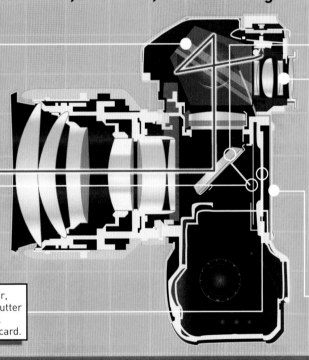

The top of the camera has a special shape that bounces the light coming from the mirror into the viewfinder.

The SHUTTER is like a curtain. It covers the light-sensitive material that captures the image you're photographing. When you push the shutter button, the shutter opens really fast to let light in and then snaps back closed again.

When you snap your shot, the button signals the shutter to open and the mirror to flip out of the way so your camera can make the exposure.

A light-detecting SENSOR, behind the shutter, captures your image when you push the shutter button. It turns the light rays into electrical signals and saves the image on a memory card.

An SLR has a MIRROR that reflects the image that the camera "sees" up into a viewfinder, so you can see the same thing. The mirror is on a hinge and flips out of the way when you press the shutter button, so light can hit the back of the camera instead.

When you look through the VIEWFINDER, you see exactly the same image as your camera does. This lets you frame your shot perfectly.

A DISPLAY on the back of the camera shows the same image that the sensor sees. Some digital cameras, especially smaller ones, don't even have a viewfinder.

FUN FACTS

● The most famous photograph used to "prove" the existence of Nessie, the **Loch Ness monster,** turned out to be fake. The photo was actually of a toy submarine with a **sea monster** head attached. But the legend lives on. Some people say the confession about the photo was itself fake.

Nessie? Is that you?

● In 2012, a rare 1923 **Leica O-series** camera, one of only a dozen known to exist, sold at auction for $2.8 million, setting a world record.

35

PROFILE: Ayanna Howard

ROBOTICS ENGINEER, INVENTOR

It wasn't just the cool, cutting-edge technology on her favorite science-fiction show that thrilled Ayanna Howard. In *The Bionic Woman*, Ayanna saw a strong, intelligent female. A heroine—a rare sight on television in the 1970s.

"She was saving the world through robotics, through bionics," Ayanna recalls. "And I thought, I want to make a bionic woman."

Ayanna has a lot in common with the Bionic Woman. No, she can't run 60 miles an hour (96

> ## 66 DREAM BIG, AND DON'T GIVE UP. 99

km/h), but she does have awesome powers. She has smarts, grit, and creativity, and she's using robotics to help the world.

Ayanna is a professor at the Georgia Institute of Technology ("Georgia Tech") and a former robotics engineer for NASA. She makes robots smarter—not just so they can do more things on their own, but so they can do more things with us.

Like play with kids. (Yes!)

PLAYING AT WORK

To be good playmates, robots need to interact with kids, getting feedback from them and responding to them. Ayanna is teaching two robots, Darwin and Avatar, how to do that.

Darwin might challenge you to a game of soccer. He'll run on his tiny robot feet to wherever

you kick the ball, and he'll kick it back to you. Except sometimes he'll kick it somewhere crazy on purpose.

He's not trying to lose. He's trying to help you get stronger.

Ayanna is designing Darwin to help kids who are recovering from an injury or who have a condition, like cerebral palsy, that makes it hard to move their muscles in some ways. To get better, those kids need to do a lot of special exercises. So when Darwin makes you go after a ball he kicked too far, he's actually getting you to strengthen a weak muscle. Sneaky, eh?

Avatar doesn't have a secret mission. This little robot is just intended for play.

Darwin and Avatar aren't quite ready to come over to your house for a play date. They're working in Ayanna's lab and "learning" how kids like to play.

"It's the most exciting work I've done," Ayanna says. "It's the most challenging."

And that's coming from someone who's designed robots to navigate on Mars.

SCIENCE FICTION BECOMES FACT

NASA had a problem to solve: how to get a rover, a robotic vehicle that explores planets, to move around on the planet's surface without getting stuck.

Engineers first tried to give it a lot of instructions like, 'If you see a rock, turn left and go around it.' But that took "a lot of hand-holding," Ayanna says. And what if the rover came to a

crater, instead of a rock?

Ayanna had a better idea. She "taught" the robot to scan the planet's surface, figure out what sort of obstacles it had to avoid, and decide for itself the best path to follow.

"As people, we do it automatically," she says. "We look, and we say, 'Oh, there's a patch of snow, and there's no snow.' Obviously, we're going to take the area with no snow." (Unless you love snow. Then you'd probably just plow right through it, right?)

Ayanna taught the rover to pick its path the same way a human would. In fact, she thinks the key to making robots smarter is getting them to mimic people. She wants her robots to think, make decisions, and act more like us.

It's not easy making robots that intelligent, but Ayanna doesn't give up when faced with a challenge.

TRUE GRIT

Growing up, Ayanna was a good student—years ahead in math. When she was in third grade, she figured out how to program computers. In high school, she hacked a car and controlled it remotely through a computer. (No worries. It was for a science competition.) It was hard to do, but she didn't stop until she did it.

It's that kind of grit that has made her so successful.

When she went to college at Brown University, a famous Ivy League university in Rhode Island, U.S.A., she struggled at first. How could that be? She was "the smart girl," the one who got all A's in high school. But some of the other students at Brown had gone to better high schools than hers.

"My starting line was way behind the starting line of these other students," Ayanna recalls. "It wasn't that I couldn't compete against them, it's that I just had to run faster to catch up."

Catch up, she did. She got her engineering degree at Brown and went on to earn a doctorate at the University of Southern California.

Learning to navigate challenges made her a better engineer.

"What Brown taught me was: How do you figure out things? How do you think about things? How do you study real hard to solve these problems, these difficult problems?"

That's a lesson she wants everyone to learn. You have to tackle problems to get where you want to be.

"Dream big," she says, "and don't give up."

Just like the Bionic Woman.

IN 2001, AYANNA FORWARD FOR HER LEADERSHIP AND TECHNOLOGICAL INNOVATION WHILE WORKING AT NASA'S JET PROPULSION LABORATORY.

WHEN SHE WAS A GIRL, AYANNA LOVED PLAYING WITH AN **EASY-BAKE OVEN** AND AN **ERECTOR SET.** "I WOULD BUILD WITH THE ERECTOR SET ALL THESE **CREATIVE THINGS,** THEN I WOULD GO OFF AND BAKE MY LITTLE CAKE AND EAT IT," SHE SAYS.

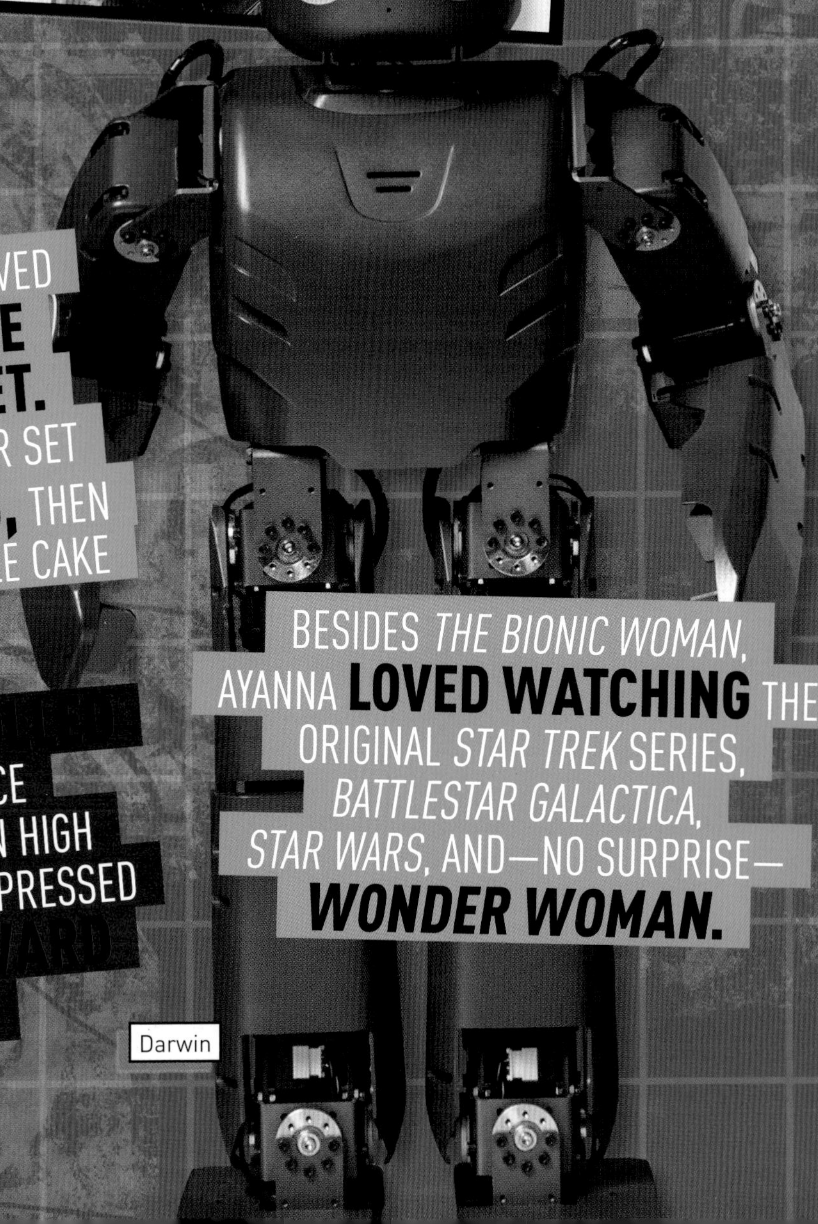

AYANNA'S WONDER ON FORGOTTEN CAR DIDN'T WIN THE SCIENCE COMPETITION WHEN SHE WAS IN HIGH SCHOOL. THE JUDGES WEREN'T IMPRESSED BECAUSE IT ONLY WENT FORWARD AND BACKWARD.

BESIDES *THE BIONIC WOMAN,* AYANNA **LOVED WATCHING** THE ORIGINAL *STAR TREK* SERIES, *BATTLESTAR GALACTICA, STAR WARS,* AND—NO SURPRISE— **WONDER WOMAN.**

Darwin

37

HELPING HANDS

How do KITCHEN GADGETS make life easier?

The Inside Scoop

Where would you be without handy kitchen gadgets? Probably a lot hungrier—or a lot messier. You'd have trouble opening cans and bottles. You couldn't flip pancakes. You'd have to mix cake batter with your hands, and then your hands would be coated with the stuff. (Hmm, maybe that last one's not so bad.) Prepare to mix it up with inside info about the way kitchen gadgets help out.

How do simple machines help **?**

Can a gadget be more than one simple machine **?**

Why are can openers awesome **?**

JUST THE FACTS

Simple

There's a reason that kitchen gadgets are so helpful. Most of them are simple machines—basic devices that take whatever force you put into a job and make it stronger. They make doing all sorts of things a lot easier. Here's how: The work required to open a can doesn't change, whether you use a fancy-schmancy can opener or a pocket knife. But the amount of force that you, yourself, personally need to put into that work can change a lot. It's easier if you spread your effort out over a longer distance, so you don't have to use as much effort all at once. Simple machines—the lever, wheel and axle, pulley, inclined plane, wedge, and screw—let you do that.

POWER  AIDES

Kitchen gadgets make cooking a lot faster and easier. Many of them are simple machines, which take whatever force you put into a job and make it stronger. They get you faster to your food.

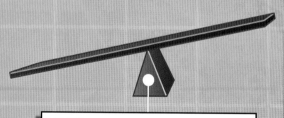

LEVER
A lever is a stiff thing that moves on a fixed support, called a fulcrum. It helps you lift and move loads, like the cap off a bottle or a scoop of food off your plate.

INCLINED PLANE
An inclined plane is a slanted surface that lets you move stuff up or down between different levels. It makes it easy to slide your freshly chopped veggies onto your plate or to make thin apple slices on a mandoline.

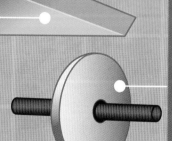

WHEEL AND AXLE
A wheel and axle—a rod going through the center of the wheel—let you move things with less friction, like a pizza cutter through a fresh pie or a rolling pin over cookie dough.

PULLEY
A pulley is a grooved wheel with a rope around it. It moves things, like the blinds on your windows, up or down. (Or, if you have a really, really fancy old house, maybe you have a dumbwaiter, which works like a little elevator to carry food up and down between floors.)

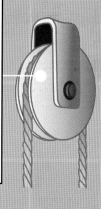

WEDGE
A wedge, which has an edge that tapers to a point, lets you separate portions of things—like using a knife to slice a piece of cake for yourself. When you chomp into an apple, you're also using wedges—your teeth!

SCREW
A screw is like an inclined plane that spirals downward. It turns your twists into an up or down force. If you've ever watched your parents use a corkscrew to open a bottle, you've seen one in action.

You can put several simple machines together in one package. For example, the humble can opener. It contains four—count them, four!—simple machines: a wedge, a screw, a lever, and a wheel and axle. When you combine simple machines, you get a ... drum roll ... complex machine. Next time you see a can opener in action, be amazed.

The blade that cuts into the can is a **WEDGE**.

A **SCREW** holds the can opener together.

The handle you close is a **LEVER**.

The **WHEEL AND AXLE** is the part you turn to make the cutter move along the rim.

Cans were invented half a century **BEFORE CAN OPENERS.** The inventor of the can suggested a way to open them: "cut around at the top with a **CHISEL AND HAMMER."**

OPENING OVER THE AGES

Food was **canned** as early as the late 1700s, but **can openers** didn't come along until the mid-1850s. Here's how they evolved.

1855
A claw-shaped opener with a lever design is invented by a British cutlery and surgical tool maker. The opener, which looks a bit like a stubby bayonet, does the job—then and now. This design is one that has stuck around.

1870
The first rotating-wheel opener is invented. You have to pierce the center of a can with the opener's sharp metal rod, adjust the length of the lever to fit the can, put a wing nut on the lever, press the cutting wheel into the can near the edge, and rotate the cutting wheel along the rim. Yep, too complicated. It doesn't last.

1925
The rotating-wheel opener is greatly improved with the addition of a second, serrated wheel, called the "feed wheel," which firmly grips the can's rim. The double-wheeled opener is fast, efficient, and still used today.

1956
The first commercially successful electric can opener hits the market in a variety of colors in time for Christmas. But, wait, there's more! It has a knife sharpener on it, too.

1980s
A new style of can opener solves the problem of sharp edges. Instead of cutting through the lid, the side-cut, or smooth-edge, can opener cuts along the side of the lid, splitting the seam where it joins the can. The result: smooth edges on both pieces.

COACH

The Inside Scoop

It hangs out with you 24/7. It "knows" if you're on the move, taking a snooze, or just sitting around. Yes, your fitness tracker can tell all that—and more. It measures a lot of things you do, like how far you walk or run, how many times you toss and turn in your sleep, and maybe even how fast your heart beats. It keeps those statistics so you have information about how fit you are. Keep moving to find out how a fitness tracker works.

How does it know what you're doing ?

What kind of information does it tell you ?

Why does it tally up steps when you're on a bumpy car ride ?

A Moving Experience

Fitness trackers work by measuring how you move—not *if* you're moving, but *how*. It's not as simple as it sounds. Most fitness trackers measure your movement in three directions: forward or backward, side to side, and up and down. They know which direction you're going and how fast you're moving. They use that information to figure out *what* you're doing. Small up-and-down bounces plus fairly slow forward motion means you're walking. Big bounces and faster forward motion? You must be running. Smooth bobs and zooming forward fast—you're on a bike. They take that information, add up how long you do it, and keep a running total of your activities for the day. Many fitness trackers will tell you how you're doing on a display on the band itself, and almost all of them beam larger amounts of data to an app on your smartphone.

"Mathemagical"

Translating a bunch of bobs and motions into data seems like magic, but it's actually serious math. Your fitness tracker uses special formulas, called algorithms, to figure out how much energy you burn when doing various activities. Exactly how your tracker crunches all those numbers is a secret. (The companies that make fitness trackers all have their own algorithms. That's why some trackers shine at tracking running while others beat them in the gym.)

Fitness isn't only about being on the move. One tracker monitors whether you're **SITTING UP STRAIGHT.** It buzzes if you start to slouch.

SNOOZE-METER

Many fitness trackers give you a readout of how well you slept. The logic goes like this: The less you thrash around during your sleep, the deeper—and better—it is. It's a fun statistic, but many sleep experts say you can't judge sleep quality based on how much your wrist moves at night. It's better to measure your brain waves, eye movement, and heartbeat, in addition to muscle movements.

FUN FACT

IF THE LOOKS OF A FITNESS TRACKER LEAVE YOU SAYING, **"MEH,"** NO WORRIES. SOME TRACKERS SPORT SERIOUS BLING. THEY'RE HIDDEN IN NECKLACES AND **FANCY BRACELETS.**

FEEDBACK

Your fitness tracker records what you're doing and how long you're doing it. It keeps statistics so you can monitor your fitness.

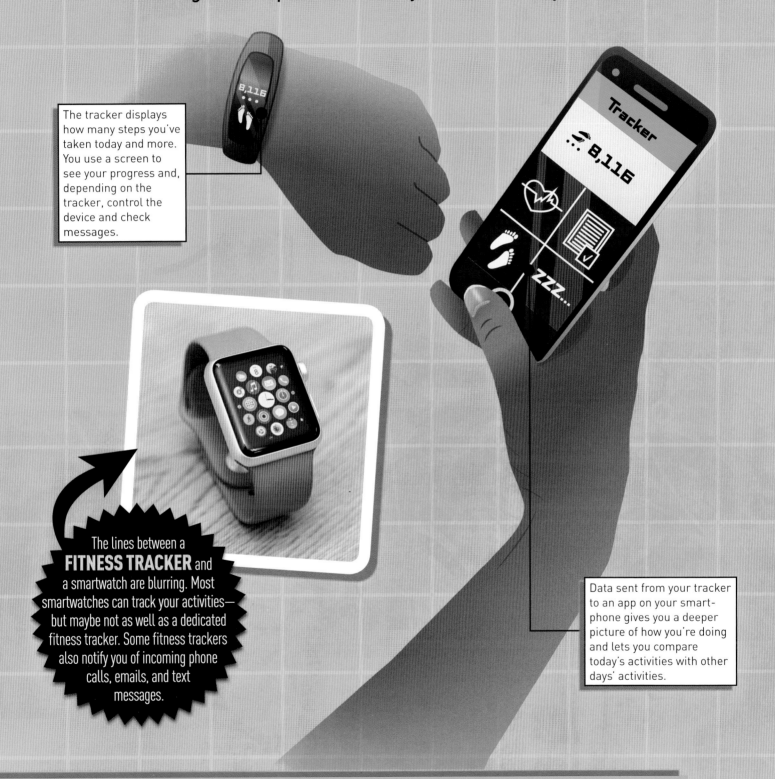

The tracker displays how many steps you've taken today and more. You use a screen to see your progress and, depending on the tracker, control the device and check messages.

The lines between a **FITNESS TRACKER** and a smartwatch are blurring. Most smartwatches can track your activities—but maybe not as well as a dedicated fitness tracker. Some fitness trackers also notify you of incoming phone calls, emails, and text messages.

Data sent from your tracker to an app on your smartphone gives you a deeper picture of how you're doing and lets you compare today's activities with other days' activities.

FUN FACT

ONE COMPANY IS MAKING A FITNESS TRACKER YOU STICK ON YOUR CHEST **LIKE A BANDAGE. IT'S STICKY** ENOUGH TO HOLD TIGHT THROUGH VIGOROUS SWEATING AND, THANKFULLY, THE SHOWER AFTERWARD.

WANT TO KNOW MORE?

TELL ME MORE

KEEPING IN TOUCH

A fitness tracker has a bunch of sensors on board to record your activities. Almost all good trackers have a three-axis acceler-ometer to pick up movements in every direction, and some add a gyro-scope to capture when you lean or rotate your body. The trackers that can tell when you climb stairs mea-sure your altitude, too. Some track-ers measure your heart rate either by using an electric current—don't worry, it's too weak to notice—or light sensors, which see blood pump-ing through your tiniest blood ves-sels. The more sensors your tracker has, the better job it does.

HOW ACCURATE ARE THEY?

A lot of fitness trackers do a great job; others, not so much. Sensors can be tricked. A tracker may give you credit for walking when you're really sitting in a car on a bumpy ride. Or it may miss the hundred steps you take in a store if your hand is too still on the shopping cart's handle. Even when they're doing their job, trackers vary in their accuracy. If you strap half a dozen different trackers on your wrist and go for a run, you'll probably end up with half a dozen different step totals. But here's the thing: It really doesn't matter. Tracking your activity can keep you fit because it motivates you to move and reach goals. Most trackers give you badges or other prizes for meeting goals. And, as long as you use the same tracker, you can compare day to day. It doesn't matter if you took 10,000 steps or 9,879, as long as you're consistent and hit a healthful goal. So get moving!

FUN FACTS

● Don't want to strap a fitness tracker on your wrist? There are lots of **other options.** Some trackers strap to your **shoes**, others clip to your **waistband.** A few transform to be worn multiple ways.

● Want even more data than a fitness tracker gives you? **"Smart shorts"** may be on the way. With **sensors** on major muscle groups in your legs and thighs, they'll measure how you move, balance, **and more.**

How Things Worked

Before high-tech fitness trackers, people used simpler gadgets, called pedometers, to count how many steps they took. The secret to how they work is the way you walk. You don't glide perfectly straight forward. Every time you take a step, bringing a leg forward, your body tilts slightly. As you step with your other leg, your body tilts slightly in the other direction. A pedometer can capture that motion with a simple device: a pendulum—the same kind of swinging arm you see in a grandfather clock, only a whole lot smaller. You clip the pedometer to your waistband, and the pendulum rocks back and forth as you walk. For every swing of the pendulum, the pedometer counts a step. To figure out how far you walk, it takes a little math:

multiplying the number of steps by how much ground you cover in a typical stride. The earliest pedometers were all mechanical. The pendulum moved a lever, which turned a gear one notch. The gear displayed numbers, which moved past a pointer arrow showing you your progress. More modern pedometers are partly electronic. The metal pendulum is wired into an electric circuit. As the pendulum swings, it turns the electric current on and off again, with the pedometer counting how many times that happens. The pedometer shows you your total steps on a screen, and most will do the math for you so you know how far you walk. Of course, if all that is still too high-tech, there's the old-fashioned way of keeping track of your steps—just count them.

WORKOUT BUDDY

While you're working out, your fitness tracker is working to measure your performance.

A rechargeable **BATTERY** powers your fitness tracker for several days.

Many trackers display running totals of your activities, like how many steps you take, on a display. Some displays also include controls for the tracker or your smartphone, while others even display messages like a smartwatch.

Multiple **SENSORS** on the underside of the tracker detect how you move. Most good trackers have accelerometers that measure the speed of at least three motions: up and down, back and forth, and side to side. Other trackers add gyroscopes that sense when you lean or rotate your body.

A small **MOTOR** vibrates to remind you to move, if you've been still too long, or to notify you of incoming messages. You can also set an alarm to vibrate to wake you up or alert you about things you need to do.

The tracker beams information to your smartphone using a special wireless technology known as **BLUETOOTH**.

The "brains" of your tracker is a **MICROPROCESSOR**, which takes all the data from the sensors and figures out what it means. It also is the control center for what the tracker does.

Some trackers measure your heart rate using optical scanners that shine light into your skin to see the blood pumped through your tiniest vessels. A few trackers use a different sensor, which uses a weak electrical current—too weak to notice—to measure how your body tissue responds. It gives a readout of how fast your heart is beating and how fast you're breathing.

The tracker's **COVER**, often a rubbery material that can handle sweat, protects both your skin and the parts inside the band.

When you need to recharge your fitness tracker, you hook it up to a charger using a special port.

TRY THIS!

It doesn't take a fancy gadget to track your fitness. A pencil and paper will work just fine. Try tracking your activities for a week. Make a chart with columns for each day of the week. Set a goal for each day, and record how long you walk, run, or play sports that day. Give yourself a star (or some treat) if you reach your goal. At the end of the week, examine your progress. Did you meet your goals? Did you see any change in your activity level? Many people are motivated to reach goals, so tracking their activity—either on paper or with a fitness tracker—can help them stay fit or train for a sports competition. How'd you do?

TRY THIS!

CAMERA MAGIC

MAKE A PINHOLE VIEWER

The ancestor of the tiny camera in your smartphone was the size of an entire room! It was the camera obscura, a completely darkened room where light passed through a small hole and projected an image onto the opposite wall. It was a cool trick, and you can see how it worked—even if you don't have a spare room to convert into a huge black box. In this experiment, you'll make your own pinhole viewer, a small camera obscura, and see like a camera sees. You can do it with stuff that's probably lying around your home. Now that'll get you to smile.

WHAT TO DO

1. USING YOUR RULER, measure two inches (5 cm) up from the bottom of the chip can and mark the spot. Do it several times until you get a dotted line around the bottom of the can.

2. ASK YOUR GROWN-UP TO CUT along the dotted line, so you end up with two pieces. Set the long piece aside for a moment.

3. USE YOUR RULER to find the center of the can's metal bottom and mark it. (Tip: Take a measurement, then rotate your ruler and take another measurement. If you come from different angles, it's easier to find the center.)

4. USE YOUR PIN to make the tiniest, smoothest hole possible in the can's metal bottom. Just use the tip of the pin, and turn it as you push it in. (If you're using a paper towel roll, put a hole in a small piece of aluminum foil and tape the foil to the end of the short tube.)

5. CUT A SMALL PIECE of waxed paper and tape it over the top of the short piece of can. Make it as flat and smooth as possible, because it's your viewing screen. (Tip: To fold the sides of the waxed paper down more easily, use scissors to make cuts from the edge of the paper to where it meets the can.)

6. PUT THE LONG PART of the can on top of the short part and tape them together, so it looks like one tube again.

7. WRAP YOUR TUBE in aluminum foil (enough to go around two or three times) and tape the edge. If necessary, trim the foil at the bottom of the tube and tuck the foil at the top inside the tube as smoothly as possible. The foil will make sure no outside light sneaks into your tube where you cut it.

8. ROLL THE PIECE of black construction paper into a tube and slip it part-way into the open end. This is your eyepiece.

9. PUT SOMETHING—A TOY, your hand, whatever—in bright light, like under a lamp, and look at it through your viewer. You'll need to experiment with how close you need to be to see the object. (Tip: Remember, you don't want other light to get into your viewer. You may want to cup your hand around the eyepiece, so no light gets in there.)

WHAT TO EXPECT

You should see an image of your toy or hand projected on the waxed paper screen inside your viewer. But it'll be upside down and reversed!

WHAT'S GOING ON?

Photography is an art, but capturing an image is all science. When light hits an object (like the toy you placed under the lamp or your hand), light rays bounce off every part of it. The rays go in every direction and overlap with rays from other parts of the scene. Some light rays enter your viewer, and your pinhole narrows them down so each hits only one tiny spot on the screen.

TRY THIS TOO!

CAMERA MAGIC

MAKE YOUR OWN SUN PRINTS

You don't need an expensive camera with all those buttons, dials, and fancy lenses—or even a cell phone—to make some serious photographic art. You can show off your creativity by making a cyanotype, or sun print, a type of blue photograph using special light-sensitive paper. It's awesome to watch your print "magically" appear before your very eyes. And it's easy. It only takes a few steps to turn a blank sheet of paper into a cool piece of art.

WHAT YOU NEED

TIME: about 20 minutes

1. Sun print paper (from a craft store or online)

2. A sturdy base, like cardboard, a cutting board, or a big book

3. Cool, sort of flat things to print, such as feathers, leaves or other stuff with interesting edges

4. A clear acrylic sheet (or piece of glass with smooth edges) a bit bigger than the sun print paper

5. A plastic basin—big enough to hold a sheet of sun print paper—filled with water

6. Lemon juice (optional)

WHAT TO DO

1. MAKE YOUR ROOM AS DARK as possible before you get out your sun print paper. Sun print paper is sensitive to ultraviolet light, which comes from the sun, and a big open window or even a shady spot outside may let in enough UV light to affect the paper.

2. PUT A PIECE OF SUN PRINT paper on your sturdy base and arrange your cool things on top. This is the time to get all artsy and show off your creativity.

3. CAREFULLY PLACE THE ACRYLIC sheet (or glass) on top of the objects to flatten them and hold them to the sun print paper. Flattening them will make sharper edges on your print because it'll keep sunlight from creeping between your stuff and the paper. But experiment! Try some prints without flattening the objects, too.

4. TAKE YOUR SUN PRINT arrangement outside and place it in direct sunlight for two to five minutes—until most of the color disappears from the paper. Cloudy day? No worries. It'll still work, but it may take up to 20 minutes.

5. REMOVE THE ACRYLIC (or glass) sheet and all your cool stuff, and then rinse the sun print paper in a tub of water for one to five minutes, however long it takes for the paper to turn deep blue. Adding a little lemon juice to the water will speed this part up.

6. PUT YOUR SUN PRINT on a flat, absorbent surface, such as a paper towel or piece of cardboard, to dry.

7. SHOW OFF YOUR AWESOME ART.

THE FIRST BOOK ILLUSTRATED ENTIRELY BY PHOTOGRAPHY FEATURED SUN PRINTS OF ALGAE. IT WAS CREATED IN 1843 BY BRITISH BOTANIST ANNE ATKINS, WHO IS CONSIDERED THE FIRST WOMAN PHOTOGRAPHER, AND IS A MILESTONE IN THE HISTORY OF SCIENTIFIC ILLUSTRATION.

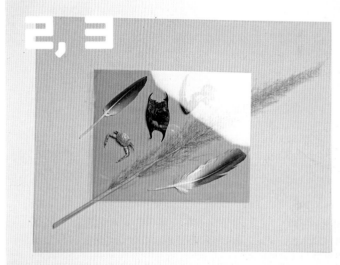

2,3

WHAT TO EXPECT

THE PARTS OF THE PAPER NOT COVERED UP BY COOL STUFF SHOULD TURN WHITE IN THE SUNLIGHT. WHEN YOU RINSE THE PRINT, THE WHITE PARTS SHOULD TURN BLUE, AND THE BLUE PARTS SHOULD TURN WHITE.

WHAT'S GOING ON?

IT LOOKS LIKE MAGIC, BUT IT'S NOT. MAKING A SUN PRINT—LIKE OTHER TYPES OF PHOTOGRAPHS—TAKES A SERIES OF CHEMICAL REACTIONS. LIGHT-SENSITIVE BLUE MOLECULES IN THE PAPER REACT TO UV LIGHT, MAKING A NEW, COLORLESS MOLECULE THAT LETS THE WHITE BASE OF THE PAPER SHOW THROUGH. THE PARTS OF THE PAPER COVERED UP BY YOUR COOL STUFF DON'T GET EXPOSED, SO THEY KEEP THEIR ORIGINAL BLUE MOLECULES. THEN, THE WATER DOES TWO THINGS. IT WASHES AWAY THE ORIGINAL BLUE MOLECULES WHERE YOUR OBJECTS WERE, LEAVING THE WHITE PAPER UNDER-NEATH. IT ALSO CAUSES ANOTHER CHEMICAL REAC-TION, TURNING THE COLORLESS MOLECULES INTO DEEP BLUE. YOU USE SCIENCE TO MAKE YOUR ART!

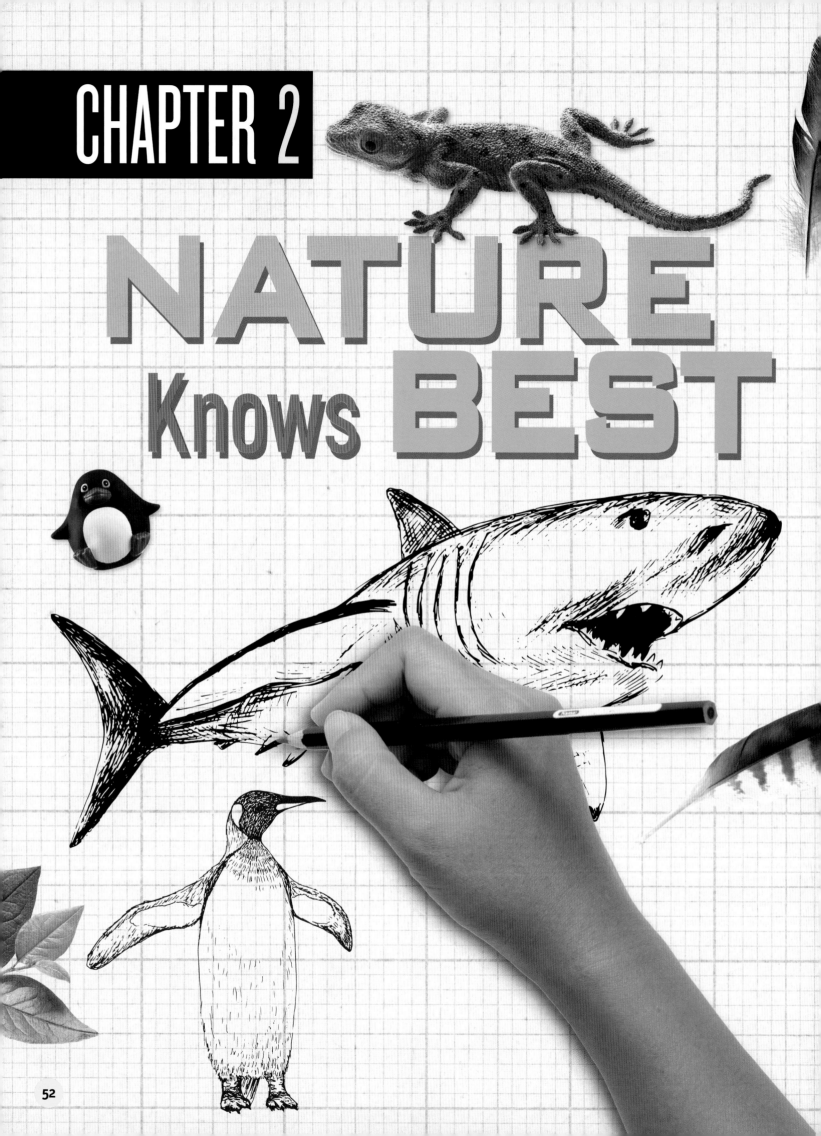

CHAPTER 2

NATURE Knows BEST

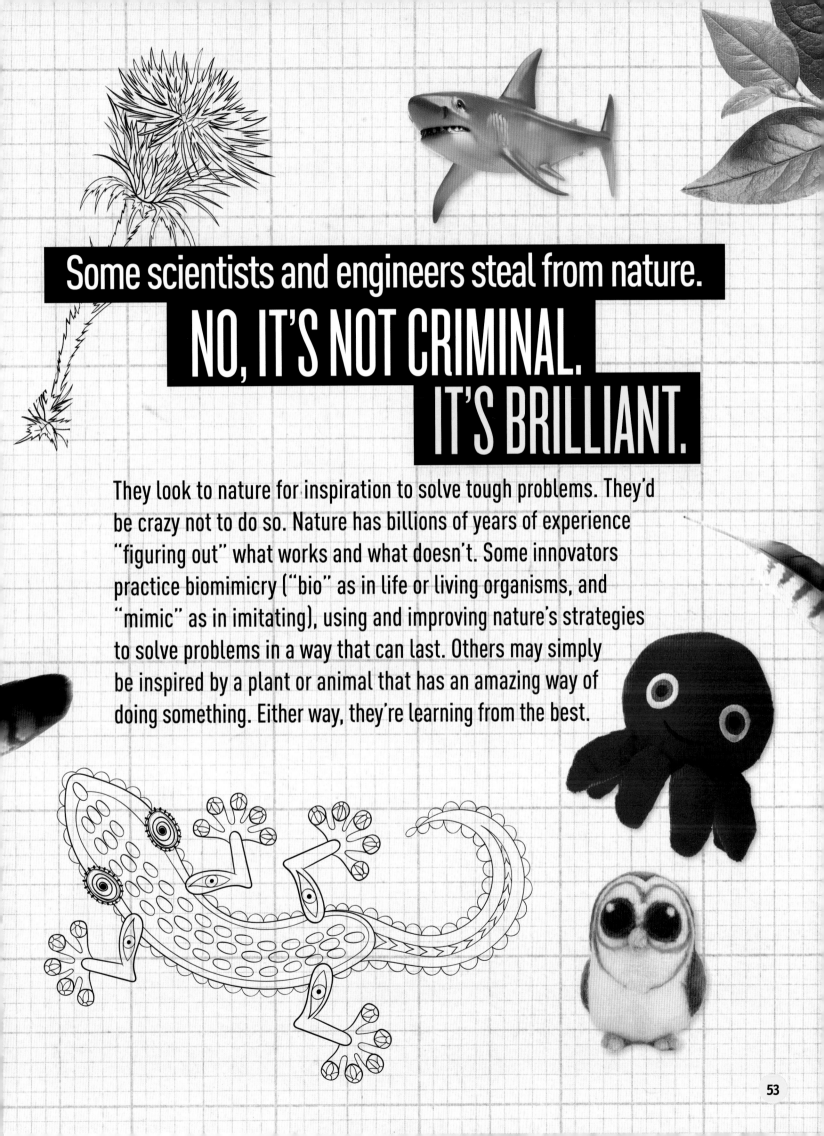

Some scientists and engineers steal from nature.
NO, IT'S NOT CRIMINAL.
IT'S BRILLIANT.

They look to nature for inspiration to solve tough problems. They'd be crazy not to do so. Nature has billions of years of experience "figuring out" what works and what doesn't. Some innovators practice biomimicry ("bio" as in life or living organisms, and "mimic" as in imitating), using and improving nature's strategies to solve problems in a way that can last. Others may simply be inspired by a plant or animal that has an amazing way of doing something. Either way, they're learning from the best.

SUPER STICKERS

How can GECKOS improve our adhesives?

The Inside Scoop

Geckos have amazing sticking power. The little reptiles scamper up walls and across ceilings as if gravity didn't even exist. And, unlike common glues and tape, they don't leave sticky goo behind. Just imagine if you could do that, you'd scale walls like Spiderman... or, maybe, Geckoman? Whatever. It's no wonder that geckos have inspired scientists to create better, stronger adhesives. Stick around for the inside scoop on how they work.

How do geckos stick to walls?

How do geckos get unstuck?

Will we ever be able to climb walls like geckos?

JUST THE FACTS

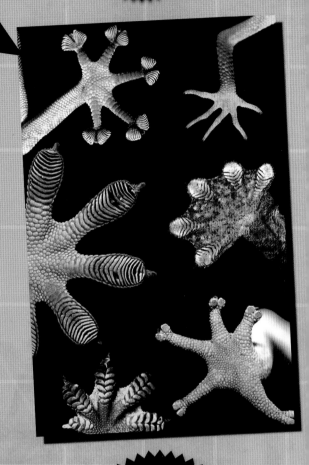

Geckos make **CHIRPING SOUNDS.**

Goo-Less Glue

If you shook hands with a gecko, you'd notice something strange. Its foot isn't sticky the way tape or glue is. No slime, no gooeyness, nothing. It's dry. So where does all that sticking power come from? Tiny hairs on the gecko's toes—millions of them. When the gecko wants to stick to a surface, it takes a step. Its toe hairs flatten down and cling to the surface. They only grip in one direction—what scientists call directional adhesion—so it's easy for the gecko to keep moving. It simply curls its toes upward, lifting the hairs off the surface, and its foot is free. No tugging required. A gecko can stick and unstick its feet as many as 15 to 20 times per second. That's some serious scampering!

Going Gecko Style

So who would want a strong, dry gecko-inspired adhesive that you could use over and over without leaving a sticky residue behind? Um, pretty much everyone—at least that's what many scientists and engineers think. Some have made tape or sticky pads that use ridges designed like the hairs on gecko toes. Like a gecko, they use directional adhesion. Sliding them on a surface presses the ridges down, creating the superclose contact that makes them stick. The adhesives are strong. A dinner-plate-size piece can hold a grown-up man off the floor. Engineers have made "gecko robots" that use sticky pads on their feet to climb walls. NASA is testing "gecko grippers" that could hold satellites for repair or grab space garbage to clear it out of the way. Someday, gecko robots may crawl around inspecting satellites, planets, or even planetary rovers.

Most geckos can **SHED THEIR TAILS** to escape from predators.

STICKY ANIMALS

Geckos aren't the only creatures with **incredible equipment for clinging.** Check out these examples of how creatures can hang out.

FLY: Hairs on its footpads produce a sticky "glue" of sugar and oil.

SPIDER: Thousands of tiny, flexible hairs increase surface contact, and opposite legs help it brace.

SNAIL: Mucus—lots of special, slimy mucus—helps it stick.

TREE FROG: Footpads create friction on a surface and mucus helps it stick.

GECKO GLUE

Geckos stick to just about any surface. They don't use claws or suction. They use millions of special hairs on their toes. When a gecko takes a step, the hairs flatten and cling to the surface.

GECKO-INSPIRED

a gecko robot foot

SPACE GECKO
In the future, NASA may use a robot called LEMUR (Limbed Excursion Mechanical Utility Robot) to inspect the International Space Station (ISS). A gecko-inspired gripping system, designed at NASA's Jet Propulsion Laboratory, would let the robot do its work.

SNAKE: Each tiny scale can be controlled to increase friction.

SQUIRREL: Its back ankles swivel so its back and front claws can always dig into tree bark.

SPIDER MONKEY: A strong, prehensile tail—one that can grasp—acts like a fifth limb, and long, hook-shaped hands allow it to swing from branches.

SLOTH: Long claws and a powerful grip help it hang from branches.

KOALA: Paws with rough pads, sharp claws, and opposable digits (like our thumbs) help it cling to trees.

PANGOLIN: Curved claws clasp around tree limbs.

CLOUDED LEOPARD: Large paws feature strong, retractable claws and specialized padding that conforms to a branch's shape. Flexible back ankles let rear paws rotate for climbing down.

TELL ME MORE

HAIRY SITUATION

When we say the hairs on geckos' toes are tiny, we mean it. One of your hairs is probably 12 or more times thicker than these special gecko hairs, called setae. Every square millimeter of a gecko's foot packs in about 14,000 of these tiny hairs. The tip of each hair has lots of split ends—as many as 1,000—that fan out to grip whatever surface the gecko wants to climb. The sticky power of each little hair isn't much by itself. But working all together, they add up to a powerful hold.

HUMAN-MADE "HAIRS"

Engineers and scientists work on a microscale—at sizes you can only see with a microscope—to create gecko-inspired adhesives. They've made fibers that mimic the way geckos' toe hairs cling to surfaces. One product uses elastic "micro-hairs" inspired by the geckos' setae. A patch of the synthetic fibers is strong. It can support hundreds of pounds (kg) of weight. Engineers see several uses for it, including improving a robot's grip.

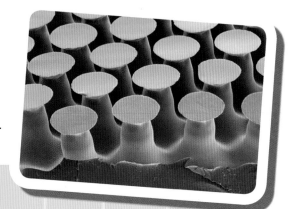

FUN FACTS

● Geckos' feet **stay clean.** The hairs shed dirt, so a gecko never loses its sticking power. Scientists are working on inventions that mimic geckos' **self-cleaning abilities.**

● The **dwarf gecko** is the smallest lizard. It's just over **half an inch** (16 mm) long and is small enough to curl up on a dime.

● Most geckos **can't blink.** They lick their eyes to keep them moist and clean.

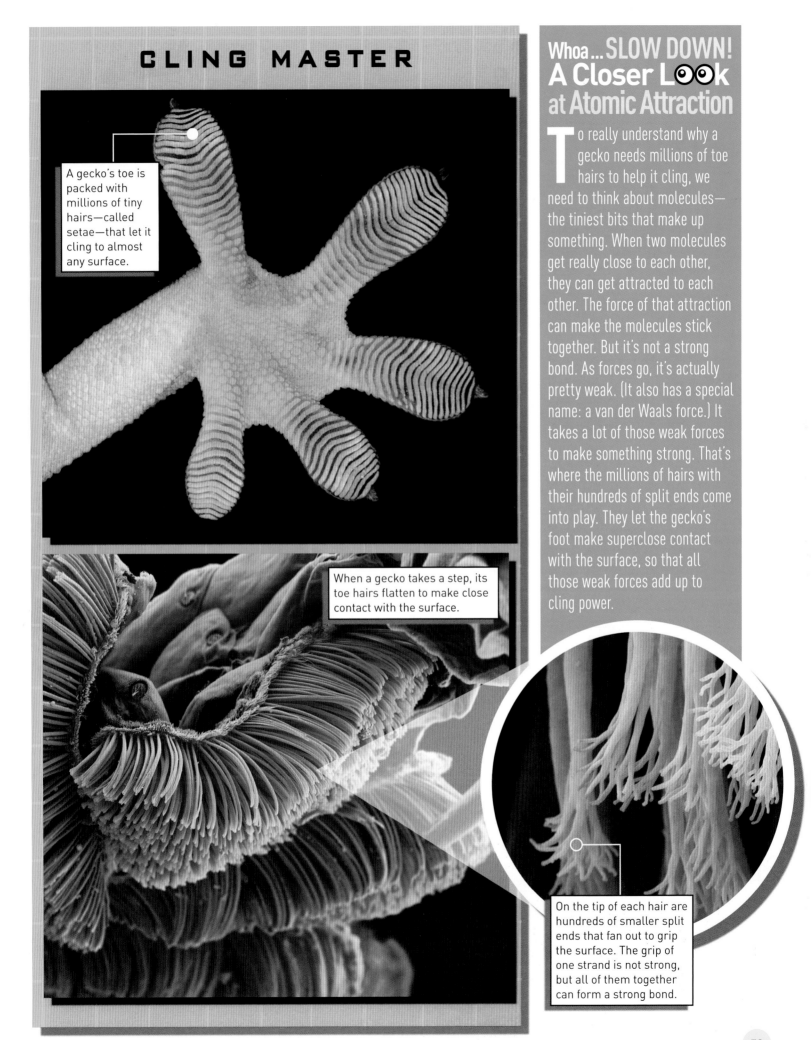

CLING MASTER

A gecko's toe is packed with millions of tiny hairs—called setae—that let it cling to almost any surface.

When a gecko takes a step, its toe hairs flatten to make close contact with the surface.

Whoa...SLOW DOWN! A Closer Look at Atomic Attraction

To really understand why a gecko needs millions of toe hairs to help it cling, we need to think about molecules—the tiniest bits that make up something. When two molecules get really close to each other, they can get attracted to each other. The force of that attraction can make the molecules stick together. But it's not a strong bond. As forces go, it's actually pretty weak. (It also has a special name: a van der Waals force.) It takes a lot of those weak forces to make something strong. That's where the millions of hairs with their hundreds of split ends come into play. They let the gecko's foot make superclose contact with the surface, so that all those weak forces add up to cling power.

On the tip of each hair are hundreds of smaller split ends that fan out to grip the surface. The grip of one strand is not strong, but all of them together can form a strong bond.

POWER PLAY

How can a **PENGUIN** help submarines move better underwater?

How can a **PENGUIN** help submarines move better underwater?

The Inside Scoop

Ever seen a penguin waddling around on land? Cute, but seriously awkward. But put the penguin in water and it's a different story. It darts back and forth and makes sharp turns with ease. Next to a penguin, our advanced submarines look ... well, seriously awkward. Researchers are trying to change that. They're uncovering the secrets of penguin propulsion to help improve human-built underwater craft.

How do penguins turn so fast **?**

Do penguins have wings or flippers **?**

How would penguin-inspired propulsion be used **?**

JUST THE FACTS

Underwater Acrobats

Put a rocket and acrobat together (and dress it up really fancy), and you've got a penguin. An emperor penguin can blast off from a standstill and hit 15 miles an hour (24 km/h) in only one second. It changes directions as fast as you blink. It's not only the penguin's streamlined shape that makes it so speedy underwater, it's also the penguin's wings. A penguin's flipperlike wing is pretty rigid and sticks out from its body—unlike most birds, which fold their wings and tuck them close to their bodies. What's really amazing is how the penguin's wings move. They don't just flap up and down. The penguin adds little twists, angling each wing so more of it pushes against the water. That's the secret to the penguin's underwater speed and acrobatics.

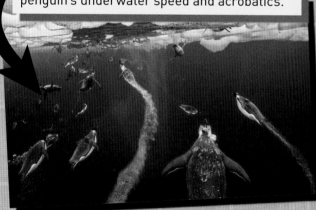

STUNT ARTIST

A penguin can rocket through the water, making sharp turns with ease. The secret to its amazing ability is its special shoulder and wing.

A penguin's shoulder can rotate, angling its wing so more of it pushes off the water. That creates more thrust, the force that pushes the penguin through the water.

A penguin's wing is rigid, more like a flipper on a dolphin or sea lion than the wing of a flying bird.

Unlike many swimming birds, a penguin does not paddle with its feet.

A penguin's wing produces thrust when it flaps both up and down. In flying birds, wings produce thrust only on the downward flap.

TOP PENGUINS

Penguins generally cruise along at four to seven miles an hour (6 to 11 km/h) in the water, but **speeds vary a lot** among penguin species. Some also are capable of short bursts of amazing speed. See how fast these top penguins swim. **Biggest isn't always best.**

LARGEST

EMPEROR:
45 inches (115 cm) tall, 48 to 88 pounds (22 to 40 kg), 6.8 miles an hour (11 km/h) average with bursts up to 14 miles an hour (22.5 km/h)

UNUSUAL DIVER (FEET FIRST)

ROCKHOPPER:
22 inches (55 cm) tall, 4.4 to 6.6 pounds (2 to 3 kg), 5 miles an hour (8 km/h)

FASTEST

GENTOO:
30 inches (76 cm) tall, 12 pounds (5.5 kg), 22 miles an hour (36 km/h)

SMALLEST

LITTLE BLUE:
13 inches (33 cm) tall, 2.2 pounds (1 kg), 4 miles an hour (6.5 km/h)

HUMAN

OLYMPIC SWIMMER:
70 inches (183 cm) tall, 190 pounds (86 kg), 5 miles an hour (8 km/h)

Most birds produce thrust, the force that pushes them forward, only when their wings flap downward. But, thanks to that handy twisting motion, penguins create thrust while flapping both up and down. Voilà! Extra speed and turning power. Penguins' special shoulder joints allow that twisting movement. They're simple but strong. Their muscles, tendons, and bones work together to rotate the joint, creating the extra thrust.

LESSON LEARNED

Researchers in Switzerland built a robotic "wing" that moves like a real penguin wing underwater. Most modern robotic arms use a series of joints to get the desired movement. But these researchers learned from the penguin. They made a spherical joint—one with a ball that moves every which way—that's compact, rigid, and precise, like a penguin's. And it paid off with more thrust. They hope the design will give propellers the ability to thrust in different directions with greater control. That would help unmanned underwater vehicles, the kind used in exploration, maneuver with more precision.

ROBO-PENGUIN

It's not as cute as a real penguin, but a device inspired by a penguin's shoulder and wing may someday give unmanned submarines the ability to thrust in precise directions. That will make them maneuver underwater much better.

The robotic joint is compact and rigid, like a penguin's, so it makes a more precise thrust. That's different from many modern robotic arms, which use a series of joints to move.

The spherical, or ball-shaped, joint lets the wing rotate and move in all directions. It improves on an actual penguin's wing, which can't rotate as far around.

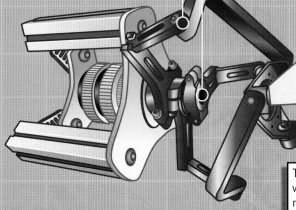

The structure of the robotic wing makes it stronger and more rigid, so it works more like a penguin's wing.

FUN FACTS

● There are **17 to 19 species** of penguins alive today, depending on whom you ask.

● Penguins have **two celebrations:** January 20 is Penguin Awareness Day, and April 25 is **World Penguin Day.** Send a penguin a card!

● A penguins black-and-white **"tuxedo"** is really camouflage! From above, the penguin's black back **blends into the dark ocean** making it less likely to be a snack.

● As penguins' wings **evolved** to get better at swimming, they **lost their ability** to fly.

BIRD-BRAINED?: SOLVING THE SHINKANSEN "BULLET" TRAIN'S PROBLEM

Speed wasn't the problem. Japan's new high-speed Shinkansen "bullet" train could hit 200 miles an hour (320 km/h). But it would never be allowed to run that fast. It was too noisy. The train's designers had a dilemma: It was 1989, and their new 500-series Shinkansen electric train needed to be on the tracks for testing within five to six years. It was to carry passengers between western Japan's two biggest cities, Osaka and Fukuoka. But how would they meet Japan's strict limits on noise pollution? The faster the train went, the more noise it made.

> ## " THEY BORROWED A STUFFED OWL AND RAN TESTS IN A WIND TUNNEL. "

One of the problems was the train's pantographs, the parts that reach up to the overhead electrical wires that power the train. Air swirled around the pantographs from one side to the other, creating big vibrations and noise.

And then there were the sonic booms after the train emerged from a tunnel. When the train rushed into a narrow tunnel at high speeds, it created a wave of air pressure that it pushed out the other end. The sudden change in air pressure caused a huge pop. The huge thunderclaps could be heard for a quarter mile (400 m).

Eiji Nakatsu, the engineer in charge of technical development for the 500-series, told his team to engineer a solution. They tried decreasing the number of pantographs and adding special shields to make the wind go around them. But the shields made the train heavier, increasing its energy usage. Worse yet, they created new, noisy vibrations. The usual engineering approach was causing as many problems as it was solving.

They had to look at the problem in a new way.

WINGING IT
One day in 1990, Eiji, a bird lover, saw a notice in his local newspaper about a lecture at the Wild Bird Society of Japan. The lecturer was an aircraft design engineer.

Intrigued, Eiji went and learned how bird flight and anatomy had influenced aircraft technology.

Most interesting was the fact that owls, unlike other birds of prey, fly silently, giving their prey no warning that they're about to strike. It was a lightbulb moment. Eiji's team needed to discover the owl's secret.

They borrowed a stuffed owl specimen from the local zoo and ran tests in a wind tunnel. They found that the front edge of an owl's wing has serrated feathers that look a bit like bristles on a comb or teeth on a saw. The special serrated feathers—unique to owls—change the way air flows over the wing, breaking up the large swirls that create noise.

It took four years, but Eiji's team developed a new pantograph with edges like the owl's feathers. It worked! It reduced vibrations and noise.

But what to do about the sonic booms?

A young engineer on Eiji's team observed that when a train rushed into a tunnel, it almost felt as if the train had shrunk. Eiji realized it was because of the sudden change in air resistance. He thought about living things that manage similar transitions as part of their daily life.

They found their answer in another bird, the kingfisher. To catch its prey, the bird dives at a high speed from the air, which has low resistance, into water, which is 800 times more dense. And the kingfisher barely makes a splash.

It had to be the long, pointy beak, he thought.

His team got to work. They built a model of a tunnel and shot bullets of various shapes through it to mimic a speeding train. They also ran computer simulations to find out which train shape was best.

It wasn't even close. The kingfisher shape won every time.

The team lengthened the nose of the 500-series train to 50 feet (15 m) and shaped it like the streamlined kingfisher beak.

Problem solved! Not only was the 500-series quiet enough to run at top speeds, it encountered 30 percent less air resistance and used 13 to 15 percent less electricity than earlier models.

These bird-brained solutions turned out to be very wise, indeed.

WHEN THE 500-SERIES SHINKANSEN ELECTRIC TRAIN WENT INTO SERVICE IN 1997, IT SET A **WORLD RECORD** FOR AVERAGE RUNNING SPEED. IT CRUISED ALONG AT A MAXIMUM SPEED OF 143 MILES AN HOUR (230 KM/H), WITH BURSTS UP TO 186 MILES AN HOUR (300 KM/H).

THE KINGFISHER GOT ITS NAME FROM ITS AMAZING ABILITY TO DIVE INTO WATER AND CATCH FISH. BUT THERE ARE SOME SPECIES OF KINGFISHERS THAT RARELY GO NEAR WATER—AND DON'T EAT FISH.

OWL-INSPIRED TECHNOLOGY MAY SOON QUIET MORE THAN SPEEDY TRAINS. THE OWL'S **SPECIAL WING STRUCTURES** INSPIRED SCIENTISTS TO DEVELOP A COATING TO **REDUCE THE NOISE** OF GIANT WIND TURBINES.

JAPAN'S HIGH-SPEED TRAIN GOT ITS "BULLET" NICKNAME BECAUSE OF ITS SHAPE AND SPEED.

Make It BETTER!

The owl-and-kingfisher design of the 500-series Shinkansen train made it the fastest train in the world when it hit the rails in 1997. But it could have been even better. The spaces between train cars create a lot of air resistance and noise—and not only on the Shinkansen trains.

Eiji Nakatsu wondered if it would be possible to reduce these problems with a special covering between the cars. Train cars can't be connected with conventional materials that would tear or break when the train goes around a tight curve. Could an animal inspire a solution? He thought so, but he wasn't able to find an affordable solution at the time. Another team of engineers had to tackle the challenge later.

But what about you? How would you solve that problem? Could you develop a "train skin" that mimics an animal's? It would need to stretch and contract without wrinkling. (Wrinkles increase air resistance.) It also would have to be strong but lightweight and let the train go really fast.

Which animal would be a good model? What shape would your "train skin" have? Get out some pencils and start sketching. You just might solve one of the biggest engineering challenges confronting trains.

65

AWESOME ARMOR

What can SHARKS teach us about giving pests the brush off?

The Inside Scoop

Probably the last word you'd use to describe a shark is "angelic." The ocean's top predator is one fearsome fish. But it also has an amazing ability that can help us. Algae and barnacles can't stick to it—unlike many other marine animals (and ships), which get covered with the stuff. Sharkskin has a unique texture, and researchers have copied it to keep germs from sticking to surfaces. Sharks may be our guardian angels! Plunge in to find out how.

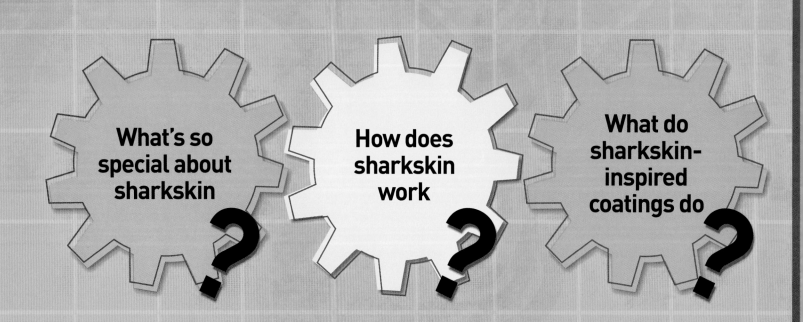

What's so special about sharkskin ?

How does sharkskin work ?

What do sharkskin-inspired coatings do ?

JUST THE FACTS

Smooth Sailing

Sharks have a secret weapon. No, it's not their rows of jagged teeth or even that superkeen sense of smell that lets them detect blood in the water miles (km) away. (Eww.) It's their skin. To be more precise, it's the texture of the scales on their skin. While whales, manatees, ships, and other ocean-goers travel through the water picking up barnacles, algae, and other hangers-on, sharks slip through water without those unwanted passengers. Nothing sticks to their skin. That's some awesome armor.

Shark Power

If you take the texture of sharkskin and shrink it down—smaller than you can see with your naked eye—you can give other surfaces shark powers. Researchers have made a sharkskin-inspired coating you can use wherever you don't want germs—like on surfaces in hospitals, so infections don't spread from one person to another. Other researchers are looking to use 3-D printed sharkskin-inspired coating for ships so they can shed barnacles, the little sea critters that glom onto ship hulls with their sticky cement, slowing the ships down and costing lots in extra energy. Boatbuilders have used a special paint to prevent barnacles and algae from sticking, but a lot of it is toxic. So using sharkskin-inspired coating wouldn't only be good for the ships, it would also help the ocean.

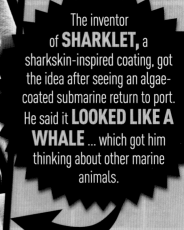

The inventor of **SHARKLET,** a sharkskin-inspired coating, got the idea after seeing an algae-coated submarine return to port. He said it **LOOKED LIKE A WHALE** ... which got him thinking about other marine animals.

FUN FACT

SHARKS ARE UNIQUE IN **USING TEXTURE** TO KEEP PESTS OFF. MOST FISH DO THE JOB USING **SLIME** OR **TOXIC SUBSTANCES**— OR EVEN BY SHEDDING SOME SKIN.

SQUEAKY CLEAN

Unlike other marine animals, sharks have the power to keep algae and barnacles from clinging to their skin and slowing them down.

Sharkskin has a patterned texture that makes it hard for anything to stick to the shark.

FUN FACT

SHARKS HAVE BEEN AROUND FOR **450 MILLION YEARS.** THEY BEAT DINOSAURS BY **200 MILLION YEARS!**

WANT TO KNOW MORE?

>TELL ME MORE

SUPER SHAPE

If you pet a shark (and you might want to think twice before doing that), make sure you go from its head to its tail. If you go the other way, its smooth skin will feel rough and prickly. That's because sharkskin is covered with layers of hard, diamond-shaped scales, called denticles, that have tiny spines or bristles that poke up from the surface. They are more like teeth than fish scales. The scales, which cover the shark's elastic skin, flex against each other as the shark moves. They help the shark swim with less effort by making it hard for stuff to stick to it. It's a brilliant adaptation.

MICRO-SHARKSKIN

The same pattern that works for sharkskin also works for human-made coatings, but on a much smaller scale. The sharkskin-inspired coatings that repel germs have a microscopic diamond pattern with ridges. The pattern is similar to a real shark's, but the tiny ridges on the human-made coating are only three micrometers tall—way too small to see without a microscope or even to feel rough when we touch them. (A strand of your hair is probably 10 to 60 times thicker than one of those ridges!) But that's just the right size for bacteria, which are microorganisms. Bacteria can't attach or grow on the sharkskin-inspired surface. If germs can't stick to a surface, they die. Thanks for the idea, sharks!

- Sharks range wildly in length. The **spined pygmy** shark is only **11 inches** (28 cm), while the whale shark is a whopping 50 feet (15 m).

- Sharks **have no bones!** Their skeletons are made entirely of **cartilage**, the firm but flexible stuff our ears and nose are made of.

- The mighty **megalodon shark,** which went extinct **2.6 million** years ago, may have reached lengths of 67 feet (20 m)—about the length of one and a half school buses.

- **The basking shark,** which swims with its mouth open to gather food, inspired an artist to create **a hydro-power** (water-powered) **generator** based on the shark's design.

- Most sharks live **20 to 30 years,** but the **spiny dogfish** and **whale shark** can live to be **more than 100.**

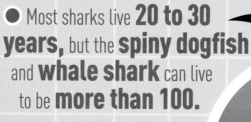

FUN FACTS

FEARSOME PROTECTION

Sharkskin has a pattern of scales, or denticles, with tiny spines that stick up off the surface. Algae and barnacles can't get a good grip on the texture, so sharkskin stays free of the pesky passengers.

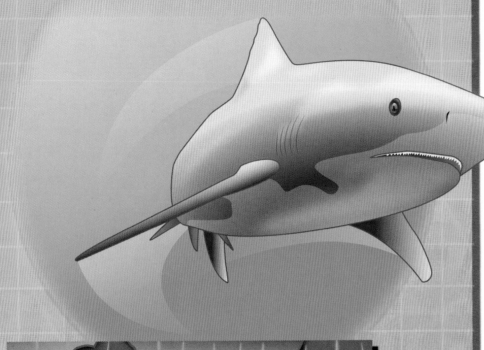

A sharkskin-inspired coating has a micropattern with tiny ridges that stick up off the surface. Bacteria, such as nasty germs that can cause infections, can't get a grip on the texture, so they can't grow.

Myth vs. FACT

MYTH: Sharkskin-inspired suits give swimmers an unfair advantage.
FACT: Yes, they would—if they really existed. In the 2008 Olympics, much ballyhoo was made about a shark-inspired swimsuit. The suit's fabric included ridges to help swimmers speed through the water. The idea was that they'd work like the grooves on a shark's denticles, which—in addition to shedding clingy critters—do two things to help a shark swim: They disrupt turbulent swirls of water, so the water passes by the shark faster, and they decrease drag, the force pushing against the shark's forward movement. The swimsuit design was credited for helping swimmers crush 23 world records at the 2008 Olympics in Beijing, China. It was considered such a technological advantage that in 2010 the International Swimming Federation banned the suits in official competitions. But a Harvard University researcher studied the suits and said that, while the suits have other qualities that may enhance a swimmer's speed—like helping a swimmer's posture and circulation—they don't reduce drag. Human bodies aren't as flexible as a shark's, so they can't benefit as much from the denticles' help. But if swimsuit makers ever do manage to imitate sharkskin, the Harvard professor is certain those suits would be banned, too.

TRY THIS!

To see how a textured surface can keep things from sticking, try this quick experiment. Get something with a suction cup and stick it on a variety of clean surfaces. Make sure some are smooth, like glass, and others are rough, like sandpaper. The rough surfaces are more similar to denticle patterns on sharkskin. How well does your suction cup stick to different surfaces?

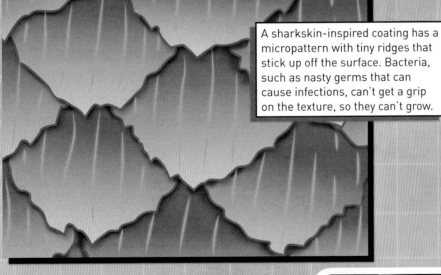

PROFILE: Joanna Aizenberg

CHEMIST, MATERIALS SCIENTIST

When Joanna Aizenberg walks along the beach, she doesn't just look at the ocean. She studies it. She analyzes the patterns the waves form as they come to shore. She examines the lines they leave behind on the sand.

> ❝ I WANT TO LOOK FOR INTERESTING THINGS THAT OTHERS HAVEN'T STUDIED. ❞

She marvels at the creatures that live in the ocean's depths.

It's not only their beauty that inspires her. It's what they do and how they do it.

Take the example of the brittle star, a close relative of the sea star and sea urchin. Scientists used to think it was blind, but then they discovered that part of its skeleton is coated with lenses. It sees through its shell!

If that's not weird enough, it does this trick: It turns dark during the day and light again at night. That's not like other animals, which try to blend in with their environment. What's going on?

It's all part of a brilliant design. "It's like the brittle star is using sunglasses," Joanna says. "And the lenses are better than we can make."

It's not just a curiosity. It's an important lesson. It shows us that in nature, materials are perfectly adapted to do many things, not only one. The brittle star's shell protects it, but it also lets the creature see.

"These are almost unrelated functions, from an engineering point of view," Joanna says. "But this organism is able to combine them in a single structure."

Joanna is not only a student of nature, she's also a chemist and professor of materials science at Harvard University. She takes nature's best ideas and uses them to create new materials and devices that outperform anything that we have today.

"It's pretty much stealing from nature," she says.

COOL COATING

One of the ideas Joanna "stole" from nature was super slippery.

She made a thin coating called SLIPS. You put it on a surface, and nothing can stick to it. Stuff slides right off without leaving a trace. That could be helpful in a lot of places. Imagine if nasty germs couldn't cling to hospital surfaces or graffiti to a wall—or if ketchup couldn't stain your favorite T-shirt.

Her inspiration? An insect-eating plant.

"The pitcher plant is carnivorous," she says. "It has an incredibly slippery surface. If an ant climbs on, it will just slide into the flower, where it is trapped and digested." Yum.

Joanna's interest in the pitcher plant was unique. Other scientists focused on the lotus leaf's special abilities to stay clean. But Joanna likes to take a different path. "I want to look for interesting things that others haven't studied, hidden clues that others haven't paid attention to."

STRONG ROOTS

When it comes to taking risks, Joanna had good role models when she was growing up in what was then the Soviet Union. Her father was a construction engineer who designed and built bridges and roads, and her mother was a doctor who focused on infectious disease. They both influenced Joanna's future greatly.

Her mother went to medical school in the 1950s, a difficult time in Soviet history. The country's dictator, Josef Stalin, banned work on genetics. It was dangerous to go against his wishes, but Joanna's mother led a group of students who met in secret to study genetics.

"She was fearless, the most strong-willed person I have ever known," Joanna says.

Her mother also taught Joanna to look deeply at the world around her.

When Joanna was young, she got sick with polio, which paralyzed her legs for a long time. "My mother spent so much time talking to me, showing me the world I could see out of my window. 'Look at how the trees grow, the shapes they make,' she would say. 'Look at the patterns the water makes as it rushes by.' It was really wonderful."

No wonder Joanna finds inspiration in nature.

WHEN SHE WAS IN MIDDLE SCHOOL, JOANNA EARNED MONEY BY DEVISING **MATH PUZZLES** FOR OTHER STUDENTS. THEY WERE PUBLISHED IN A JOURNAL.

JOANNA'S INTEREST IN MATH AND SCIENCE GO BACK TO HER CHILDHOOD. SHE COMPETED IN A LOT OF **MATH OLYMPIADS** WHEN SHE WAS IN MIDDLE AND HIGH SCHOOL.

AMONG JOANNA'S MANY INSPIRATIONS FROM NATURE ARE WATER STRIDER LEGS, **MOSQUITO EYES,** LEAF BRISTLES, BUTTERFLIES, BEETLES, AND, OF COURSE, BRITTLE STARS.

JOANNA HAS WORKED ON A **SELF-LUBRICATING MATERIAL** INSPIRED BY THE MUCUS IN OUR INTESTINES (EWWW!) AND THE FILM THAT MOISTENS OUR EYES WHEN WE BLINK.

JOANNA WENT TO COLLEGE AT MOSCOW STATE UNIVERSITY IN **RUSSIA** AND GRADUATE SCHOOL AT THE WEIZMANN INSTITUTE OF SCIENCE IN **ISRAEL.** AFTER THAT, SHE WENT TO **HARVARD** TO DO MORE RESEARCH.

HOLDING FAST

How did a BURR show us a new way to attach things?

The Inside Scoop

How something so annoying can become so helpful is one of the amazing stories of inventions. We're talking about burrs, those prickly little seeds that cling to your dog's fur, your socks, and your shoelaces. Wait, you do have shoelaces, don't you? Or maybe your sneakers close with hook-and-loop fasteners? See where we're going? Hold tight, we're about to see how burrs inspired our favorite fastener.

Why do burrs cling to things **?**

How do hook-and-loop fasteners work **?**

Why aren't burrs easier to get off **?**

Hitchhiker

The spiky burrs that tangle your dog's fur and prick your fingers are an amazing adaptation of nature. Burrs are seeds from cocklebur plants. There are several varieties of cockleburs, each with its own design. But in general, each plant produces hundreds of the nasty little burrs covered with stiff, prickly hooks. Why would nature make something so vicious? Plants want to spread their seeds to grow more plants. Some seeds float on the air. Some seeds drop to the ground. Burrs hold tight to fur or socks and hitchhike to a new place.

Zipperless Zipper

The burr's clinging power is amazing, so it's a natural inspiration for a fastener. (OK, so maybe it's not so bad after all.) Hook-and-loop fasteners copy the burr's action by using two strips of material. One side, with lots of tiny hooks, acts like the burr. The other side, which is made of tiny loops, takes the place of your dog's fur or your sock. When you press the two pieces together, the hooks grab the loops and hold tight. The fastener is a quick and easy way to secure all sorts of things. It's used on sneakers, jackets, backpacks, and astronauts' suits. But over time it can lose its gripping power. Sometimes the hook side gets dirty, and sometimes the loops get worn.

A **FASHION SHOW** in New York in 1959 featured clothes made with hook-and-loop fasteners. It included fancy golf jackets and diapers.

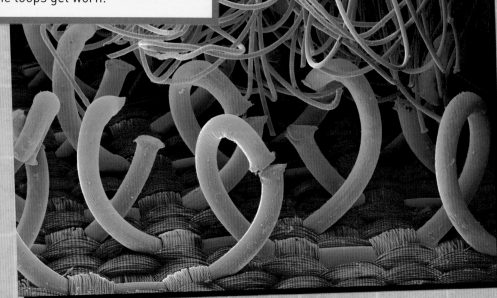

FUN FACT

WHEN **VELCRO** HIT THE MARKET IN THE 1950S, EARLY NEWS REPORTS DESCRIBED IT AS A **"ZIPPERLESS ZIPPER."** IT'S THE ONLY WAY THEY COULD THINK OF DESCRIBING THE REUSABLE FASTENER.

UNWANTED  PASSENGER

Burrs, which are the seeds of the cocklebur plant, are hitchhikers. They get dispersed by clinging to fur (or socks). It's their way of making sure they end up where they can grow into a new plant. But they're a pain to get out of your dog's fur.

The original hook-and-loop fastener, **VELCRO**, was invented by a Swiss engineer, Georges de Mestral, who, in 1941, went for a walk in the woods with his dog. They came back covered in **BURRS.** Lightbulb moment!

FUN FACT

BELIEVE IT OR NOT,
THOSE PRICKLY COCKLEBURS BELONG TO THE **SUNFLOWER FAMILY.**

WANT TO **KNOW MORE?**

Burrs come by their grip naturally. It wasn't as easy to find the right material for hook-and-loop fasteners. The first ones were made with cotton strips, but that fabric ripped under repeated use. A new invention, which hit the market in 1939, held the answer: nylon, a strong synthetic (human-made) plastic material that can be melted into shape. Nylon doesn't break down, rot or attract mold, and it holds its shape after being heat-treated. Hook-and-loop fasteners used nylon thread woven in loops, which were cut so they could be fastened and unfastened as many times as you like.

STRENGTH IN NUMBERS

Each individual hook is too weak to hold much on its own. But when you press many of them together, they hold powerfully.

The REAL DEAL

Do hook-and-loop fasteners do everything their natural inspiration does? Fortunately, no! Both the human-made fasteners and the natural burrs have amazing gripping power, thanks to small hooks that are great at grabbing things and hanging on like crazy. (Don't get your hook-and-loop fastener near a sweater.) But the similarity ends there. Real burrs come in a lot of shapes and sizes. Some, like hedge parsley, are nearly microscopic in size, while others, like the palm-size devil's claw, are large enough to make you shrink back in horror. In case that's not scary enough, some burrs, like jumping cholla, don't just hang on with hooks. They prick into their host like a mini-arrowhead. One of the most dreaded is puncture vine, which has sharp, thorny burrs that can puncture bike tires and hiking boots. Tread lightly.

FUN FACTS

● **Apollo astronauts** used hook-and-loop fasteners to secure food packets, pens, and other equipment they didn't want to **float away** in the absence of gravity.

● Securing garments using **hooks and loops** is nothing new. As early as the 1500s, people used metal hook-and-eye clasps to secure breeches and corsets. A **U-shaped clasp** was slipped into a **small metal loop.** The innovation of hook-and-loop fasteners was making them tiny and sticking them to strips of material.

● **A suit** made of hook-and-loop fasteners? Yes, it's a thing. You don a suit **covered with the little hooks** and launch yourself at a wall covered with little loops. Don't ask us how you get unstuck.

HOW TO HOOK ON

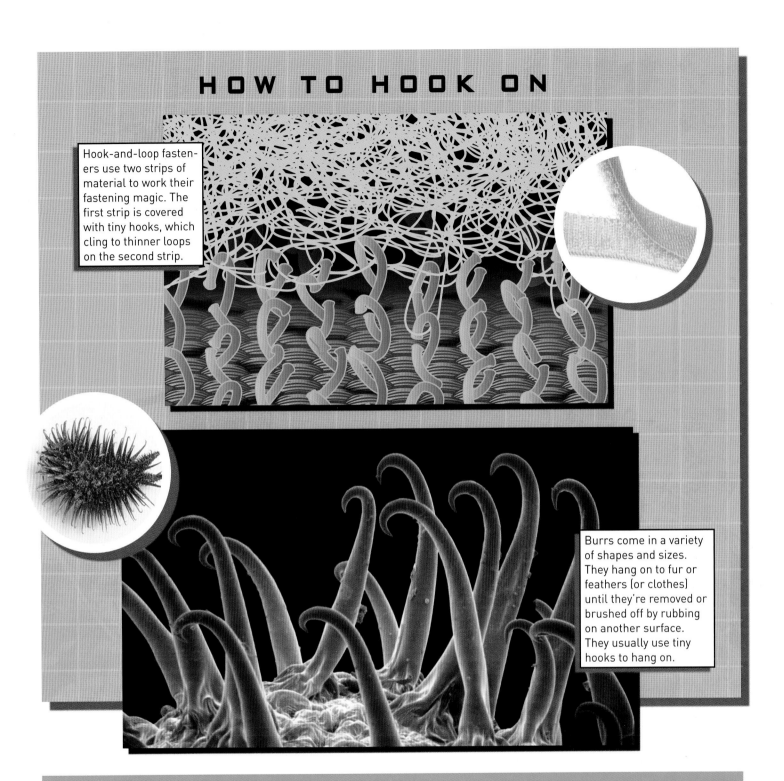

Hook-and-loop fasteners use two strips of material to work their fastening magic. The first strip is covered with tiny hooks, which cling to thinner loops on the second strip.

Burrs come in a variety of shapes and sizes. They hang on to fur or feathers (or clothes) until they're removed or brushed off by rubbing on another surface. They usually use tiny hooks to hang on.

STEEL SPIKES

German researchers made a hook-and-loop fastener out of steel. It looks like the regular fastener only a whole lot scarier. Instead of the pleasant-looking little plastic hooks, it has sharp spikes that snag something that looks like a jagged steel brush. But it has awesome strength and lasting power. A piece that is 10 feet square (1 sq m) holds 38.5 tons (35 t)—the weight of about five fully grown male African elephants. The material also can withstand heat of up to 1472°F (800°C).

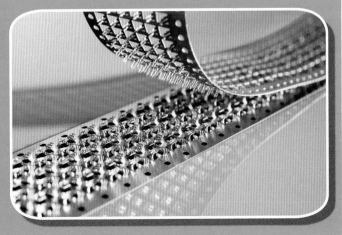

SOMETHING'S FISHY

How can **FISH** help us improve wind power?

The Inside Scoop

Fish have a lot to teach us about wind power. Yes, fish and wind. It sounds crazy—it's not like the wind blows in the depths of the ocean. But the way fish swim in a school helps them zip through the water more easily. And researchers think the secrets of fish schooling can help improve wind turbine farms. Read on to learn how—this is no fish tale.

Why do fish swim in a school **?**

Can fish schools really help wind turbine farms **?**

How much better are fishy wind farms **?**

JUST THE FACTS

Flying in a V helps geese fly efficiently.

A Little Help From Friends

Fish don't swim in schools just to be chummy or safe. They also do it to help each other swim. Inside a school, fish position themselves to get a boost from others' wakes, the paths they leave behind in the water. It's a lot like geese flying in a V-formation, only wigglier. (They're fish, after all.) Schooling helps the fish glide through the water more efficiently, using less energy to do the job.

Well-Schooled

In a typical wind turbine farm, large propeller-shaped turbines are spaced far apart. If they're too close, they mess up each other's wind currents, slowing the air and decreasing the energy they can make. But that means conventional wind farms take up a lot of land. The rotating blades on the tall turbines also pose a risk to birds and bats flying by. Using lessons learned from fish schools can change that. Researchers arranged smaller vertical wind turbines like a school of fish—closer together, so they could take advantage of each other's wakes. The result was more energy from shorter turbines—safer for birds and bats—and on less land.

Wind turbines need a lot of space.

WIND TURBINES: TWO WAYS

Check out how much space a **vertical wind turbine** uses compared to a propeller-shaped turbine.

Typical horizontal wind turbine
328 feet (100 m) tall, including 116-foot (35-m) blades on top of a 212-foot (64-m) tower. Spacing: 15 diameters* apart.

Typical vertical wind turbine
30 feet (9 m) tall. Spacing: 4 diameters* apart.

*1 diameter = the length of the wind turbine from blade edge to blade edge.

FUN FACT

A COUPLE OF U.S. STATES GENERATE A LOT OF **WIND POWER.** AT VARIOUS TIMES DURING ONE YEAR, WIND POWER PROVIDED **43 PERCENT** OF THE TOTAL ELECTRICITY IN TEXAS AND 66 PERCENT OF THE POWER IN COLORADO.

Fish get a lot of benefits from swimming in a school, including riding others' wakes to get through the water using less energy.

ENERGY MAXIMIZED

Placing vertical wind turbines close to each other—kind of like fish in a school—lets them use each other's wind currents to generate more energy.

FUN FACT

BUMBLEBEES INSPIRED A NEW TYPE OF SMALL WIND TURBINE, WHICH HAS LARGE WINGS THAT MOVE IN A **FIGURE EIGHT** PATTERN.

WANT TO KNOW MORE?

TELL ME MORE

HITCHING A RIDE

There's a lot going on when a fish wiggles through the water. As a fish swishes its tail from side to side, it creates a swirling wake, or vortex, behind it. A fish behind it and a bit to its side can catch a ride on those swirling currents—kind of like a surfer riding a wave. When all the fish position themselves in a school, the vortices reduce how much effort they use to swim. Now that's teamwork.

WIND WAKES

Vertical turbines have twirling blades that generate energy as the wind flows past them. When they're placed close together in a "school," one turbine's blades can take advantage of how another moves the air—much like the way a fish uses the wakes made by the ones swimming in front of it. The fish use the boost to move forward, but the turbines use it to make energy.

FUN FACTS

- With its **long coastlines, mountain ranges,** and **Great Plains,** the United States is a **windy** place. It produces more total wind energy than any other country—enough to power 18 million homes. But wind energy still supplies less than 5 percent of the total electricity generated in the United States.

- **Trees, mountains,** and **buildings** can slow wind down, so wind farms often work better near the coast and even offshore.

- **China** has the greatest wind farm capacity in the world—**more than twice** that of the United States—but the United States takes better advantage of wind resources.

- **Denmark,** which, as of 2015, meets 42 percent of its energy needs with wind power, is the world's leader. Wind energy is also the **third largest source** of electricity in Spain, which met 19 percent of its energy needs with wind in 2014.

- The bumps on a **humpback whale's** flippers inspired improvements in the blades of horizontal wind turbines. The bumps **increased the turbines' performance** by channeling air flow across the blades more effectively.

TEAMWORK

Fish save energy by riding the wakes of others while swimming in a school. They position themselves in a staggered formation to get a boost from their neighbors' wakes.

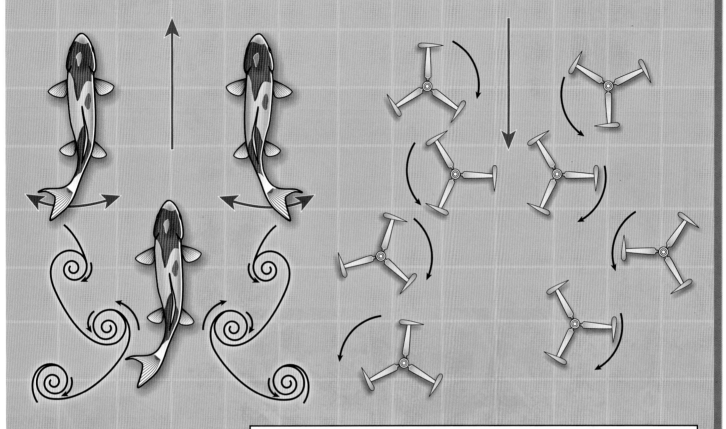

Vertical wind turbines maximize energy production by being close together so they can work with each other's air currents. Researchers at the California Institute of Technology found that two vertical turbines spinning in opposite directions produced the most power.

How Things Worked

Wind turbines seem like a new way to produce energy, but wind power has a long past. Wind filled the sails of ships going back to 5,000 B.C. The earliest windmills appeared in about the 10th century A.D. in Persia and were used by the Persians and then the Chinese to pump water and grind grain. When windmills made it from the Mediterranean to Northern Europe, the Dutch developed them further than others. Their windmills had separate floors for grinding grain, removing chaff, and storing grain. The "windsmith" and his family lived on the bottom floor of the mill. The windsmith had to manually turn the sails toward the wind by pushing a large lever at the back of the mill. Mills powered a lot of activities in Europe, including sawmills and factories that processed spices, cocoa, and paints and dyes. In the 1800s, steam engines replaced many of the European mills. But in the mid-1800s in the United States, small-scale wind turbines started dotting the American Midwest and West. They pumped water and generated electricity. In fact, over 120 years, more than six million small wind turbines were installed around the United States. In the late 1800s, large, individual electricity-generating wind turbines appeared in the United States and Europe, but the technology wasn't developed. A major shortage of gas and oil in the 1970s was a wake-up call to the U.S. government, which then supported research and development of wind power. In 1980, the first large wind farms were installed in California.

TRY THIS!

FLOWER POWER

MAKE SOMETHING INSPIRED BY NATURE

Can you make something inspired by nature if you don't know how the thing works? Of course not! Biomimicry takes two steps. First, you learn nature's secrets. Then, you use them in your own design. That's what you'll do now. You'll "reverse engineer" a flower—that is, take it apart to see how it works. Then you'll use your new expertise to design something amazing. You'll never look at a flower the same way again.

WHAT YOU NEED

TIME: 30 minutes to a couple of hours

1. 1 or 2 tulips or daisies (or one of each!)

2. Magnifying glass

3. Water in a glass

4. Straw or dropper

5. Paper towels

6. Reverse-engineering tools, like scissors, tweezers, toothpicks, etc.

7. Paper

8. Colored pencils, markers, or crayons

Optional: Building materials (modeling clay, tape, rubber bands, cardboard, aluminum foil, etc.)

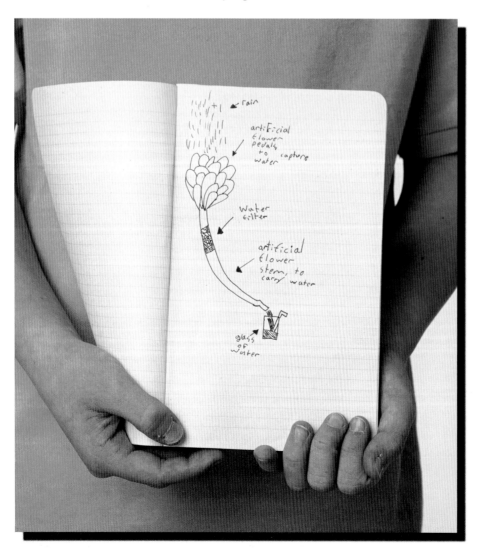

WHAT TO DO

NOTE: Scientists record their findings. As you reverse-engineer your flower, sketch what you see, make notes, marvel.

1. CHECK OUT HOW AWESOME your flower is. Really. Don't just say, "OK, it's a flower. I've seen a million of these things." Take a deeper look. How's it made? What's its shape? What colors are its parts? What do the parts feel like? Why?

2. EXPERIMENT WITH IT. Bend its parts. Which parts are more flexible? Dribble some water over different areas, and watch where the water goes. Figure out why. Hold it up to the light. Can you see through any part? Blow on the flower. How does the air move? Why?

3. NOW, DESTROY IT. Wait, wait, wait! What we mean here is: Slowly and carefully take it apart. Sketch the different parts. Sketch its insides. How does it all fit together?

4. PONDER. Why is the flower like this? What challenge in nature does the flower solve by being like this—having this shape, this structure, this strength or flexibility?

5. PONDER SOME MORE. How could you mimic the flower to design something new? Would you use its color or its shape? Does its strength or flexibility inspire you? Does the way it channels water give you any ideas? Or maybe you want to mimic the entire structure and how it's put together?

6. BRAINSTORM. Think of a new product you'd make based on the flower, or ways to improve an existing product. Would it look a lot like the flower, like a tulip-shaped cup? Or would it be totally different? A new waterproof coating for something, or a system for moving water around a building? Could you make a building with the strength and flexibility of a flower stem?

7. DESIGN. Sketch your flower-inspired innovation or invention. Amaze your family and friends.

8. IF YOU WANT (and can), build a model of your innovation or invention. Use whatever you can get your hands on. (No, not your family's things—unless you ask permission.)

9. TEST YOUR MODEL. Does it work like you thought it would? How would you tweak your design? Can any other plant—or animal—give you ideas for improvements?

WHAT TO EXPECT

IF YOU THOUGHT ABOUT ALL THE QUESTIONS ALONG THE WAY, YOU PROBABLY CAME UP WITH AN AMAZING DESIGN—MAYBE SOMETHING YOU WOULDN'T HAVE THOUGHT ABOUT BEFORE. IT'S NOT SURPRISING. NATURE HAS BEEN SOLVING CHALLENGES LONG BEFORE WE CAME ALONG. SCIENTISTS AND ENGINEERS GET GREAT IDEAS BY STUDYING PLANTS AND ANIMALS. THE COOL THING IS THAT TWO INVENTORS CAN LOOK AT THE SAME FLOWER AND COME UP WITH COMPLETELY DIFFERENT FLOWER-INSPIRED DESIGNS. HOW'D YOU DO?

WHAT'S GOING ON?

FLOWERS AREN'T JUST PRETTY. THEY'RE AMAZING. DAISIES PACK THEIR SEEDS TOGETHER IN A REALLY EFFICIENT WAY, AND THEIR STEMS HAVE SPECIAL FIBERS THAT REINFORCE THEIR STRENGTH. TULIPS CLOSE THEIR PETALS WHEN IT RAINS TO PROTECT THEIR POLLEN FROM GETTING WET. THESE FLOWERS CAN INSPIRE ENGINEERS AS MUCH AS ARTISTS.

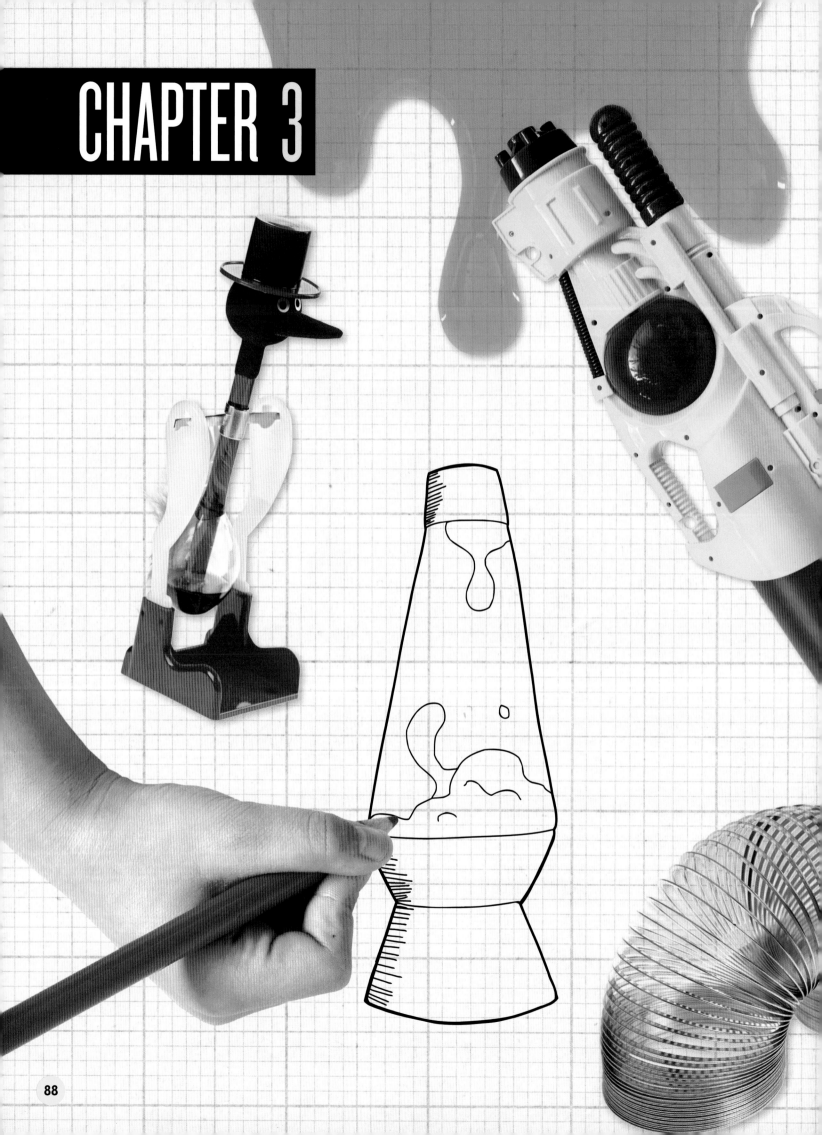

CHAPTER 3

HAVE A BALL!

Some inventions are WEIRD, WACKY, AND DOWNRIGHT CRAZY.

They amaze and amuse us. Sometimes they trick or surprise us. They make us wonder, Who in the world thought of that?
Answer: probably a scientist or engineer. Yep, some of the silliest inventions aren't just fun and games. They're science and engineering at their best. What?!

PARTY PRANKSTER

How do TRICK CANDLES light back up?

The Inside Scoop

The lights dim, the anticipation builds. It's your special day, and here comes your birthday cake. You take a deep breath and blow. Yes! All the candles are out. But, wait ... they flare up again. What?! You've just been pranked. Those aren't ordinary candles. They're trick candles. Read on—we'll illuminate how they work.

How do they light on their own **?**

How are they different from regular candles **?**

Will they ever go out **?**

JUST THE FACTS

Enlightened

Candles are a nifty package of portable light. As long as you light them where there's air (so, not in outer space), they have everything else they need to burn: fuel and a wick. The fuel is the candle wax itself. The wick, the string running down the middle and peeking out on top, heats up the wax and helps it burn. When you light a candle, the wax near the candle's flame melts into a liquid and gets sucked up the wick, which is super absorbent so it can hold a lot of liquid wax. The closer the wax gets to the flame, the hotter it gets. When it reaches the flame, it's so hot that it vaporizes, turning into a gas. That's what burns.

Fired Up

The secret to a trick candle is in the wick. It's not a normal candle wick. It contains magnesium powder, a metal that can ignite at extremely low temperatures. When you blow the flame out, the wick still has glowing embers, which are hot enough to ignite the magnesium. The magnesium sparks, igniting the wax vapor and relighting the wick. It's ready for your next (futile) attempt to blow it out.

HOT STUFF

Have you ever noticed that flames are a mix of colors? Each color is a different temperature. The brightest part of the flame is not the hottest! The exact temperatures vary depending on lots of things, like the type of candle wax, amount of oxygen present, and surrounding air temperature. **Here are some ballpark figures:**

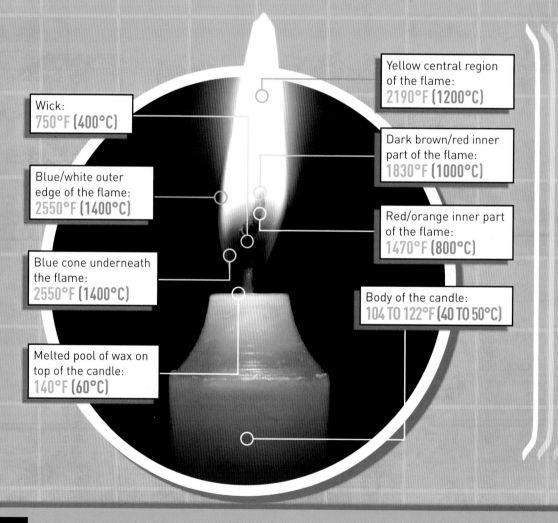

Wick:
750°F (400°C)

Yellow central region of the flame:
2190°F (1200°C)

Dark brown/red inner part of the flame:
1830°F (1000°C)

Blue/white outer edge of the flame:
2550°F (1400°C)

Red/orange inner part of the flame:
1470°F (800°C)

Blue cone underneath the flame:
2550°F (1400°C)

Body of the candle:
104 TO 122°F (40 TO 50°C)

Melted pool of wax on top of the candle:
140°F (60°C)

FUN FACT

A **QUARTER OF THE ENERGY** CREATED BY BURNING A CANDLE IS RELEASED **AS HEAT.**

DO-OVER

Trick candles are mostly like regular, old candles. They both need fuel (wax), wicks, and oxygen to burn. But there's one big, surprising, and often hilarious difference.

Trick candles light up right after you blow them out. Unlike regular candles, their wicks contain a little bit of powdered magnesium, which is ignited by the glowing embers of the wick.

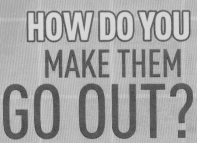

HOW DO YOU MAKE THEM GO OUT?

How do you **extinguish** a candle that you **can't blow out?** You have to cut off its air supply, so it can't get any oxygen. A good way to do that is to **run it under water.** Even after it's out, let it sit in your sink for an hour or two before throwing it in the trash. In fact, that's a good practice with regular candles, too. You know the rule: **Better safe than sorry.**

FUN FACT

YOU'D THINK THE INVENTOR OF TRICK CANDLES WOULD BE FAMOUS, BUT NO. WE'RE NOT SURE WHO CAME UP WITH THE IDEA. IT MAY HAVE BEEN A JAPANESE INVENTOR WHO IN 1983 PATENTED A **"SELF-IGNITED CANDLE."**

WANT TO KNOW MORE?

TELL ME MORE

WICKS AND WAXES

The wick and wax of a candle work together as a clever system. When you light the wick, heat travels quickly down to the wax body of the candle. Wax has a low melting point, so the top of the candle's wax body melts, turning into a hot liquid. The rest of the candle remains comfortable to touch because wax is a poor conductor of heat, meaning it does not transfer heat well from one point to another. The liquid wax at the top of the candle vaporizes, traveling up the wick and catching fire.

FUN FACTS

Other novelty candles include some that **burn with colored flames.** Adding different types of powdered metals into the wicks creates the different colors—similar to the colors of **fireworks.**

The wisp of smoke you sometimes see when a candle flickers is caused by **soot particles** that weren't burned up in the flame.

CANDLE CHEMISTRY
A trick candle takes advantage of chemistry to relight—and surprise you.

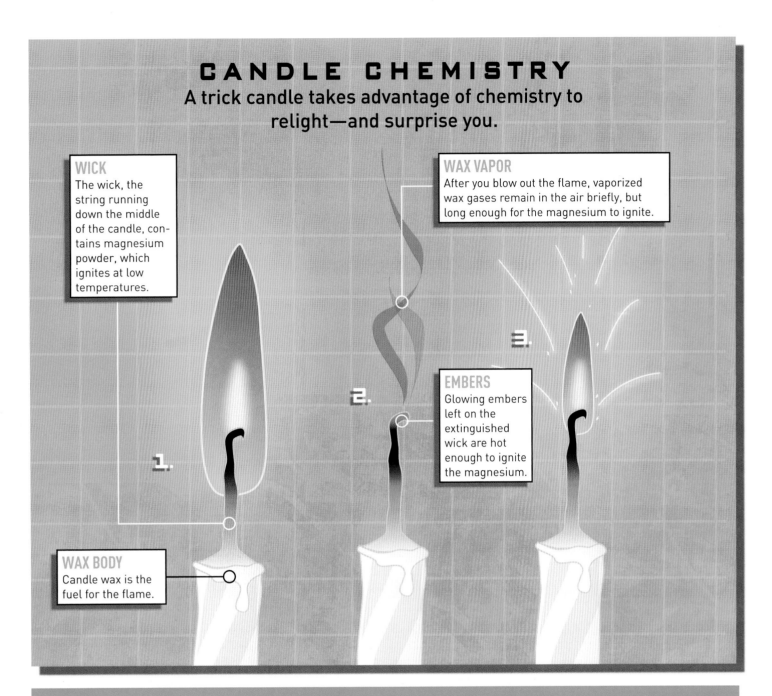

WICK
The wick, the string running down the middle of the candle, contains magnesium powder, which ignites at low temperatures.

WAX VAPOR
After you blow out the flame, vaporized wax gases remain in the air briefly, but long enough for the magnesium to ignite.

EMBERS
Glowing embers left on the extinguished wick are hot enough to ignite the magnesium.

WAX BODY
Candle wax is the fuel for the flame.

1.

2.

3.

Whoa ... SLOW DOWN!
A Closer Look at Fire

To appreciate how a candle burns, it's helpful to know some fire basics. It takes three things to make a fire: fuel, oxygen, and heat. Candles use liquefied wax for fuel, but there are lots of other fuels: wood, paper, charcoal, and so on. The fuel reacts with oxygen (from the air) in a chemical reaction, called combustion, which creates heat. The heat keeps the fire going. The heat must be strong enough to ignite the fuel. That's why flames, like from matches, are needed to get it going.

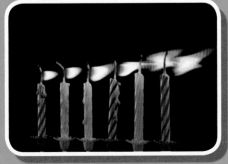
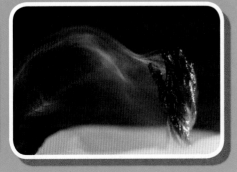

LIGHTNING UNDER GLASS

How does a PLASMA BALL shoot out light?

The Inside Scoop

If you've ever seen a plasma ball, you know it's an amazing display. It looks like a colorful lightning storm trapped inside a glass globe. A plasma ball lets you see electricity in action—and even play with it! How does it work? Read on to find out. You'll get a charge out of this.

What's inside the glass ?

How does it make the lightning bolts ?

Why does the lightning chase my finger ?

JUST THE FACTS

Light Show

Electric currents usually flow through wires, but that's not how they work in a plasma ball. A plasma ball is a simple apparatus: a clear glass globe with an electrode at its center. (An electrode is a device that conducts electricity.) The globe is filled with gases at a lower pressure than the outside air. When you turn the plasma ball on, electric current flows through the electrode and charges the gas, creating threads of glowing plasma like little lightning bolts.

How Touching

If you touch the plasma ball, a colorful lightning bolt streams from the electrode to your finger. (No, it doesn't hurt—not enough electricity gets through the glass.) So, what's the attraction? People can conduct electricity; it can flow through us. If you've ever gotten a shock after scuffing your feet on carpet, you already know that. In fact, you conduct electricity better than the glass and gas in the plasma stream do. So, when you touch the plasma ball, the "lightning bolt" heads your way. It wants to travel through you to the ground, but the glass blocks most of it.

TRY THIS!

If you have a fluorescent lightbulb, you can do a cool trick—with or without a plasma ball. If you have a plasma ball, turn it on and move the bulb near it. The bulb will light up! Although you can't see it, the electric current extends beyond the surface of the plasma ball's globe. When you bring the fluorescent bulb close to it, mercury atoms inside the fluorescent bulb get excited. They emit ultraviolet light, which hits phosphors (a light-emitting substance in the white coating inside the bulb) and make the bulb light up. Don't have a plasma ball? No worries. You can use a balloon as your source of electricity! Give an inflated balloon an electrical charge by rubbing it vigorously on your hair or a wool sweater. Then hold it near the bulb. You didn't know you were so bright, did you?

Z A P !

Nothing makes you feel more like a mad scientist than a plasma ball! You can actually see electric currents, like mini lightning bolts, streaming through the gas inside the glass globe. Even better, you can control where they go just by touching the globe.

The colors of the lightning bolts inside a plasma ball **DEPEND ON THE GASES** used inside it. Neon is red with pinkish orange ends, and argon is purple.

Normally, gases don't conduct electricity well. But if they get a big enough zap of electricity, that situation can change. To understand why, we need to see what happens to electrons, the charged particles that zip around atoms (the tiniest unit of matter). The high voltage from the electrode heats the gas quickly, giving the electrons in the gas more energy. They zoom around and smack into other electrons and gas atoms, freeing even more electrons. Atoms that gain or lose electrons are called ions. The ions blaze a trail through the gas, creating a plasma stream.

BRIGHT IDEA

But what makes the stream of plasma light up? All those energetic particles crashing into one another!

When the atoms and ions get smacked around, their electrons jump up a level in energy. Scientists say they're "excited." (Yes, that's the highly technical scientific term.) When the electrons relax and return to their normal level of activity, they let go of the extra energy. It comes out as a burst of light, known as a photon. It's like their little sigh when they relax. A really bright sigh.

LIGHT BURSTS

Atoms are really excited to give off light—literally.
Check out how they emit light photons.

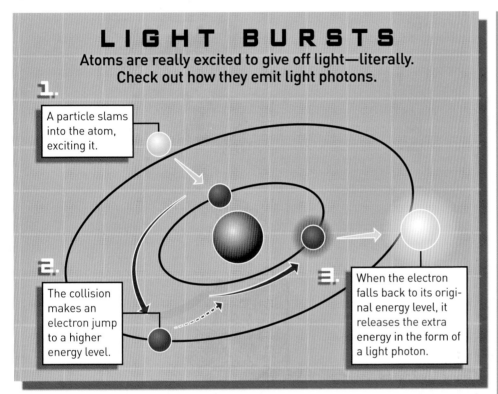

1. A particle slams into the atom, exciting it.

2. The collision makes an electron jump to a higher energy level.

3. When the electron falls back to its original energy level, it releases the extra energy in the form of a light photon.

INSIDE THE GLOBE

A plasma ball provides a rare opportunity to see electricity with your own two eyes.

ELECTRODE
Electric current passes through the electrode and oscillates, or moves back and forth, really fast. Electrons from the electrode move into the ionized gas.

PLASMA
Streams of plasma, which look like tiny lightning bolts, form when ions blaze a trail through the gases inside the globe. They glow brightly because their atoms give off bursts of light, called photons.

GASES
Inert gases, which don't react chemically to other things, fill the globe. Gases, like all matter, are made of atoms.

GLOBE
The glass of the globe doesn't conduct electricity well. The lightning bolt stays inside the globe, but a little current does move through. (You can't see that.)

TRANSFORMER
The power supply gets things started by sending electricity to the electrode inside the globe.

Whoa ... SLOW DOWN! A Closer Look at Plasma

What is plasma? It's the most common state of matter in the universe—more common than solids, liquids, or gases, the states of matter you already know and love. (In case you need a little refresher on those, think about water: It's a liquid, right? But when you freeze it, it becomes a solid: ice. When you boil it, it becomes a gas: water vapor or steam.) Plasma is a fourth state of matter. So why haven't you heard much about it? It's a bit unusual. It's formed when gas is ionized, meaning the gas atoms get so excited (like when they're heated up) that they lose some of their electrons. In regular gases, the electrons are bound to their atoms; they zip around the atoms. In plasma, the electrons are free to move around. You see plasmas when you look at the stars, the northern lights, or lightning. Plasma is also at work inside fluorescent lights, neon signs, and, as the name suggests, plasma televisions. Because electrons move around easily in plasmas, they're great at conducting electricity.

PROFILE: Lonnie Johnson
INVENTOR, ENGINEER, ENVIRONMENTALIST

Don't tell Lonnie Johnson that something can't be done. He'll prove you wrong.

Consider the Super Soaker, Lonnie's most famous invention. He tried for seven years to interest toy companies in his super-powered water squirter, but they all turned him away. (What?! Were they crazy?)

Lucky for us, Lonnie didn't give up. In 1989, he went to a toy fair and met someone from the Larami toy company. Lonnie told him that he had invented an awesome water squirter but couldn't find a company to make it.

> ## "NOT BAD FOR SOMETHING THAT STARTED OUT AS AN ACCIDENT."

The man felt bad for Lonnie. He told Lonnie to stop by Larami headquarters if he ever happened to be in Philadelphia.

Lonnie wasted no time. Two weeks later, he made a special trip to Philly. When it was time to meet the company's executives, he didn't say much. He opened a pink suitcase he brought and pulled out a water squirter he made from white PVC pipe, Plexiglas and a plastic bottle.

The company's president was skeptical. He asked if it worked.

Lonnie pumped it and pulled the trigger. Water blasted across the room and soaked the far wall.

The company's executives sat stunned. The president said only one thing: "Wow."

"They could see what I had seen in the water gun all along," Lonnie recalls.

Larami jumped at the chance to make the Super Soaker, and it became one of the top-selling toys of the 1990s. It was inducted into the National Toy Hall of Fame in 2015.

Not bad for something that started out as an accident.

NOT JUST FUN AND GAMES

As a child growing up in Mobile, Alabama, Lonnie was fascinated with how things worked—a trait his five siblings didn't always appreciate. He once tore up his sister's doll to see what made its eyes close. He built his own toys, miniature rockets and go-carts.

In high school, he decided to build a robot like the one on his favorite television show, *Lost in Space*. "Nobody told me that the other robots I was watching had people inside," he says. "But I didn't know any better than to try."

Using salvaged parts from an old jukebox, barbecue grill and tape recorder, he got to work. He powered the robot's arms using compressed air—a technology he later used in the Super Soaker. He entered his robot in a regional engineering fair.

It was 1968, during the civil rights movement, and the engineering fair was at the University of Alabama, where only five years earlier, the governor had tried to block the first African-American students from enrolling.

Lonnie was the first student from his all-black high school class to enter the fair. He won first prize.

Lonnie went to college and became an engineer. He worked on NASA's Galileo mission to Jupiter and Cassini mission to Saturn. He also helped develop the U.S. Air Force's stealth bomber. He spent his free time working on his own projects.

In 1982, Lonnie was working on an environmentally friendly heat pump that would use water instead of freon, a gas that hurts the ozone layer surrounding Earth's atmosphere. He was experimenting with the pump in his bathroom when a stream of water shot out. Cool! If only a water squirter could do that ...

He put the "hard science stuff" on hold and developed the Super Soaker. It made so much money, he started his own lab.

Once again, he's working on environmentally friendly inventions. He's figured out a new way to convert heat energy, like from the sun, directly into electricity. If his invention works as planned, the Johnson Thermoelectric Energy Converter, or JTEC ("jay-tek"), will be twice as efficient as existing technologies. It's potentially a "world-changing innovation," according to *Popular Mechanics* magazine.

Lonnie hopes his technology will replace energy from fossil fuels, like oil and coal, which harm the environment. He'll keep working at it until he succeeds. "Just like with the robot, I don't know any better than to try."

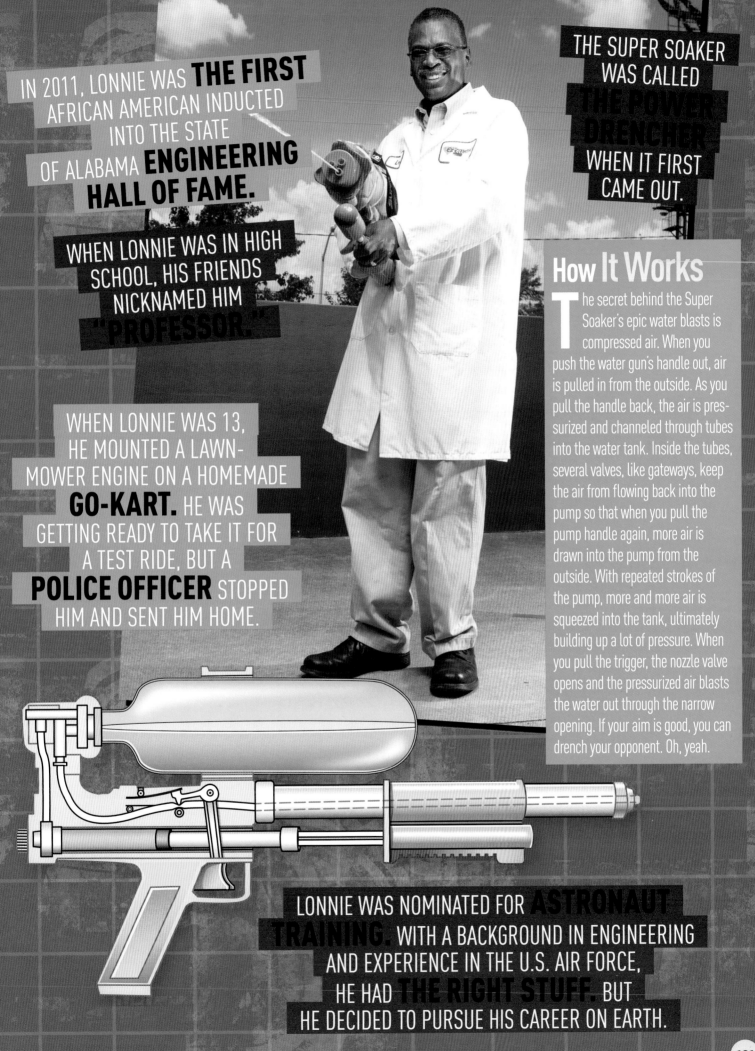

IN 2011, LONNIE WAS **THE FIRST** AFRICAN AMERICAN INDUCTED INTO THE STATE OF ALABAMA **ENGINEERING HALL OF FAME.**

THE SUPER SOAKER WAS CALLED **THE POWER DRENCHER** WHEN IT FIRST CAME OUT.

WHEN LONNIE WAS IN HIGH SCHOOL, HIS FRIENDS NICKNAMED HIM **"PROFESSOR."**

WHEN LONNIE WAS 13, HE MOUNTED A LAWN-MOWER ENGINE ON A HOMEMADE **GO-KART.** HE WAS GETTING READY TO TAKE IT FOR A TEST RIDE, BUT A **POLICE OFFICER** STOPPED HIM AND SENT HIM HOME.

How It Works

The secret behind the Super Soaker's epic water blasts is compressed air. When you push the water gun's handle out, air is pulled in from the outside. As you pull the handle back, the air is pressurized and channeled through tubes into the water tank. Inside the tubes, several valves, like gateways, keep the air from flowing back into the pump so that when you pull the pump handle again, more air is drawn into the pump from the outside. With repeated strokes of the pump, more and more air is squeezed into the tank, ultimately building up a lot of pressure. When you pull the trigger, the nozzle valve opens and the pressurized air blasts the water out through the narrow opening. If your aim is good, you can drench your opponent. Oh, yeah.

LONNIE WAS NOMINATED FOR **ASTRONAUT TRAINING.** WITH A BACKGROUND IN ENGINEERING AND EXPERIENCE IN THE U.S. AIR FORCE, HE HAD **THE RIGHT STUFF.** BUT HE DECIDED TO PURSUE HIS CAREER ON EARTH.

GET A GRIP

How do STICKY TOYS hang on walls?

The Inside Scoop

There's more than one way to stick. Wacky wall walkers and suction-cup balls are amazing ways to defy gravity—at least for a while. These stretchy, sticky toys adhere to vertical surfaces using two different scientific mechanisms. Stick around to find out more about them.

Why do wall walkers feel a little gooey?

Can a suction-cup ball stick to any surface?

Which one can defy gravity the longest?

JUST THE FACTS

An Attractive Style

To see these toys in action, you have to wind up and hurl them at a wall or other vertical surface. The wall walker will cling to the vertical surface and then start crawling down it. How fast it goes depends on the type of surface it's on and how clean it is.

That Sucks—Really

The suction-cup ball works differently. When you throw it hard against a wall, some of its suction cups hit hard enough to stick and support the weight of the entire ball for a while. How long? Like with the wall walker, it depends on several factors, especially how tightly it's adhered and how smooth and clean the surface is.

TRY THIS!

It's time to experiment. Get a wall walker and suction-cup ball. (You may have some already. They're popular party gifts.) Throw them against a variety of surfaces, including wood doors, metal appliances or filing cabinets, and tile walls. Time how long they stick to the surfaces. Which one is the winner? Does it always win, or does it depend on the surface?

SUPER SUCKERS

Animals don't have to be made of gooey plastic to have amazing sticking power. These **real, amazing sea creatures** set the bar high for suction power.

Northern clingfish
Its pelvic and pectoral fins form a disc on its belly, allowing it to grip slimy, wet, or rough surfaces with super strength.

Remora
This suckerfish has a modified dorsal fin that works like an oval, suckerlike organ to hold on to larger marine animals.

Giant squid
The suckers on its tentacles are ringed with razor-sharp "teeth" that can dig into the skin of its only predator, the sperm whale.

Octopus
Its eight tentacles are lined with hundreds of "suction cups" that change shape and sense food.

TELL ME MORE

TAKE THAT, GRAVITY

The wall walker gets its grip mainly from its material. It's made of polymers, plastic materials created of many small molecules that join to form a larger mass, with an additional sticky substance added. You can tell by playing with it that it's stretchy and slightly sticky. When you throw it against a surface, it has a weak attractive force that holds it to the surface for a while. But gravity eventually overcomes the attraction, pulling the wall walker down in its characteristic crawl.

SO PUSHY

The suction-cup ball defies gravity for a while because enough of its cups form an airtight seal with the wall surface it hits. The cup initially hits the surface with enough force to push out some of the air. When the cup regains some of its natural shape, the trapped air expands to fill the larger area inside the cup. The pressure of this air inside the cup is lower than the pressure of the outside air, which pushes the suction cup against the wall. This difference in pressure creates suction and allows the cup's edges to hold tight using friction.

GRAVITY-DEFYING

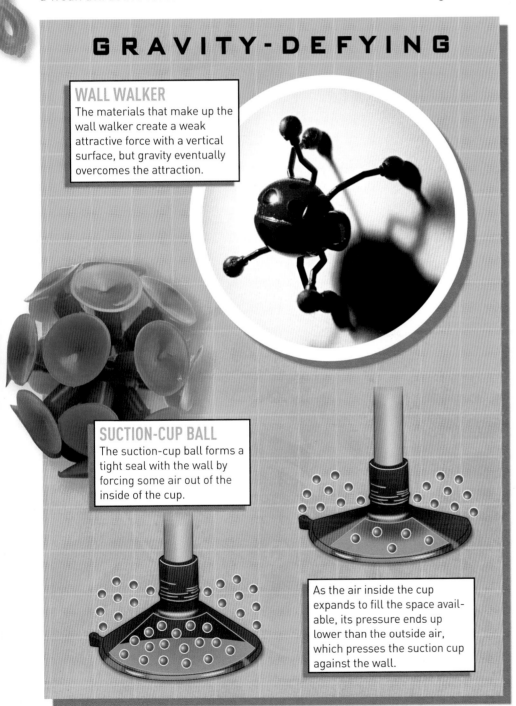

WALL WALKER
The materials that make up the wall walker create a weak attractive force with a vertical surface, but gravity eventually overcomes the attraction.

SUCTION-CUP BALL
The suction-cup ball forms a tight seal with the wall by forcing some air out of the inside of the cup.

As the air inside the cup expands to fill the space available, its pressure ends up lower than the outside air, which presses the suction cup against the wall.

FUN FACTS

● In one episode of *The Simpsons* cartoon, **an alien** hit a tree and crawled down it like a wall walker.

● Wall walkers were popular in **Japan** before being sold in the United States.

● **Wetting the edge** of a suction cup helps make a tight seal.

● **Bigger** suction cups suck more, so they stick better.

● To **remove** a suction cup, peel it up from the side instead of trying to pull it straight off. The peeling action will let air in.

PERPETUALLY PARCHED

How does a DRINKING BIRD keep going?

The Inside Scoop

It's a bizarre little creature: a little glass bird with a long fuzzy beak, startled eyes, a rather large rear, and a dapper top hat. And it's thirsty—constantly. It dips over to take a drink, straightens back up, and does it again—over and over and over. You can't help watching, mesmerized, wondering if it'll ever stop. Dive in to find out what's going on with the drinking bird.

Why does it keep going back for more ?

What's the liquid inside ?

Will it ever stop ?

JUST THE FACTS

THE BIRD'S BUILD

The drinking bird dips and stands as a liquid shifts in its body.

Thirsty Bird

The drinking bird seems to defy logic. After it sips water, it flips back upright, rocking back and forth. You wait for the rocking to die down, leaving the little guy upright. But it doesn't. The bird, which is made of two hollow glass bulbs connected by a glass tube, tips over and takes another drink. As long as water's available, the bird will continue to drink.

Tipping Point

If you suspect the bird's perpetual thirst has something to do with the red liquid inside, you're right. When the fluid moves up into the bird's head, it causes the bird to become top-heavy and dip forward. When that happens, fluid moves back into the abdomen, causing the bird to become bottom-heavy and tip back up. The movement of the fluid changes the bird's center of mass, the point where an object's mass seems to be concentrated. Gravity does the rest.

The bird's body is two glass bulbs connected by a tube.

The legs are attached at a pivot point, allowing the bird to dip down and stand back up.

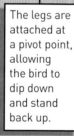

FUN FACT

THE **EARLIEST VERSION** OF A DRINKING BIRD DEVICE APPEARS TO HAVE BEEN **MADE IN CHINA** BETWEEN 1910 AND 1930.

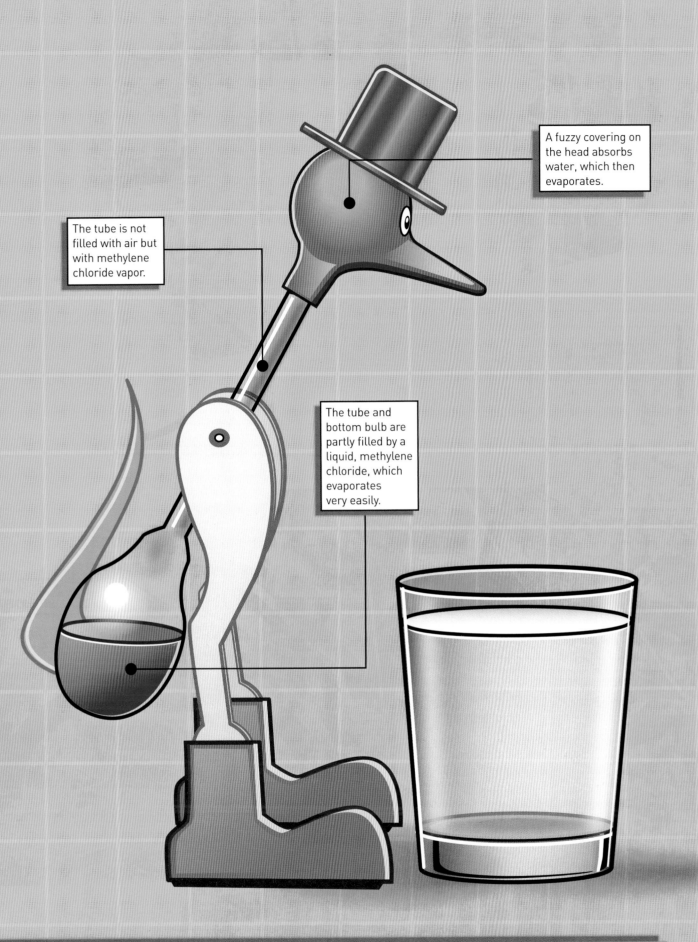

A fuzzy covering on the head absorbs water, which then evaporates.

The tube is not filled with air but with methylene chloride vapor.

The tube and bottom bulb are partly filled by a liquid, methylene chloride, which evaporates very easily.

FUN FACT

RUMOR HAS IT THAT **ALBERT EINSTEIN** AND HIS WIFE, **ELSA,** WERE FASCINATED BY A DRINKING BIRD DURING A VISIT TO SHANGHAI, CHINA, IN 1922.

KEEPING A COOL HEAD

It looks like magic, but it's actually solid science powering the drinking bird. The little device is a heat engine. It works because of temperature changes. When it dips its beak into the water, the fuzzy covering on its beak gets wet. As it rocks back and forth, water evaporates from its beak, causing the temperature in the bird's head to fall. The decrease in temperature also lowers the pressure inside the bird's head. The higher pressure in the bottom bulb pushes the liquid upward and into the bird's head. The bird keeps bobbing, with some help from gravity.

● Drinking bird toys are also known as **dippy birds** and **insatiable birdies.**

FUN FACTS

● Most drinking bird toys wear **top hats.** No one is sure why.

TRY THIS!
Here's an easy way to get a firsthand feel for the cooling effects of evaporation. Put a little rubbing alcohol on your skin. You'll feel a chill. Here's why: When the rubbing alcohol evaporates, changing from a liquid to a gas that floats away, it takes along some of the heat from your skin. It leaves the chill behind. That's what happens with the bird's head.

Myth vs. FACT

MYTH: The drinking bird is a perpetual motion machine—one that goes on and on all by itself.
FACT: A perpetual motion machine goes on indefinitely without any external source of energy. Creating a true perpetual motion machine is something people dream about. Could the drinking bird be it? Many people say so. It keeps dipping into its drink and never stops, as long as water's available. It bobs up and down—no batteries required! And there's no external source of power, right? Wrong! It gets its energy from the water evaporating off the bird's head, which creates the temperature change that drives the motion. So, the drinking bird is not a perpetual motion machine. Sorry.

SCIENCE AMBASSADOR
The drinking bird shows chemistry and physics as it sips its water.

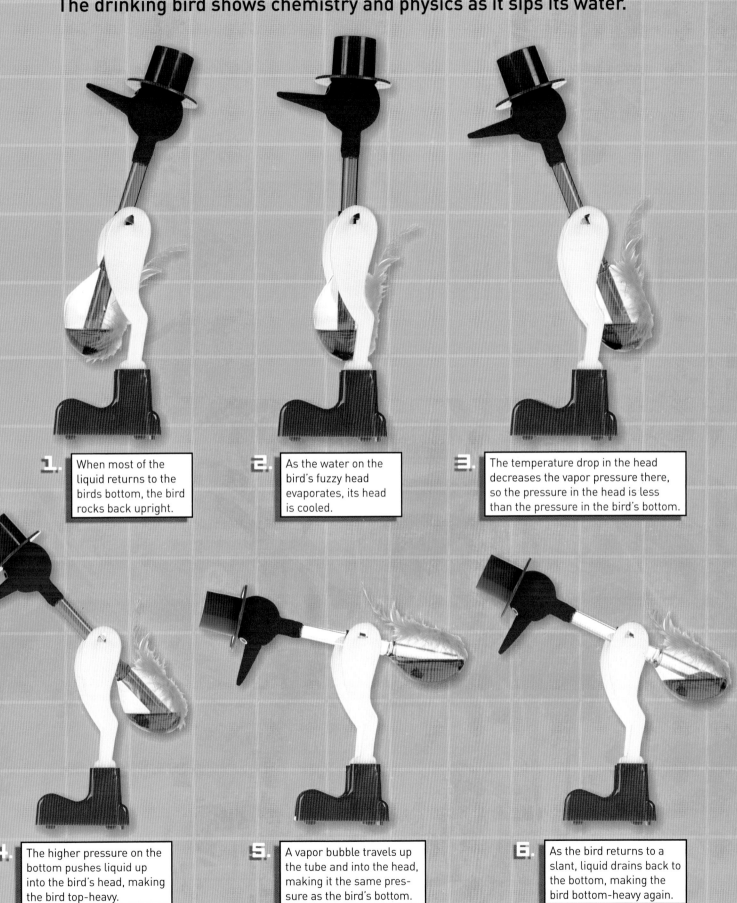

1. When most of the liquid returns to the birds bottom, the bird rocks back upright.

2. As the water on the bird's fuzzy head evaporates, its head is cooled.

3. The temperature drop in the head decreases the vapor pressure there, so the pressure in the head is less than the pressure in the bird's bottom.

4. The higher pressure on the bottom pushes liquid up into the bird's head, making the bird top-heavy.

5. A vapor bubble travels up the tube and into the head, making it the same pressure as the bird's bottom.

6. As the bird returns to a slant, liquid drains back to the bottom, making the bird bottom-heavy again.

IT'S GROOVY, BABY

How does a LIQUID MOTION LAMP make those blobs float around?

The Inside Scoop

OK, so this "lamp" doesn't light up your room. But a liquid motion lamp is still out of sight. Colorful blobs float around inside, twisting and contorting into different shapes. It's the ultimate way to hang loose. You want to be cool? Get one for your crash pad. If you're wondering what's the deal with these psychedelic lamps, hang tight, man. We'll illuminate you.

What's that goop inside?

How do the blobs move around?

Will it work if the light's off?

JUST THE FACTS

The Science of Goop

Two kinds of goop work their magic inside the lamp. One goop makes the blobs, and the other goop is what the blobs float around in. Sound simple? Hang on a minute. The two goops have to be almost the same density and immiscible. (Whoa. It just got complicated.) Actually, it's simpler than it sounds. Density is how much mass is in a certain amount of something. The "magic" happens when the two compounds are about the same goopiness (density). If one were more dense than the other, it would sit at the bottom the whole time. Not much fun to watch. "Immiscible" means they can't mix together or dissolve in each other. If they did, there'd be no blobs. Even less fun to watch.

Flick on the Switch

The light in the bottom of the lamp makes the blobs look cool. It also makes them float. Have you heard that heat rises? When a blob is close to the light at the bottom, it heats up and floats up the lamp. It gets to the top and cools down, so it sinks back to the bottom. While one blob's at the top, a lower one starts its journey. As if taking turns, they do this over and over and over.

TRY THIS!

Let's zero in on immiscibility. Remember, that impressive word just means things can't be mixed or blended together. If you try, it might look like you succeeded. But don't be fooled, you really didn't. The things will eventually separate back out again. A classic example of immiscible compounds is oil and water (or, for you salad lovers, oil and vinegar). Here's a way to see it yourself. Get a clear glass and pour a little cooking oil into it. Pour to a depth about the width of your thumb. Now pour about twice as much water into the same glass. If you have some food coloring, add a couple of drops, but don't stir! Watch what happens. After a few minutes, give it a good stir, then let it sit. Again, check it out. Can you dig it?

A liquid motion lamp is a simple device based on some out-of-sight science. Light heats up the blobs at the bottom, making them float to the top. They cool down and then sink back to the bottom. It's hypnotic to watch.

The two goopy compounds—both the blobs and the liquid surrounding them—are similar in density so they can move past each other. They're also immiscible, meaning they can't mix together.

A clear globe displays the show.

WHAT exactly is that goop in the lamps? It's **A SECRET.** The companies that make them won't tell.

A bulb in the base lights up the lamp and heats the blobs nearest the bottom.

It's really cool how heat makes the blobs float up. Heat changes their density! The less dense substance will float up, while the denser substance will sink. Heat works at the molecular level to change a substance's density. Molecules are the smallest units of a substance. These little particles are made of atoms bonded together. If we could see the molecules inside the goopy liquids, we'd see them moving around. If you heat them up, they move even more, bumping into and bouncing off everything nearby. They need more room to do that, so they spread apart. That makes the goop less dense. When the molecules chill out, they get closer together, so the goop gets more dense again. The density doesn't change much, so it's slow moving. *Mellow.*

NEATO!

A lava lamp creates its groovy display by using heat to move two goopy compounds around in a glass globe.

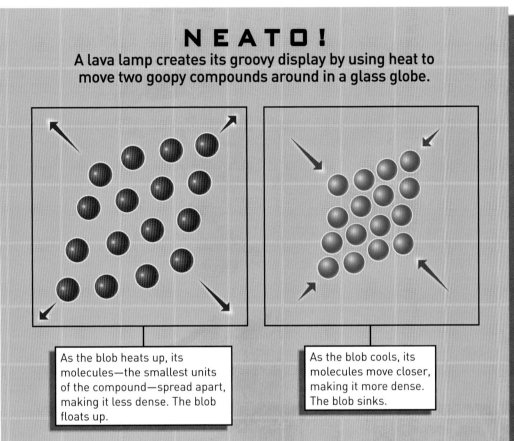

As the blob heats up, its molecules—the smallest units of the compound—spread apart, making it less dense. The blob floats up.

As the blob cools, its molecules move closer, making it more dense. The blob sinks.

FUN FACTS

● In 2002 the town of **Soap Lake, Washington**, decided to build a 60-foot (18-m)-tall liquid motion lamp to attract tourists to the small town. They're still figuring out how to do it.

Artist's concept

● The **rocket shape** of the original lamps was an appealing design in the 1960s, the early days of space travel.

How Things Worked

When the Lava Lite became popular in the 1960s, it worked like the lamps do today. End of history lesson. No, no, there's more to be said. But it's not about changes in the lamp's technology. It's about society. The lamps first came out at a time when youth in the United States were rebelling against the culture of the time. They protested war and pushed for civil rights and women's rights. They embraced creativity and different lifestyles. Some became hippies. The lamps, like peace symbols, became something of a symbol of this 1960s–'70s counterculture. And, it seems, that came as a surprise to the company that made the lamps. At one point in 1968, the company tried marketing an "executive" version of the lamp to lawyers. It came mounted on a polished walnut base along with a fancy pen in a holder. It doesn't get further from hippie culture than that!

TALES FROM THE LAB

GREAT GOO:
THE ACCIDENTAL INVENTION OF SILLY PUTTY

It was supposed to be a substitute for rubber, but the gooey invention turned out to be a big flop. Or a big bounce. Or a big stretch, or ... plain goofy. Whatever. The putty was supposed to replace rubber, but it just wouldn't do that.

In 1943, rubber was in short supply because of World War II. The United States needed rubber to make tires, boots, gas masks, and rafts. It usually got its natural rubber from Asian producers. But Japan, which at the time was fighting with the United States, had cut off the supply.

The rubber shortage was so bad that the U.S. government asked citizens to donate their spare tires, rain boots, and anything else made of rubber. It also asked U.S. companies to invent a synthetic rubber that could replace the real deal.

Scientists raced to make a rubberlike substance out of easy-to-get ingredients. One day,

> ## 66 THE PUTTY MAY NOT HAVE BEEN THE ANSWER TO AMERICA'S RUBBER SHORTAGE, BUT IT SURE WAS FUN. 99

James Wright, an engineer at General Electric in Connecticut, mixed boric acid and silicone oil in a test tube. The result was fascinating. It was a putty that bounced and stretched. It didn't get moldy, and it was hard to melt.

But you couldn't make tires or boots out of it.

James couldn't just throw away the goo, though. He thought it might be good for something; he just didn't know what. He sent samples to other scientists, but no one else could think of a use for it either.

FUN FACTOR
The putty may not have been the answer to

America's rubber shortage, but it sure was fun. Scientists shared it with friends and family, who had a blast stretching, molding, and bouncing it. They discovered it lifted copies of their favorite comics off newspapers. They took it to parties to amuse their friends.

In 1949, a glob of the goo made it to Ruth Fallgatter, who owned the Block Shop toy store in Connecticut. Advertising consultant Peter Hodgson convinced her to sell the bouncing putty in her catalog of toys. At two dollars, a tidy sum back then, it outsold everything except a 50-cent pack of crayons.

Peter, who was $12,000 in debt, saw an incredible opportunity. He borrowed $147 and bought more of the putty, as well as the rights to make it. He hired college students to divide it into small globs and pack it into red plastic eggs. He named the goo Silly Putty and started to sell it for a dollar.

In 1950, Peter went to a toy fair in New York. The toy makers didn't see the putty's potential, but Peter still convinced the department store Neiman-Marcus and Doubleday bookstores to stock it.

As it turned out, that was all it took. Well, that *and* a bit of good luck.

A writer for the *New Yorker* magazine was browsing at Doubleday and came across Silly Putty. The writer thought Silly Putty was amazing and wrote an article about it. "It not only bounces like a rubber ball, but stretches like taffy, flies into a thousand pieces when hit with a hammer & goes right back again."

Within three days, Peter received more than a quarter million orders for Silly Putty. At first, adults bought most of it. But by 1955, kids were molding and bouncing Silly Putty and, of course, using it to twist and stretch pictures of their favorite comic characters, lifted off newspapers.

Silly Putty became one of the fastest selling toys in U.S. history and was inducted into the National Toy Hall of Fame in 2001.

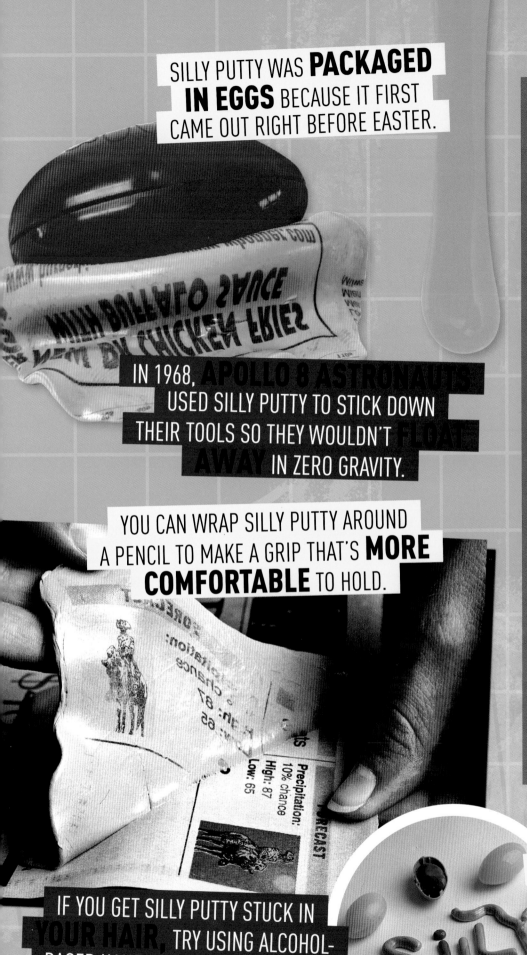

SILLY PUTTY WAS **PACKAGED IN EGGS** BECAUSE IT FIRST CAME OUT RIGHT BEFORE EASTER.

IN 1968, **APOLLO 8 ASTRONAUTS** USED SILLY PUTTY TO STICK DOWN THEIR TOOLS SO THEY WOULDN'T **FLOAT AWAY** IN ZERO GRAVITY.

YOU CAN WRAP SILLY PUTTY AROUND A PENCIL TO MAKE A GRIP THAT'S **MORE COMFORTABLE** TO HOLD.

IF YOU GET SILLY PUTTY STUCK IN **YOUR HAIR,** TRY USING ALCOHOL-BASED HAND SANITIZER ON IT. SILLY PUTTY DISSOLVES IN **ALCOHOL.**

Make It BETTER!

Silly Putty originally was beige, but now it's available in a whole rainbow of colors. You can even get glow-in-the-dark and metallic putty.

If those aren't enough options, putty comes in a wide range of stiffness. Silly Putty is on the firmer side. It's easier to mold and keeps its shape pretty well. But if you prefer something on the slimier side, there are plenty of gooey options.

Playing with putty isn't just fun. It can be good exercise. Special putties are sold in different levels of firmness to strengthen fingers, hands, wrists, and forearms. People recovering from injuries and surgery use those to get back in shape. Rock climbers and other athletes exercise with putty to get a stronger grip. Some people swear that squishing putty helps them relax.

Can you think of any better uses for putty? If you wanted to invent a new putty, would it be firm or slimy? How would you use it? What would it look like? Put on your thinking cap and try to invent the perfect goo.

MORE THAN 99 PERCENT OF THE WORLD'S NATURAL RUBBER COMES FROM **LATEX,** A MILKY WHITE LIQUID FOUND IN **RUBBER TREES.**

COOL COILS

How does a **SPRING** walk down a slope?

The Inside Scoop

It looks so simple—a compressed spring. What can you do with that? As it turns out, quite a lot. You can watch it bounce and swirl and make waves. But best of all, you can watch it walk down stairs or a slope. Read on to find out what makes a walking spring toy do its most amazing trick.

How does it keep going **?**

Why doesn't it fall over or roll away **?**

How steep of an incline can it handle **?**

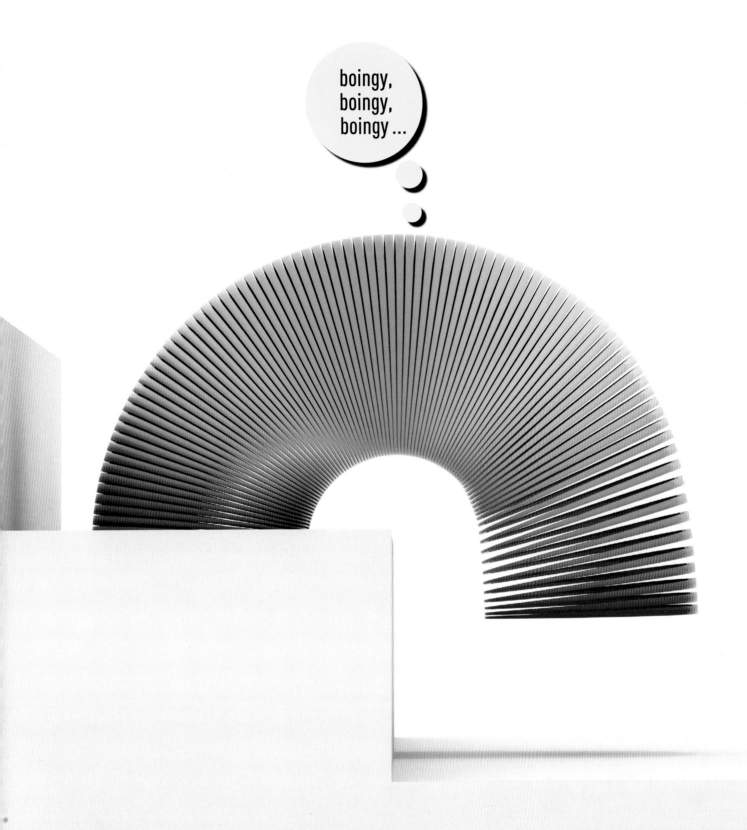

JUST THE FACTS

Taking a Walk

Walking isn't the only thing the spring does, but it's one of the most amazing tricks to watch. The spring stretches down a step, reforms itself, and then reaches for the next. It travels down the stairs, end over end, under its own momentum and the influence of gravity. All you have to do is get it started at the top.

The Slinky **WAS NOT** originally **INTENDED TO BE A TOY.** Richard James, a retired navy engineer, thought bouncy springs could cushion sensitive instruments on ships during rough seas. When the navy wasn't interested, Richard and his wife, Betty, decided in 1945 that the springs would make great toys. **BETTY THOUGHT UP THE NAME.**

MADE IN U.S.A.

TRY THIS!

You have to play around with one of these springs. Stack some books to make a shallow staircase or, better yet, find a board you can use for an inclined plane. Don't start too steep. Put the spring at the top and give it a start by pulling it over into an arch shape, then let it go. Experiment by angling the board more or less, or making the steps higher or lower.

TELL ME MORE

There's a lot of science in the spring's trip. Before it takes off, it has potential energy, energy that's stored up. When it gets under way, that potential energy is converted to kinetic energy, the energy of motion. As it moves from step to step, it transfers its energy along its length in a compression wave. In a compression wave, also called a longitudinal wave, the waves travel forward (or backward) along the spring, compressing and then expanding, like an inchworm.

OUT FOR A STROLL

Once you get it started, a walking spring toy heads down stairs under its own momentum—with some help from gravity, of course.

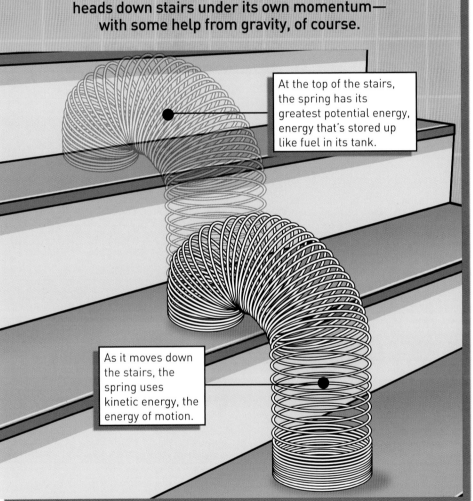

At the top of the stairs, the spring has its greatest potential energy, energy that's stored up like fuel in its tank.

As it moves down the stairs, the spring uses kinetic energy, the energy of motion.

FUN FACTS

● People have been trying to make the Slinky Pennsylvania's **official state toy** since 2001. It also was inducted into the **National Toy Hall of Fame** in 2000.

33 USA

Slinky Craze Begins 1945

1999

● **Making crafts** out of the metal or plastic springs is a thing. People have used the springs to make business card holders, ornaments, squirrel feeders, and flower-shaped garden decorations, **among other things.**

Peanut-filled squirrel feeder

● In 1999, the Slinky was featured on a **U.S. postage stamp.**

TRY THIS!

A GREEN THUMBS-UP!

MAKE AND GROW YOUR OWN FLORA FRIEND

It's fun! It's easy! It's almost like the Chia Pets you see on TV—the little terra-cotta figurines that grow plant "fur" or "hair." Millions have sprouted since the novelty gained popularity in the 1980s. Now you, too, have the chance to raise something kinda-sorta like one: your own little mud creature with bright green hair! This is one little buddy who'll grow on you.

WHAT YOU NEED

TIME: about 30 minutes

OPTIONAL: A grown-up's help (if you want to use hot glue)

1. Knee-high nylon stocking or a panty hose leg cut off at the knee (ask your mom before you raid her drawers)

2. A terra-cotta pot (small-to medium-size)

3. Potting soil

4. Grass seed

5. Rocks

6. Rubber bands

7. Scissors

8. Decorating stuff: googly eyes, craft foam, permanent paint markers, fabric, colorful pipe cleaners, whatever

9. Glue: either white glue or hot glue with a glue gun (Tip: Hot glue works faster, but check with an adult first.)

10. Spray bottle filled with water

1. STRETCH THE NYLON stocking (or panty hose leg) over the top of the terra-cotta pot, with the toe part pointed into the pot.

2. SPREAD A THIN LAYER of potting soil on top of the stocking. It only needs to be about as thick as the peanut butter in your favorite sandwich.

3. SPRINKLE THE GRASS SEEDS on top of the soil.

4. ADD MORE POTTING SOIL until you have enough to make a ball a little bigger than the top of your pot. Tie a knot in the open end of the stocking next to the ball.

5. LIFT THE STOCKING and pat the soil into a nice shape.

6. PLACE A COUPLE ROCKS in the pot to help support the ball.

7. TURN THE BALL OF SOIL OVER so the knot hangs down. Place it inside the pot, so that most of the ball is above the rim.

8. TO MAKE EARS OR ARMS for your creature, pull parts of the stocking and soil out and secure with rubber bands.

9. TO GIVE YOUR CREATURE some personality, glue on googly eyes and a mouth made from craft foam—or draw them on with permanent paint markers. Decorate the pot, too, if you want.

DECORATING TIP: If your soil ball is too wet, it may be easier to glue googly eyes and other decorations onto pipe cleaners or thumbtacks and stick them into the ball.

10. PLACE THE POT ON a sunny windowsill.

11. KEEP THE SOIL MOIST by spraying your creature with water. Don't let it dry out!

WHAT TO EXPECT

The grass seeds should sprout and grow a nice green head of "hair" (or "fur"?) for your creature. It usually takes about four to seven days, depending on the time of year and amount of sun and heat in your room. Uh-oh, did your buddy stay bald? Maybe the soil wasn't moist enough for the seeds to sprout. Or, if you used a really fancy nylon stocking with a tight weave, the sprouts may not have been able to push through the nylon. Try again—this time, snipping little holes on top of the nylon to help the sprouts out. Don't forget to water!

WHAT'S GOING ON?

You already know the basics: You planted seeds and made sure they had light and water. You might not have thought about it, but you also provided the warmth, air, and nutrients they also need to grow. (The nutrients came from that good potting soil you used.) That's all plants need.

THE FIRST CHIA PET, IN 1982, WAS A RAM. SINCE THEN, YOU COULD FILL A ZOO WITH THE VARIETY OF CHIA ANIMALS. THERE EVEN ARE CHIA DINOSAURS AND CHIA PEOPLE, INCLUDING A CHIA PRESIDENT OBAMA.

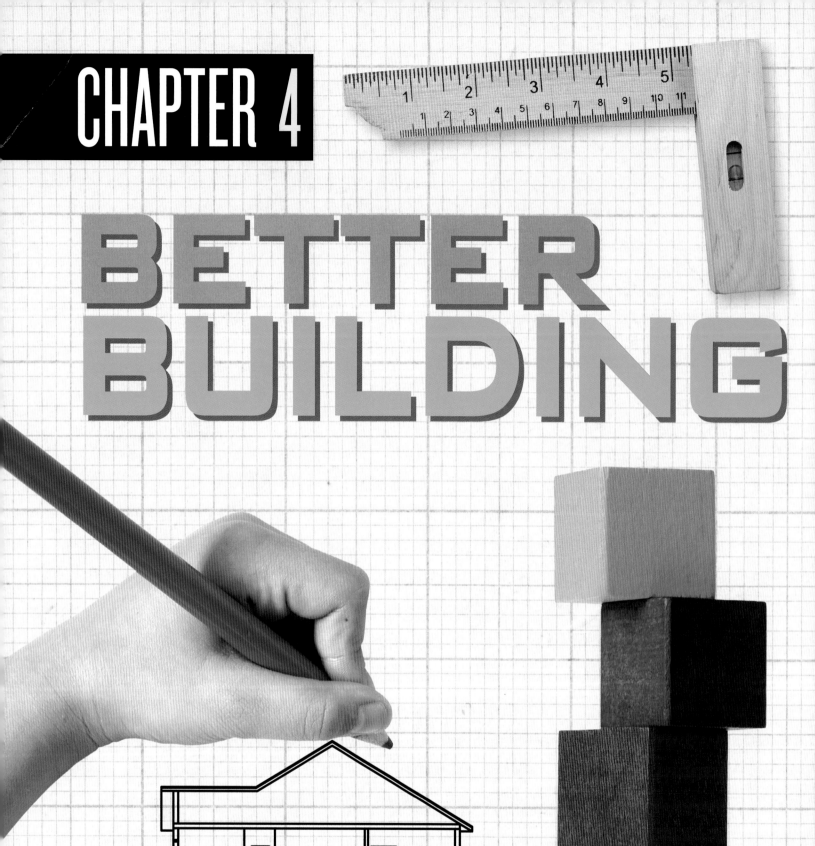

CHAPTER 4

BETTER BUILDING

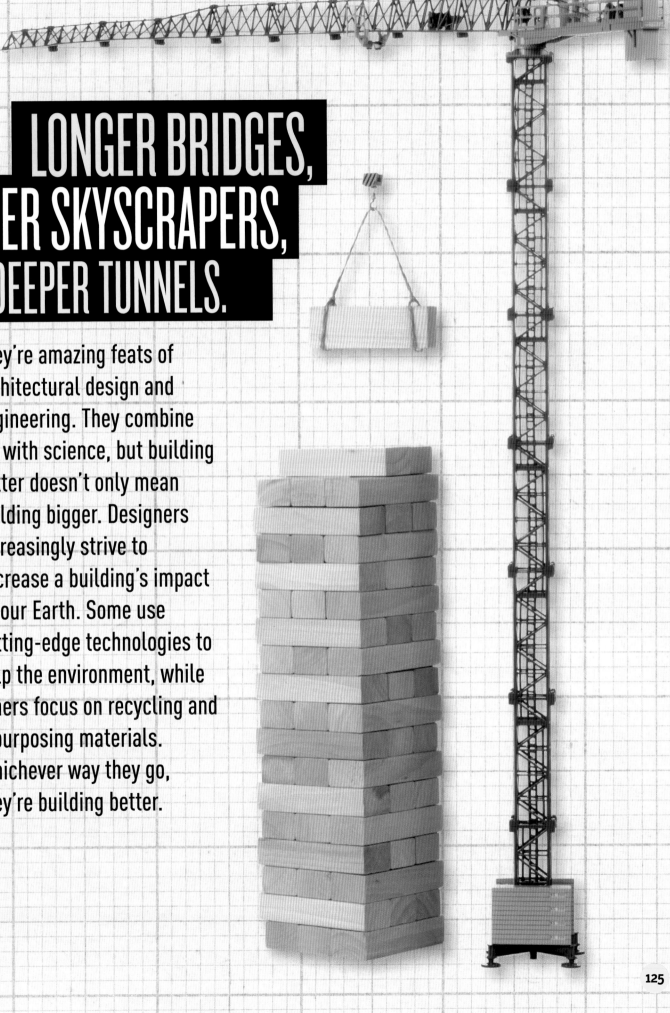

LONGER BRIDGES, TALLER SKYSCRAPERS, DEEPER TUNNELS.

They're amazing feats of architectural design and engineering. They combine art with science, but building better doesn't only mean building bigger. Designers increasingly strive to decrease a building's impact on our Earth. Some use cutting-edge technologies to help the environment, while others focus on recycling and repurposing materials. Whichever way they go, they're building better.

DON'T LOOK DOWN

How do SKYSCRAPERS rise to dizzying heights?

The Inside Scoop

The Burj Khalifa building in the United Arab Emirates soars half a mile (0.8 km) up into the clouds—a world record it's held since 2010. But the new Jeddah Tower in Saudi Arabia will shoot past it, probably to be dwarfed later by a mile-(1.6-km)-high super-skyscraper planned for construction in Japan. World records fall every time you blink now. Compare that to 1931, when the Empire State Building opened in New York City. It was the world's tallest building for four decades. Chicago's supertall Willis Tower (formerly, Sears Tower) held the title for nearly 25 years after it opened in 1974. Want to know how buildings rise to record-breaking heights? Get ready to learn the secrets of superhigh skyscrapers.

How can buildings get so tall?

Why don't they blow over in the wind?

How do they support all that weight?

127

JUST THE FACTS

Defying Gravity

Climbing high into the sky is not a simple feat. The higher a building goes, the more weight it has—and the more it feels the downward tug of gravity, the force that holds us to the Earth. Without a strong foundation, the building would collapse right into the ground. But that's not the only problem gravity presents for skyscrapers: Because they're so tall, buildings have a high center of gravity. If the building is straight and nothing pushes it to the side, its center of gravity should be smack dab over its foundation. But if something—like a really strong wind—pushes the top of the building, shifting its center of gravity to the side, that's a problem. Gravity pulls on it, creating a turning force that tries to tip the whole building over. To deal with these problems, skyscrapers have strong foundations extending deep into the ground so they can resist the downward and tipping forces. The foundations push back, keeping the building standing tall.

Building Blocks

A skyscraper's foundation isn't the only part keeping the building upright, of course. Each skyscraper is unique, but they generally have inner skeletons of vertical steel columns and horizontal girder beams working together to support the building and handle the forces of gravity. All parts channel the force of gravity downward. The horizontal girders transfer the force sideways to the walls and vertical columns, which support the skyscraper's weight. Unlike buildings of old, a modern skyscraper's outside covering, its "curtain wall," does not support the building's weight.

REACHING HIGH

The **100 tallest buildings** in the world all stand at least 300 meters (984 feet, or 60-plus floors) tall. That's about **three football fields** end to end. At that height, they're no longer mere skyscrapers. They're considered to be "supertall." Take a look at how the top ten stack up as of 2016.

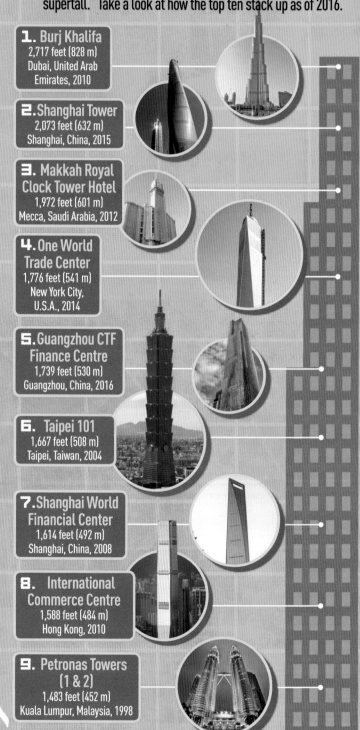

1. Burj Khalifa
2,717 feet (828 m)
Dubai, United Arab Emirates, 2010

2. Shanghai Tower
2,073 feet (632 m)
Shanghai, China, 2015

3. Makkah Royal Clock Tower Hotel
1,972 feet (601 m)
Mecca, Saudi Arabia, 2012

4. One World Trade Center
1,776 feet (541 m)
New York City, U.S.A., 2014

5. Guangzhou CTF Finance Centre
1,739 feet (530 m)
Guangzhou, China, 2016

6. Taipei 101
1,667 feet (508 m)
Taipei, Taiwan, 2004

7. Shanghai World Financial Center
1,614 feet (492 m)
Shanghai, China, 2008

8. International Commerce Centre
1,588 feet (484 m)
Hong Kong, 2010

9. Petronas Towers (1 & 2)
1,483 feet (452 m)
Kuala Lumpur, Malaysia, 1998

FUN FACT

MORE SKYSCRAPERS **ARE BUILT IN CHINA** THAN IN ANY OTHER COUNTRY. IN 2016 ALONE, 84 SKYSCRAPERS AT LEAST 656 FEET (200 METERS, OR ABOUT 40 TO 45 FLOORS) TALL WERE BUILT—**67 PERCENT OF THE WORLD'S TOTAL.**

The Empire State Building, completed in 1931, was crowned with an ornamental spire to make sure it'd be taller than the **CHRYSLER BUILDING.** But people claimed it was intended to be an anchor **FOR DIRIGIBLES,** the inflated airships flying the skies at the time.

GIANT CRANES hoist construction materials up to workers building skyscrapers. But how do they reach the top of the **WORLD'S TALLEST** buildings? To build the Burj Khalifa in Dubai, workers used cranes that could jack themselves up. The cranes grew along with the building.

STRENGTH IN NUMBERS

Each skyscraper's design is unique, but in each case, many parts must work together to support its immense height. Here are some common structural elements.

A steel skeleton of vertical columns and horizontal beams provides the main support for the skyscraper.

Reinforced concrete—concrete strengthened with steel rebar—forms a skeleton behind the outside walls.

The exterior, or "curtain walls," do not bear weight. Finished with panels of various cladding materials, such as glass, metal, stone, or concrete, the curtain wall—as its name suggests—hangs on the side.

At each floor level, horizontal beams, or girders, run between the vertical columns and provide additional strength, as well as support for floors.

Diagonal beams may provide extra support.

Vertical beams, called piles, are driven through the soil and, if possible, into bedrock deep below. If bedrock is closer to the surface, holes, called footings, are drilled or blasted in the bedrock to hold steel or reinforced concrete columns.

Vertical steel columns along the building's perimeter rise the entire height of the skyscraper to support its weight.

A platform of reinforced concrete sits on top of the columns or piles and provides support for the building.

FUN FACT — IF YOU TOOK THE 128 TALLEST SKYSCRAPERS COMPLETED IN 2016 AND **STACKED THEM ON TOP OF EACH OTHER,** THEY'D STAND ABOUT **18.8 MILES** (30.8 KM) TALL.

WANT TO KNOW MORE?

TELL ME MORE

PUSHED AND PULLED

Buildings must handle multiple forces. When a lot of weight is placed on a vertical column, it's squeezed, or compressed, between the weight and the ground below it. When a horizontal beam is weighed down in the middle, it experiences two forces. As it sags under the weight, the top of the beam is compressed, while the bottom is stretched, or subjected to tension. If the beam isn't strong enough to bear the load, the portion under tension will snap. For the tallest skyscrapers, wind is a more difficult challenge than the building's

weight. Wind blowing on the top of skyscrapers creates twisting forces, or torsion. Very slender buildings also can experience wind vortices, whirlwinds that can pull the buildings side to side. Even if the wind effects only produce a gentle swaying, that can be enough to make people inside very uncomfortable.

BEARING UP

How can a skyscraper deal with all these forces? Two ways: Engineers use superstrong building materials and design the skyscraper's shape to minimize these problems. Builders

reinforce concrete with steel bars, called rebar, to help it withstand both tension and compression. They brace the horizontal girders, which may be shaped like a capital "I" for extra strength, with additional steel supports. Strong foundations help the skyscraper resist the forces of gravity, wind, and earthquakes. Engineers also test skyscraper designs in wind tunnels to see how they react to winds in the area. The results of wind-tunnel testing can help engineers modify the building's design and position it on its property so that winds are less of a problem.

NOT GETTING RATTLED

Earthquakes pose a big challenge for buildings, especially supertall skyscrapers. If quakes only moved the ground up and down, they wouldn't be much of a problem. Skyscrapers are built to handle vertical forces. But earthquakes ripple through the ground, creating horizontal forces that shake buildings sideways. That sideways movement stresses the building's structure and, if bad enough, can damage it or make it collapse. Luckily, engineers and architects have come up with innovative ways to help supertall buildings absorb movement, so they don't get too rattled during earthquakes.

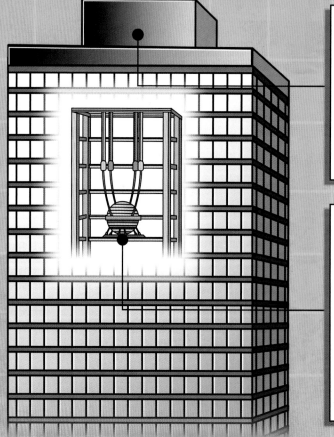

GENERAL DESIGN
The building's design is symmetrical—with each side mirroring the others—to distribute forces equally throughout the structure. Unusual shapes twist more during earthquakes.

DAMPER WEIGHTS
Giant, heavy weights, called tuned mass dampers, work like a pendulum to reduce the sway of a building. When the building tries to sway to one side, the damper counterbalances the movement by swinging to the other side.

● A sculptor in Missouri spent months sculpting a swan, only to have it crack and shatter. She wanted to make sure that never happened again. So she invented an **indestructible, fireproof,** and **nontoxic building material** in her basement.

● September 3 is **National Skyscraper Day.** Go hug a skyscraper.

● In 2015, the **total number of buildings** that were at least 200 meters (656 feet) tall reached 1,040—the first time it ever broke the 1,000 mark. The total was almost four times as many as in 2000, when only 265 buildings reached that height.

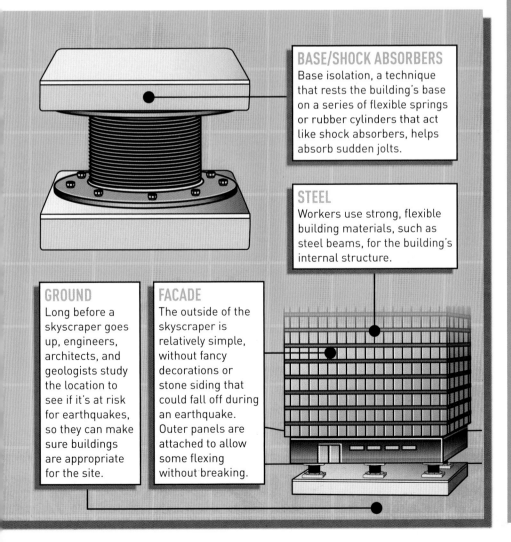

BASE/SHOCK ABSORBERS
Base isolation, a technique that rests the building's base on a series of flexible springs or rubber cylinders that act like shock absorbers, helps absorb sudden jolts.

STEEL
Workers use strong, flexible building materials, such as steel beams, for the building's internal structure.

GROUND
Long before a skyscraper goes up, engineers, architects, and geologists study the location to see if it's at risk for earthquakes, so they can make sure buildings are appropriate for the site.

FACADE
The outside of the skyscraper is relatively simple, without fancy decorations or stone siding that could fall off during an earthquake. Outer panels are attached to allow some flexing without breaking.

How Things Worked

For a century and a half, architects and engineers have been pushing buildings ever taller. But none of it would have been possible without one great invention in 1857: the safe passenger elevator. (Who'd want to hoof it up a hundred floors?) More central to the skyscraper's structure was the development of iron and then steel production in the late 1800s. Narrow metal beams could support more weight than the solid brick walls used in older buildings. Architects soon developed steel-frame construction methods, using a rigid steel skeleton to support the building's weight. Before that major innovation, the lower walls of brick buildings had to be built thicker and thicker to support more height. A 16-floor building built in 1891 in Chicago had walls six feet (1.8 m) thick at the base. So, with limited room to expand sideways, buildings rarely rose much higher than 10 floors. Metal beams not only held more weight, but they also took up only a fraction of the space that brick walls used. With this new technology, buildings rose higher through the early 1900s, resulting in such iconic structures as the 1,454-foot (443.2-m)-tall Empire State Building, completed in 1931. But even steel has its limits. As heights increased, steel columns needed to be placed closer together, leaving less room inside. In the mid-1960s, architects developed a new way of designing skyscrapers, called a tubular system. This involved bundling multiple steel frames together to create a single strong structure. This design let skyscrapers become supertall. But each time architects want to go taller, they must invent a new structural system. For Dubai's Burj Khalifa, architects used a hexagonal core that is buttressed, or supported, by three wings. More innovations are certain to follow. When it comes to skyscraper design, the sky's the limit—or maybe not.

TALES FROM THE LAB

SEEING IN A NEW LIGHT:
TRANSFORMING SHIPPING PALLETS INTO SHELTERS

Sometimes the answer to a problem is right in front of you and you don't even know it.

Just ask Suzan Wines and Azin Valy. The two New York architects were racking their brains, trying to think of a design to enter in a 1999 competition to come up with temporary housing for refugees returning to Kosovo in Europe.

"We wanted specifically to use a material that is wasted in the developed world," Azin says. "We were looking at bottles, plastic bottles—that was our instinct—but it didn't inspire us enough. So we were exploring other possibilities."

The team wanted a modular building material, one that people could assemble quickly in a variety of ways using only hand tools. They made sketch after sketch, but nothing worked—not bottles, not tires.

Time was running out. It was a Friday evening, and they needed a design by the next morning. Otherwise, they'd have to give up on the competition.

Suzan started walking home, the deadline and competition on her mind. She didn't see the wooden shipping pallet lying in the middle of the sidewalk until she tripped over it.

It was a eureka moment. The portable wooden platforms are used to support bundles of stuff shipped all over the world—including relief supplies of clothing, food, medicine, and building materials in refugee situations. After being unloaded, the pallets are often discarded, chopped up for firewood, or thrown on a trash heap. They're cheap, sturdy, and plentiful. Perfect for shelters.

Suzan hauled the pallet up to their studio. She knew Azin would understand the second she saw it.

MULTIFUNCTION
Suzan and Azin started sketching again. They figured out how to put pallets together to make flexible, easy-to-build houses. They made small models. Their ideas worked. But they still wanted to test them with full-size materials.

There was just one problem: Their studio was too small. There wasn't enough room to build a whole house.

They found a vacant lot in the Bronx, in New York City, and experimented with different ways to assemble a house, like using nails or straps. They asked a company to donate used, unwanted pallets—and were almost overwhelmed with the response.

"They were happy to get rid of the pallets," Azin says. "They kept dumping more and more pallets on the property."

But their work paid off. Azin and Suzan developed

> ## " THEY'RE CHEAP, STURDY, AND PLENTIFUL. PERFECT FOR SHELTERS. "

simple instructions that anyone could follow to build a flexible shelter out of pallets. Four or five people could build one with power tools in less than a week, or a few days longer with hand tools.

A 250-square-foot (23-sq-m) house—about the size of a single-car garage—takes 100 pallets to make and includes a sleeping loft, dining room, kitchen, bathing area, and living room—room enough for a family of four or five.

The shelters are easy to assemble, and they can transition from temporary shelters to permanent houses. The walls can gradually be insulated and finished with locally available materials, like sand, mud, or gravel. People can even add electrical wiring and plumbing.

If refugees move, the shelters can be recycled—or shipped to another place. "You can literally take the house, or take it in large sections, and transport it to your property," Suzan says.

It's flexible. It's creative. Just like Suzan and Azin.

Their playful approach shows up in clever designs that do multiple things—both in humanitarian and commercial projects.

Today, hundreds of people have built the pallet houses, and humanitarian organizations have adapted the plans to help house people in need.

AZIN AND SUZAN FIGURED THAT THE UNITED STATES PRODUCES IN A YEAR AND A HALF

SUZAN WINES AND AZIN VALY MET AS ARCHITECTURE STUDENTS AT THE **COOPER UNION,** A PRESTIGIOUS SCHOOL FOR ARCHITECTURE, ART, AND ENGINEERING LOCATED IN NEW YORK CITY.

AS A GIRL GROWING UP IN IRAN, AZIN VALY LOVED TO DRAW AND KNEW SHE WOULD BECOME A DESIGNER. SHE JUST COULDN'T DECIDE IF SHE WANTED TO DESIGN HOUSES, AIRPLANES, CLOTHES, TOYS, OR DOORKNOBS.

Make It BETTER!

Suzan and Azin designed shelters to help people who've had to leave their homes or whose houses have been damaged in a natural disaster. Pallet houses can be built fast, easily, and inexpensively from recycled materials—features that make them a great solution in those situations. And when they're not needed any longer, the materials can be recycled.

Other architects and designers took different approaches to the problem: Some proposed portable tents that open like umbrellas, while others designed houses made from cardboard tubes. Some of the designs were more rigid, including wire frames that could be filled with rocks or cement. On the other extreme were inflatable shelters made of fabric.

Now it's your turn. Grab a pencil and paper and think like an architect. How would you design a shelter that could be assembled quickly and easily but still be strong enough to last outside? If you've ever built a fort in your home out of sofa cushions and blankets, you already have some experience.

133

NEW FROM OLD

How can **RECYCLED** materials become innovative buildings?

The Inside Scoop

Have you heard the saying that one person's trash is another's treasure? When it comes to building, used and discarded materials can be gold. Not only do they cut building costs, but they do Earth a big favor, too. And don't think that using recycled stuff will make a building look shabby. Architects and home builders are using these materials in innovative and eye-catching designs. Step inside for a look at building with recycled materials.

Does a building made of junk look junky **?**

How does using recycled materials help **?**

What kind of things can be used as building materials **?**

The Three R's

To go green, follow the three R's: reduce, reuse, and recycle. Many homebuilders take that mantra to heart when they build or remodel homes. They try to use as many recycled products as possible, and there are lots of options. Recycled plastic bottles can be turned into many different products, including wall materials, fencing, and even carpet. Recycled steel can frame a house, and recycled windshields can be used for floor tile. Some builders even use straw bales and old tires to form the structure of walls, which they coat in earthen materials. But not all recycled materials are hidden. Reclaimed barn wood is valued for its beauty. Glass bottles have turned walls and windows, and even entire buildings into works of art.

Upcycling

If using tiny bits of recycled products is too small for your tastes, why not make a home out of an entire building or structure created for a different purpose? "Adaptive reuse" is taking an abandoned old building or property and using it in a new way. It's valued as a way to preserve historic buildings, conserve land, and reduce urban sprawl (when new homes extend cities and suburbs onto rural land). A lot of people have seen barns and farm buildings turned into houses or old warehouses made into chic apartments. But reusing can get even more crazy. Homes have been made in abandoned water towers, grain silos, and billboards. Some people have put a twist on adaptive reuse—they've made homes out of structures that never stayed in one place too long: shipping containers, railroad cars, and airplanes!

REDUCE

This natural home is all about reducing waste and a building's impact on the environment. Can you guess what it's made of?

Boston's **"BIG DIG"** project, which rerouted a highway that cut through the city into a tunnel, produced a massive amount of construction waste. Architects are working to reclaim some of the steel and concrete and to reassemble it in a dramatic, contemporary **NEW BUILDING.**

FUN FACT

INTERESTED IN **LIVING ON A TROPICAL ISLAND?** GRAB SOME PLASTIC BOTTLES. THAT'S WHAT A BRITISH ARTIST DID. HE CREATED AN ARTIFICIAL ISLAND BY FILLING NETS WITH EMPTY, DISCARDED PLASTIC BOTTLES AND THEN HE BUILT ON TOP OF THEM.

REUSE
This bright, modern house was designed to capture the beautiful views of Costa Rica. Can you guess what it's made of?

RECYCLE
This awesome green-and-brown Buddhist temple in Thailand is made of a common material found throughout the world. Can you guess what it is?

FUN FACT

A LUXURY HOME IN CALIFORNIA USES **RECLAIMED PARTS** FROM A **747 AIRPLANE,** WITH THE WINGS MAKING A DRAMATIC, CURVY ROOF. OTHER AIRPLANES HAVE BEEN USED WHOLE AS HOMES, HOTELS, AND CAFES.

WANT TO **KNOW MORE?**

TELL ME MORE

ADDING UP

A building uses energy before it's even built! Making and delivering building materials use resources and energy. Wood comes from trees that are chopped down and cut into planks. Stone is blasted from mountainsides, cut into slabs, and polished. Iron ore is mined from the ground and processed in a blast furnace to make steel. Then all the materials are sent to the building site on ships, freight trains, and trucks. The energy used to do all that adds up! It's called a building's "embodied energy." People used to think that a building's embodied energy was pretty small compared to the energy of using the finished building. But now they realize embodied energy can equal the energy costs of operating a building for many years.

CUTTING COSTS

Architects and home builders look for ways to reduce a building's embodied energy. Designing a building to be useful for a long time is one way. Recycling and reusing building materials is another—especially if the building materials come from nearby.

TIRING WORK

This "Earthship" home dramatically reduces the building's impact on the environment. Construction materials come from nearby and include recycled, waste, natural, and renewable materials. The home also uses renewable solar energy and collects and treats its own water.

Old tires are stacked to form walls, which are then coated with earthen materials.

SHIP SHAPE

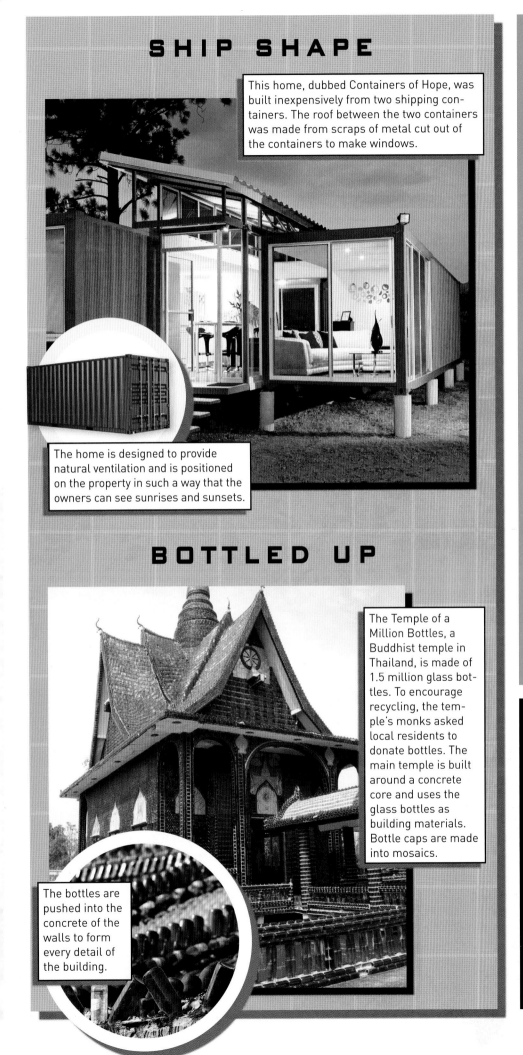

This home, dubbed Containers of Hope, was built inexpensively from two shipping containers. The roof between the two containers was made from scraps of metal cut out of the containers to make windows.

The home is designed to provide natural ventilation and is positioned on the property in such a way that the owners can see sunrises and sunsets.

BOTTLED UP

The Temple of a Million Bottles, a Buddhist temple in Thailand, is made of 1.5 million glass bottles. To encourage recycling, the temple's monks asked local residents to donate bottles. The main temple is built around a concrete core and uses the glass bottles as building materials. Bottle caps are made into mosaics.

The bottles are pushed into the concrete of the walls to form every detail of the building.

Myth vs. FACT

MYTH: Recycled materials are "green."

FACT: Recycling is a great way to help out the Earth, because you're not using new materials (and you often need less energy) to create new things. But recycled materials don't always make great building blocks. Take the case of shipping containers. They have a lot going for them: Many empty, unused shipping containers can be found on docks around the world, just taking up space, because it's too expensive to ship empty containers back to where they came from. Some innovative builders have taken advantage of this supply to create cool buildings. But sometimes preparing a shipping container to be a home can be hard on the environment. Some containers have special chemical coatings on the outside to withstand voyages across the ocean, or they may be sprayed inside with hazardous pesticides to keep nasty critters away. To become a home safe for people and pets, that stuff needs to be cleaned off or even replaced. And that can create a lot of hazardous waste. Is it worth the trade-off of not using new materials? That's up for debate.

TRY THIS!

If you like oatmeal, you'll love this idea. The next time you finish off a round carton of oatmeal, don't throw it away. Think of all the things you can do with it. Clean it out and go to work. Without any effort, you already have a drum. But think of all the possibilities: decorate the outside to make a cool storage container, stack a bunch together to make an artsy cubby. You're upcycling, recycling something in a fancy way. You're only limited by your imagination.

SUPER SPANS

How do BRIDGES carry loads across a span?

The Inside Scoop

If you've ever crossed a narrow stream by walking across a fallen log, it's easy to see how that bridge works. The stream's banks support the ends of the log, and the log is strong enough—you hope!—to support both its weight and yours. But what if you have to cross a wide river or canyon? There are different ways to span that distance, and they're all remarkable feats of engineering. Check out how bridges work.

What holds the bridge up ?

Why are bridges so many different shapes ?

Why do long bridges have towers ?

JUST THE FACTS

Getting Support

How do you support a heavy load when you can't put a foundation right under it? That's the problem that bridge builders must solve, and they do it in different ways. If the gap isn't too wide, the bridge may just lie across it, like a log over a stream. Those simple bridges, called beam bridges, are held up at each end by vertical supports called abutments. Sometimes the beams are reinforced by triangular supports, called trusses, on their sides or underneath. Another simple bridge is the classic arch bridge, which curves gracefully over a short span and is supported by large abutments on either end. Beam and arch bridges, the oldest kinds of bridges, can only stretch so far before they collapse under their own weight. If you want to cover a really long distance, you need a type of suspension bridge. Those impressive spans come in a couple of styles: The longest suspension bridges have huge cables strung over two tall towers and anchored on both ends. Thinner cables hang down from the main cables and hold the roadway. Medium spans are often covered by cable-stayed bridges, which anchor their cables directly to their towers. The cables, balanced on either side of the tall towers, fan out to hold the roadway. They're an impressive sight.

Going Long

The expertise of engineers has made it possible to design longer and longer bridges. But they can't do it alone. They need stronger and stronger materials to hold the spans. More durable concrete, reinforced with steel bars, now strengthens the tall towers of cable-stayed bridges, so they can push to lengths that only traditional suspension bridges used to cover. Spray-on coatings protect steel from corroding, and sensors monitor the condition of materials. All those innovations keep bridges strong over the long run.

 **MANY WAYS TO CROSS**

Engineers have designed many types of bridges to carry us over rivers, canyons, and other roadways.

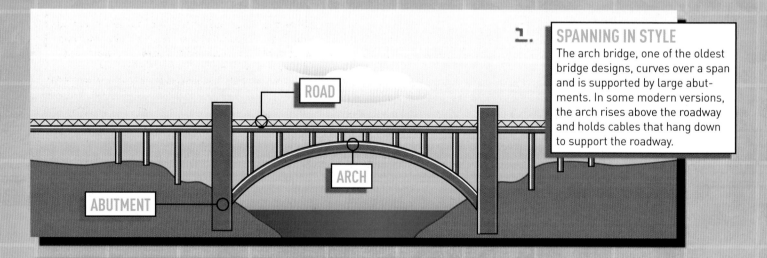

1.

ROAD

ARCH

ABUTMENT

SPANNING IN STYLE
The arch bridge, one of the oldest bridge designs, curves over a span and is supported by large abutments. In some modern versions, the arch rises above the roadway and holds cables that hang down to support the roadway.

FUN FACT — THE **BEIPANJIANG BRIDGE,** IN CHINA, IS THE **HIGHEST BRIDGE** IN THE WORLD. ITS ROADWAY IS 1,854 FEET (565 M) ABOVE A RIVER. DON'T LOOK DOWN.

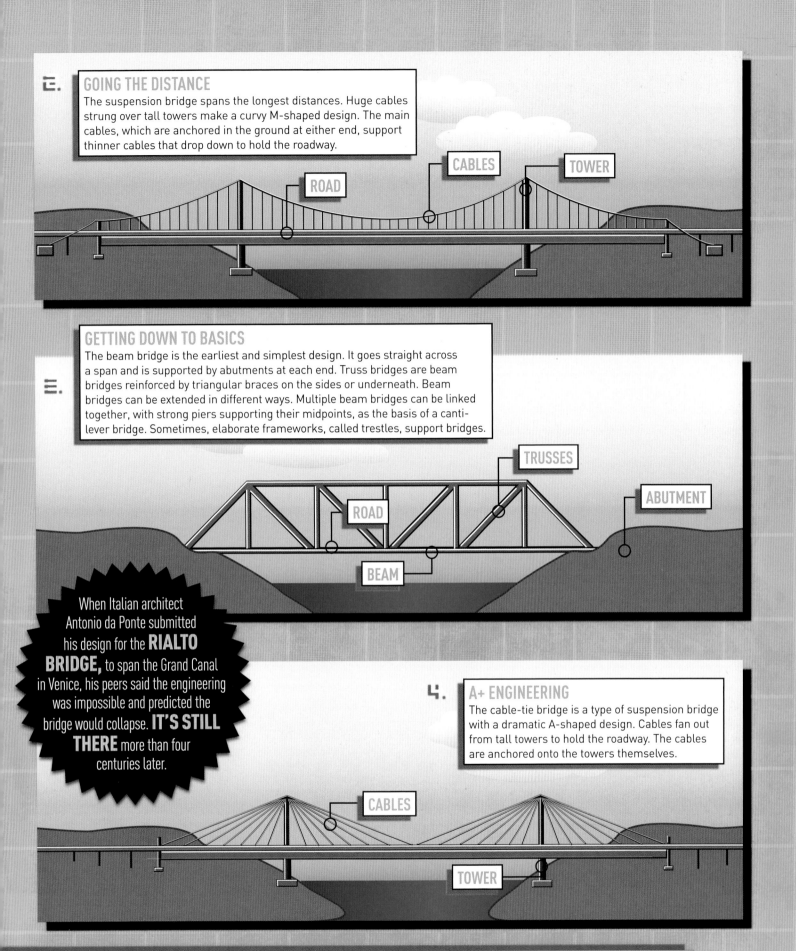

2.

GOING THE DISTANCE

The suspension bridge spans the longest distances. Huge cables strung over tall towers make a curvy M-shaped design. The main cables, which are anchored in the ground at either end, support thinner cables that drop down to hold the roadway.

ROAD

CABLES

TOWER

3.

GETTING DOWN TO BASICS

The beam bridge is the earliest and simplest design. It goes straight across a span and is supported by abutments at each end. Truss bridges are beam bridges reinforced by triangular braces on the sides or underneath. Beam bridges can be extended in different ways. Multiple beam bridges can be linked together, with strong piers supporting their midpoints, as the basis of a cantilever bridge. Sometimes, elaborate frameworks, called trestles, support bridges.

TRUSSES

ABUTMENT

ROAD

BEAM

When Italian architect Antonio da Ponte submitted his design for the **RIALTO BRIDGE,** to span the Grand Canal in Venice, his peers said the engineering was impossible and predicted the bridge would collapse. **IT'S STILL THERE** more than four centuries later.

4.

A+ ENGINEERING

The cable-tie bridge is a type of suspension bridge with a dramatic A-shaped design. Cables fan out from tall towers to hold the roadway. The cables are anchored onto the towers themselves.

CABLES

TOWER

FUN FACT — SAN FRANCISCO'S **GOLDEN GATE BRIDGE,** WHICH OPENED IN 1937, HAS BEEN CALLED ONE OF THE WONDERS OF THE MODERN WORLD. IT WAS THE LONGEST **SUSPENSION BRIDGE** IN THE WORLD UNTIL 1964 AND IS STILL THE MOST PHOTOGRAPHED.

WANT TO KNOW MORE?

BALANCING ACT

Bridges hold up tremendous weight. They're heavy structures on their own, plus they support the vehicles and people crossing them. Meanwhile, gravity, the force that holds us down on Earth, tugs at them from underneath. How do they bear it? They stand strong because they're engineered to balance two forces: compression (a squeezing force, like when you push on a spring) and tension (a pulling force, like when you stretch the spring out). The various bridge designs handle compression and tension forces differently, but they generally work to transfer the weight load onto the bridge's abutments or supports. The balancing act is important. It locks the bridge in place, so no external force, like the wind, can move it—which would be a huge problem.

ADDING A TWIST

Bridges, especially the superlong suspension spans, often contend with high winds because of where they're located. Winds can whip around the bridges' road decks, creating a twisting force called torsion. To handle that force, bridges are reinforced with trusses. They're also designed to make air flow more smoothly past them. Engineers test the bridges' aerodynamics in wind tunnels, just like they do with airplanes!

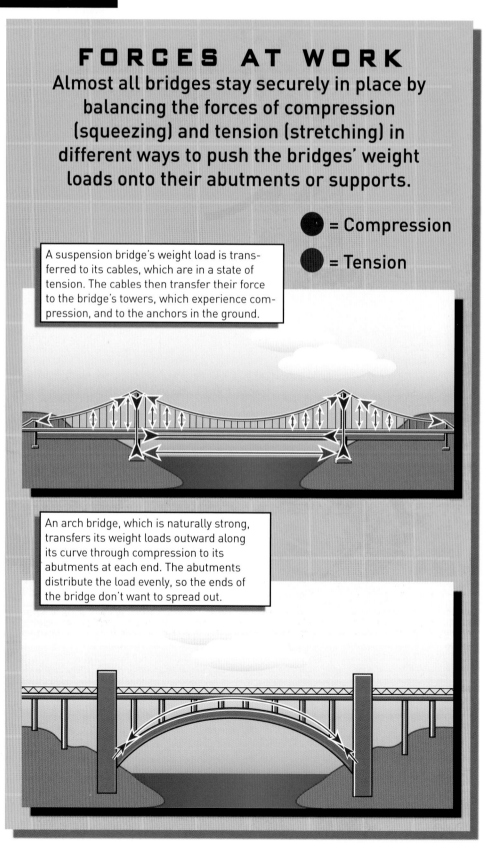

FORCES AT WORK

Almost all bridges stay securely in place by balancing the forces of compression (squeezing) and tension (stretching) in different ways to push the bridges' weight loads onto their abutments or supports.

● = Compression

● = Tension

A suspension bridge's weight load is transferred to its cables, which are in a state of tension. The cables then transfer their force to the bridge's towers, which experience compression, and to the anchors in the ground.

An arch bridge, which is naturally strong, transfers its weight loads outward along its curve through compression to its abutments at each end. The abutments distribute the load evenly, so the ends of the bridge don't want to spread out.

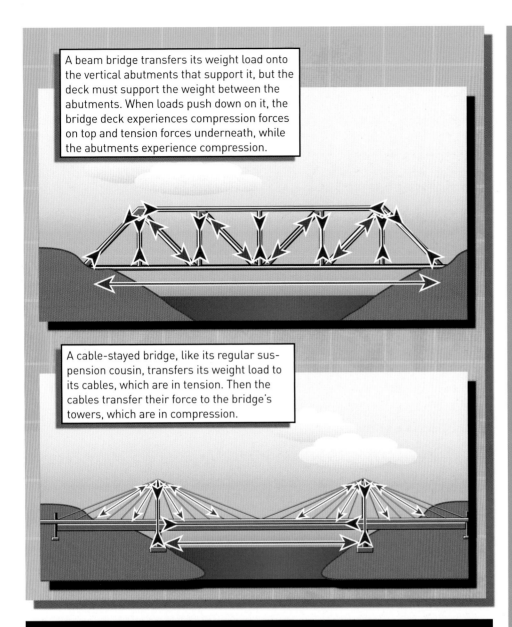

A beam bridge transfers its weight load onto the vertical abutments that support it, but the deck must support the weight between the abutments. When loads push down on it, the bridge deck experiences compression forces on top and tension forces underneath, while the abutments experience compression.

A cable-stayed bridge, like its regular suspension cousin, transfers its weight load to its cables, which are in tension. Then the cables transfer their force to the bridge's towers, which are in compression.

TRY THIS!

Here's a gooey, delicious way to learn about forces. Get a big marshmallow—the kind you toast over a campfire, not the little ones you put in hot chocolate—and a marker. Draw a grid of crossing lines, like a checkerboard pattern, all the way around your marshmallow. (And, no, you're not going to eat this one.) Now, experiment. Squeeze it together from the ends and see how the force of compression affects it. Stretch it out to see what tension does. Give it a good twist to see torsion in action. If you work up an appetite experimenting, get a clean marshmallow to eat. Toasting optional. Yum.

FUN FACTS

● The **oldest known bridge** in the world is the Caravan Bridge in Turkey. It was probably built around 850 B.C.

● In Burma, the U Bein Bridge, the longest bridge made **entirely of teak** wood, spans 4,000 feet (1,200 m) over a lake.

How Things Worked

As long as trees have fallen across streams, people have used bridges. The earliest human-made bridges probably followed the model of fallen trees: planks or branches lashed together to span a stream or small cavern. From that modest start, engineers made leaps forward over the ages. Arch bridges were one of the great achievements of the ancient Romans of the first and second centuries A.D. They fit wedge-shaped blocks of stone into an arch shape, which held together because of compression forces. Arch bridges remained the dominant design for centuries, but Europeans in the 12th century added an interesting innovation to the bridges: homes and shops. During a period when many great cities were walled, these inhabited bridges were a practical solution for a time when space for new homes was in short supply. The practice lasted nearly six centuries. Other than inhabited bridges, bridge engineering stagnated in Europe (and Asia) until the 1700s. Across the ocean, however, an early version of suspension bridges was invented in the 16th century. The Inca living in the Andes Mountains of South America built long rope bridges using massive cables of woven grass to span canyons, gorges, and rivers. In the early 1700s, Europeans began developing innovative designs for wooden bridges. But it wasn't until 1779 that a revolution in bridge building began. The first cast-iron bridge, an arch bridge named Iron Bridge, spanned the River Severn in Shropshire, England. Soon larger wrought-iron bridges were built with stronger truss designs, only to be replaced with stronger steel designs. In a short time, these bridges became the amazing spans we see today.

CUTTING EDGE

How can GREEN BUILDINGS help our planet?

The Inside Scoop

Think about a large office building on a hot summer's day. Air conditioners whir, elevators zoom up and down, and computers crank through all kinds of tasks (and cat videos). Can you imagine how much electricity the building uses? A lot! Residential and commercial buildings consume about 40 percent of the energy used in the U.S. every year. But many architects are working to change that. They're designing "green" buildings that don't hurt the environment—and may even help it. Read on to learn the secrets of making a building green—and, no, it doesn't involve paint!

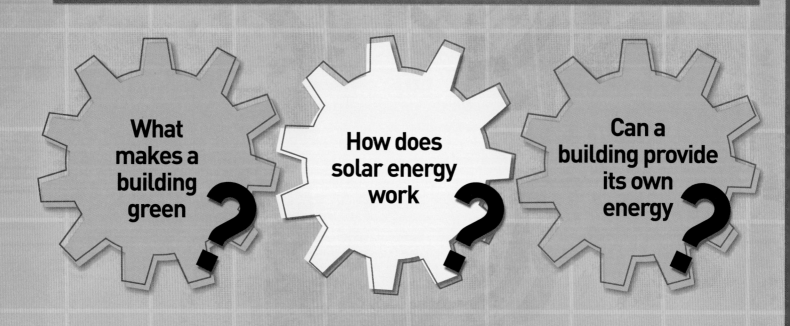

What makes a building green?

How does solar energy work?

Can a building provide its own energy?

JUST THE FACTS

Stepping Lightly

When you think of "green" buildings, what comes to mind? Solar panels? Plants growing on roofs? (Seriously green!) Those are two great ways to make a building more environmentally friendly. Solar panels capture the sun's energy—a clean, renewable source of power. Architects also can make a building energy efficient, so it needs less energy in the first place. Good insulation (including plants!) keeps heat from seeping through walls and roofs, and building materials with high thermal mass help keep temperatures steady. A building's layout can position rooms and windows to stay cool in the summer and warm in the winter. Green construction materials— recycled, reclaimed, or rapidly replaced materials (like fast-growing bamboo)—can help the building's environmental footprint, too. When architects minimize the negative impact that buildings have on the environment, they're practicing "sustainable architecture." Sustainability means doing things in a way that's not going to be harmful over the long run.

The sun's path is lower on the horizon during winter months.

Sun: Two Ways

If you've ever gotten into a hot car on a summer's day, you know about passive solar heating. Sunlight beamed through the car's windows, trapping heat inside—a lot of it! Maybe you put up a shade behind the windshield to limit the amount of sunlight that gets in. Architects can use passive techniques like this to help heat a green building. They design it to allow a lot of sunlight to stream in through windows during the winter and to limit the sunlight during the summer. The way a building is positioned on its property is really important, so it can catch maximum sun rays in the winter but less light in the summer, when the sun is higher overhead. Architects often add large overhangs or movable shades over windows to block some of the summer sun. When architects put solar panels on a building, they're using an active system—a system that uses mechanical and electrical equipment to capture the sunlight and turn it into heat or electricity. Active and passive systems both use solar energy.

Windows can be used for passive solar heating. The building is positioned on its property and designed so a lot of sunlight streams in during the winter but less streams in during the summer. Large overhangs and shades help control how much sun comes in.

FUN FACT

THE WORLD'S FIRST **SOLAR BIKE PATH** IS BEING TESTED IN THE NETHERLANDS. THE 110-YARD (100-M) STRETCH **GENERATES ENOUGH ENERGY** TO SUPPLY ONE PERSON WITH ELECTRICITY FOR A YEAR.

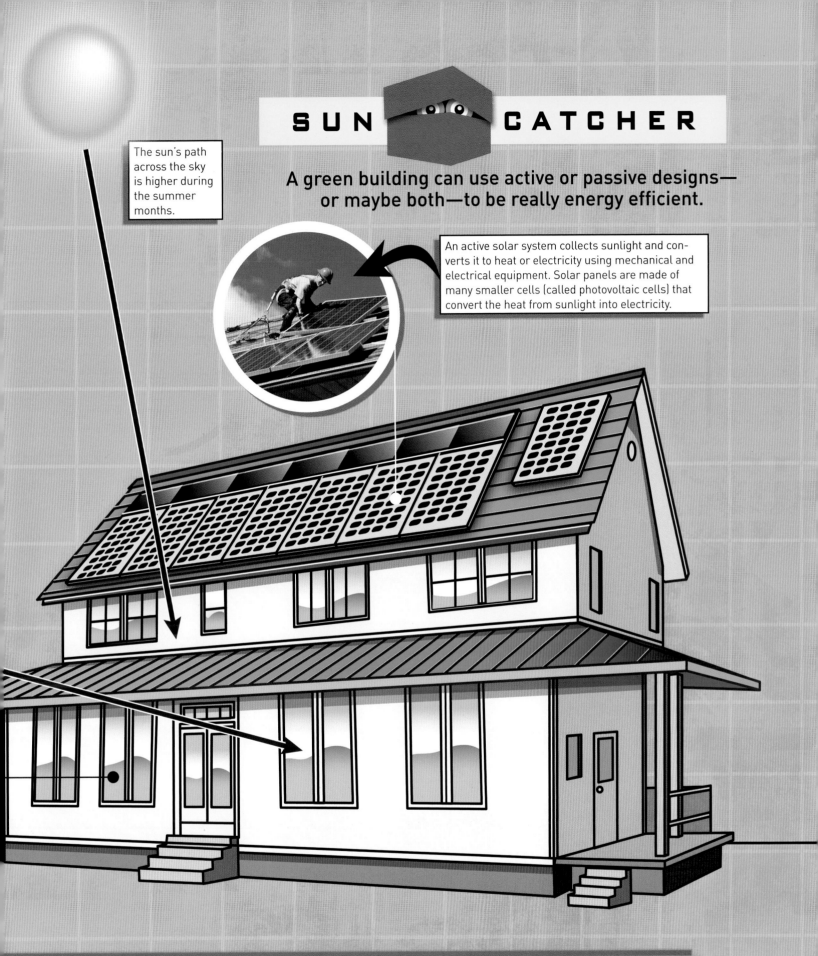

S U N ◆ C A T C H E R

A green building can use active or passive designs—or maybe both—to be really energy efficient.

The sun's path across the sky is higher during the summer months.

An active solar system collects sunlight and converts it to heat or electricity using mechanical and electrical equipment. Solar panels are made of many smaller cells (called photovoltaic cells) that convert the heat from sunlight into electricity.

FUN FACT

SMOG-EATING BUILDINGS? YEP. MEXICO CITY'S MANUEL GEA GONZÁLEZ HOSPITAL BUILT A SPECIAL HONEYCOMB-SHAPED FACADE THAT BREAKS DOWN **AIR POLLUTANTS** WITH ULTRAVIOLET LIGHT.

WANT TO
KNOW
MORE?

GIVING BACK

Architects can design a building so it doesn't harm nature at all—and maybe even helps it. A "net-zero" building creates as much energy in a year as it uses. Its own renewable energy sources—like solar, wind, and hydropower—cover all of its energy needs. Some buildings even make *more* energy than they use in a year! The way to make this work is to start with a really energy-efficient building, so architects use a lot of passive techniques to limit the amount of energy the building needs. They make the building airtight, insulate everywhere, use energy-saving systems to provide fresh air, and install high-performance doors and windows. Low energy needs are easier to meet.

WATER CYCLE
Some buildings even take care of all their water needs. They collect rainwater in a big tank, called a cistern, and may add well water, too. They treat the water on site so it's clean enough to drink, and they catch the water that goes down the drains (called gray water) to water plants or flush toilets. Some buildings use natural water filters, like sand, wetlands, and marshes, to help clean the water. Others use a special system that makes water clean enough to drink. Nothing goes to waste.

Whoa ... SLOW DOWN!
A Closer Look at Catching Heat

Taking advantage of thermal mass is a great way to make buildings more energy efficient. But what exactly is thermal mass? It's a material's ability to absorb, store, and release heat. ("Thermal" refers to heat.) It's kind of like a battery. When temperatures rise during the day, some materials can absorb a lot of that heat and hold on to it. When surrounding temperatures cool, they release the heat, warming the building inside. (Heat likes to travel to anything that's cooler.) Dense materials, like stone, brick, ceramic tiles, and concrete, have high thermal mass. But lightweight materials, like wood, have low thermal mass. Thermal mass is really helpful where there are big differences between day and night outside temperatures. It can help even out a building's temperature inside. But to work well, thermal mass needs to be used with other good passive design techniques, like insulation, shading, and positioning windows to catch sun in the winter but not the summer. If you don't do it right, it can make temperature differences worse!

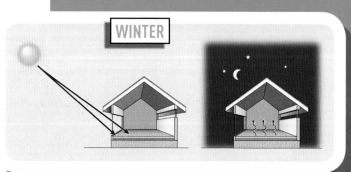

WINTER

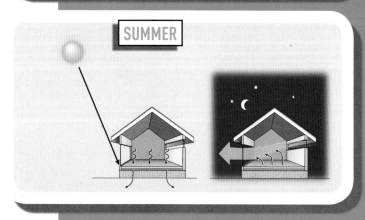

SUMMER

GOING GREEN

A net-zero building creates as much energy in a year as it uses. It combines active systems, like solar panels, with well-designed passive systems to make a high-performance building. Step inside for a closer look.

Solar panels, positioned to capture the most sun, convert sunlight into electricity. The greenest buildings create as much energy in a year as they use—and sometimes even more.

High-performance windows use multiple panes of glass and special seals to control heat and drafts passing through. Letting windows capture sunlight during the winter and shading them during the summer helps reduce energy use.

Water that goes down your shower and bathtub drains ("gray water") can be collected and reused to flush toilets or water plants (as long as you use environmentally friendly soap).

Rainwater is collected and stored in a cistern, or tank, to be used for watering plants and flushing toilets. Some green buildings can treat their own water, making it clean enough to drink, so they don't need to draw any from water supply lines.

Energy-efficient appliances and low-energy lighting reduce the amount of energy the building uses.

High levels of insulation prevent heat from going through walls, keeping heat inside during the winter and outside during the summer.

Green houses take advantage of the fact that heat rises by allowing hot air out during the summer.

Green building techniques try to use materials that are recycled, reclaimed from other buildings, or derived from sustainable sources, like fast-growing bamboo. They also try to use locally available materials, instead of shipping materials a long distance.

FUN FACTS

● An Italian company is developing UFOs—**Unidentified Floating Objects**—powered by solar, wind, and water power. The saucer-shaped houseboats will include a vegetable garden on their outer ring and an underwater window.

● The Bosco Verticale buildings in Milan, Italy, are **seriously green.** Plants cover 42 percent of its outsides. Green walls provide shade in the summer, **reducing air-conditioning** costs.

PROFILE: Arthur Huang
ENGINEER, ARCHITECT, INNOVATOR

If there's anything Arthur Huang hates more than environmental harm, it's sitting around and not doing anything to help.

People use up Earth's resources, creating tons of trash and hurting the environment. It's a problem Arthur talked about with his classmates and professors when he was studying architecture at Cornell and Harvard Universities. It's a problem he talked about with his own students after he became a professor at Tunghai University in Taiwan.

Talk, talk, talk—it didn't feel right to Arthur. "I almost felt embarrassed talking about the problem because I couldn't offer a solution," he recalls.

One day, he was walking down the hallway behind a couple of his students and overheard their conversation. They were

> ## "THE WALLS WEIGHED ONLY ONE-FIFTH AS MUCH AS CONVENTIONAL BUILDING MATERIALS."

discussing how there weren't enough answers to the environmental problem. Then they started talking about him. "They were saying, 'This guy hasn't done anything.'"

The words stung. Arthur knew they were true—and that's not the type of architect he wanted to be.

"Ever since I was young I'm always more like the doing type," he says. "I like to make things

happen. I don't like to talk about it."

So Arthur got to work. He started a company, MINIWIZ, in Taiwan to promote environmentally friendly building and sustainable products.

"How we started is actually out of spite. We were just angry," he says. "We were angry that we were talking about sustainability, we were talking about all kinds of problems with environmental issues, but there's no solution."

But anger isn't enough. Arthur had to figure out what solutions MINIWIZ could offer.

He didn't have to look far for inspiration.

UPCYCLING

"We just looked at our trash cans," he says. "And we noticed that in our office most of the trash that we have is actually PET (plastic) bottles because all our engineers love drinking bottled tea."

Arthur's team decided to make a new building material from 100-percent recycled plastic bottles. Taiwan was the perfect place to do that. It has one of the highest rates in the world for recycling that kind of plastic and is known worldwide for making plastic items.

MINIWIZ reshaped recycled plastic bottles into see-through plastic bricks. The blocks interlocked in a honeycomb design, creating walls and panels without needing any adhesives. The

walls weighed only one-fifth as much as conventional building materials, but they were strong enough to withstand hurricanes and earthquakes.

"Our idea is that if we can create something that's light, that's cheap, strong, high-performance and at the same time uses very little toxic material, then, I think, that is a very big step."

INSPIRATION FOR INNOVATION

People have called Arthur a visionary. But he's quick to point out that he hasn't invented anything new. He's an innovator, pulling together practices from other architects, nature, history, and his culture.

He rattles off some examples: A bee's honeycomb inspired the interlocking structure of his plastic bricks. He designs strength into products by incorporating folds, just as many other designers do. He reinforces materials with reused rice husks, much like the Chinese did when building the Great Wall.

He also follows the examples he saw as a young boy. "For sustainability, minimizing your waste is such a (part of) Asian culture, so that became part of my upbringing when I was growing up in Asia." His family always turned off the lights when they left a room and thought about how to conserve and reuse resources. "If everyone did that," Arthur says, "really there wouldn't be as much of a sustainability or environmental issue today."

GROWING UP, ARTHUR COMPETED A LOT WITH HIS BROTHERS. IT GAVE HIM THE DRIVE TO SUCCEED LATER IN LIFE, HE SAYS.

This building was made with recycled plastic bottles.

ARTHUR STILL WEARS A T-SHIRT FROM COLLEGE AND RESOLES HIS SHOES SO HE CAN WEAR THEM FOR LONGER THAN A DECADE. YEAH, **HE'S SERIOUS ABOUT RECYCLING.**

TO COME UP WITH THE NAME MINIWIZ, ARTHUR'S TEAM TOOK THE WORD "MINIMIZE"—AS IN MINIMIZING OUR NEGATIVE IMPACT ON EARTH. THEN THEY FLIPPED THE SECOND "M" UPSIDE DOWN TO BECOME A "W," LIKE REUSING OLD THINGS IN NEW WAYS.

GOING UNDER

How do TUNNELS take shortcuts?

The Inside Scoop

If you can't go around something, go through it. That, at least, is what a tunnel does. It's a time-saving shortcut through mountains, under rivers and bays, or even below cities. It may look like just a tube sticking through a mountain, but a tunnel is actually a bit of pure engineering genius. Take a deep look at how tunnels cut our travel time.

How do you dig out a tunnel ?

Why doesn't it get crushed under a mountain's weight ?

What can tunnels go through ?

155

Rocky Road

You don't just start digging a tunnel. You need to know exactly what the tunnel will go through, or you risk a cave-in when you're digging. Before a shovel touches the ground, tunnel builders study the geology of the site. They find out what type of rock and soil the tunnel will go through and if there are pockets of water or other hazards along the way. Long tunnels often pass through several types of rock and soil, and that affects how engineers dig it out. They use different digging techniques depending on what they must go through. Better to be safe than sorry.

Munching Like a Mole

You'd think that tunneling through rock would be the hardest, but it's not. In firm rock, tunnel builders can use huge rock-munching tunnel-boring machines, or TBMs. Nicknamed "moles," the TBMs slowly push forward, chomping through a slice of rock and sending the rubble back behind them on a conveyor system. If the rock is really hard, tunnel builders may use explosives to blast chunks away. In softer soil—like clay, mud, sand, or gravel—cave-ins are a constant danger. Tunnel builders use a shield, an iron or steel support that is slowly pushed into the soft soil. It holds up the roof of the tunnel while workers dig it out and reinforce it with a lining. When they complete a section, the shield is pushed forward, and the routine starts all over again. As workers advance through the tunnel, they may spray a coating of quick-drying concrete to hold the rock in place until they get the permanent liner built.

The **ZION-MOUNT CARMEL TUNNEL** in Utah, built in 1930, has a series of windows so visitors can look out on amazing rock formations as they pass through.

STRETCHING IT OUT

Tunnels are **engineering marvels,** especially when they push limits. Check out these record setters.

Longest subway/rapid transit tunnel: Guangzhou Metro Line 3, 37.5 miles (60 km) long, Guangzhou, China, completed in 2010.

Longest train tunnel: Gotthard Base Tunnel, 35 miles (57 km) long, Lepontine Alps, Switzerland, completed in 2016.

FUN FACT

WHEN BUILDING THE CHANNEL TUNNEL (NICKNAMED **THE CHUNNEL),** BRITISH AND FRENCH TUNNEL WORKERS RACED TO SEE WHO WOULD REACH THE MIDDLE FIRST. THE BRITISH WON.

ROCK CRUNCHER

A tunnel-boring machine (TBM) can dig as much as 250 feet (76 m) of tunnel in a day. TBMs can be massive machines, as long as two football fields and as tall as a four- or five-story building.

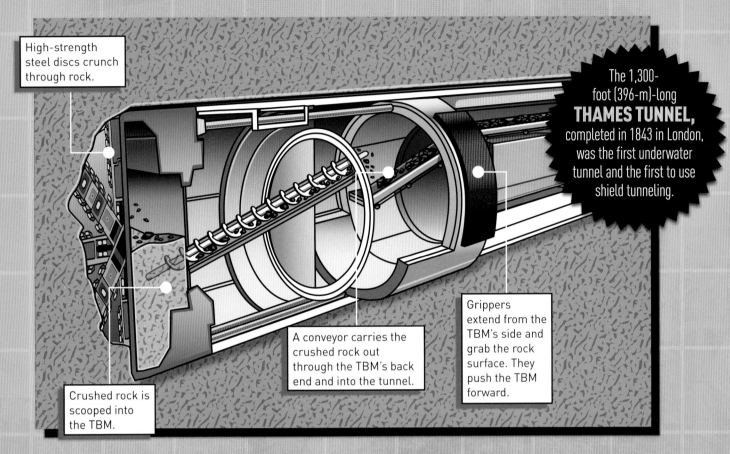

High-strength steel discs crunch through rock.

The 1,300-foot (396-m)-long **THAMES TUNNEL,** completed in 1843 in London, was the first underwater tunnel and the first to use shield tunneling.

Crushed rock is scooped into the TBM.

A conveyor carries the crushed rock out through the TBM's back end and into the tunnel.

Grippers extend from the TBM's side and grab the rock surface. They push the TBM forward.

Longest road tunnel:
Lærdal Tunnel, 15.2 miles (24.5 km) long, Lærdal-Aurland, Norway, completed in 2000.

Longest underwater train tunnel:
Channel Tunnel, 31.35 miles (50.5 km) long, with 24 miles (38 km) undersea, English Channel, England-France, completed in 1994.

Longest train tunnel running under both land and water:
Seikan Tunnel, 33.4 miles (53.8 km) long, with 14.5 miles (23.3 km) undersea, Tsugaru Strait, Japan, completed in 1988.

Longest road tunnel running underwater:
Tokyo Bay Aqua-Line, 8.6 miles (14 km) long, with 6 miles (9.6 km) undersea, Tokyo Bay, Japan, completed in 1997.

FUN FACT

CHINA HAS PLANS TO BUILD AN UNDERSEA TUNNEL **TWICE AS LONG** AS THE CHUNNEL.

WANT TO KNOW MORE?

SQUEEZING IN

How do tunnels snake through mountains without getting crushed? Their architects are masters of math and physics! Tunnels must hold heavy loads—their own weight plus the weight of the vehicles and people moving through them—and withstand any pressure from surrounding ground or water. Heavy rock isn't the problem. Dense rock walls can support themselves and don't put a lot of pressure on tunnels. But loose chunks of rock, wet ground, and water are different matters. They push hard against the sides of tunnels. Tunnels handle that pressure in two ways. They're made with really strong materials, such as steel, iron, concrete, and masonry. Their shapes are also designed to take it. Tunnels take advantage of the strength of an arch, which handles compression—or squeezing—by channeling the force around its curve. Tunnels are like continuous arches—going all the way around in a circle—a great shape for handling pressure on all sides.

WATER PLAY

Rivers and bays pose an extra challenge for tunnel construction. Sometimes, tunnels are dug under the bottom of the body of water, much like tunneling through other ground. But other times, engineers build the tunnel in the water. One of the ways they do this is to start by digging a trench in the riverbed or floor of the bay. Then long, premade tunnel sections, which are sealed to keep out water, are floated into position and sunk into the trench. Divers connect the sections and remove the water seals. Any water that seeped in is pumped out, and the tunnel is covered up so it stays buried at the bottom of the water.

● The **first undersea rail tunnel** linking two continents, Europe and Asia, opened in 2013 in Turkey. It's 200 feet (60 m) under the seabed of the Bosporus. The tunnel, first dreamed up by an Ottoman sultan 150 years ago, was begun in 2004 but delayed for four years by a series of archaeological discoveries.

● From 1927 to 2003, the British Postal Service used an **underground Mail Rail system** that ran through tunnels 70 feet (21 m) below London. The small, unmanned electric trains carried as many as 12 million items a day.

● The **Delaware Aqueduct** is the longest tunnel carrying water—and the longest tunnel anywhere at 105 miles (170 km) long. Completed in 1944, it supplies water to New York City.

FUN FACTS

HANDLING PRESSURE

A tunnel's cylindrical shape—like a continuous arch going all the way around—is ideal for handling compression, or squeezing, forces. It channels the force around its curve.

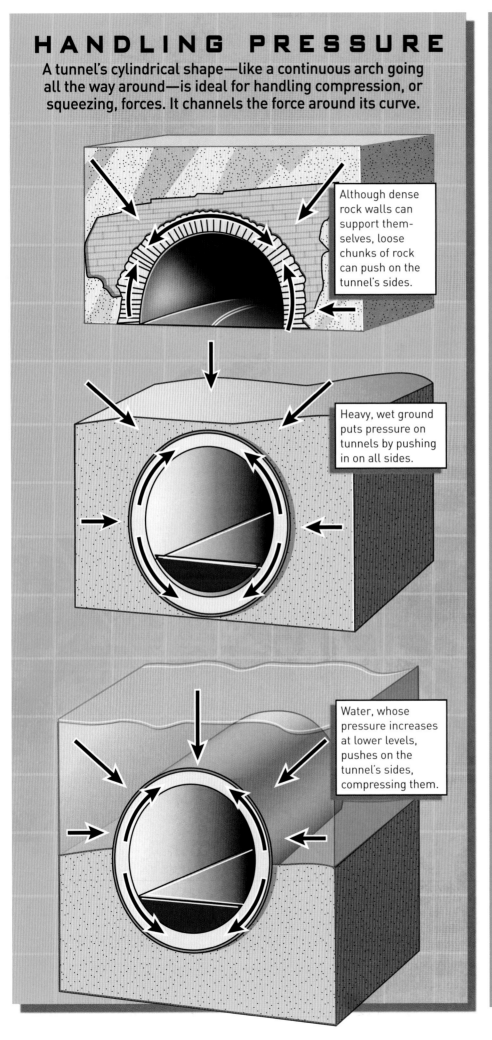

Although dense rock walls can support themselves, loose chunks of rock can push on the tunnel's sides.

Heavy, wet ground puts pressure on tunnels by pushing in on all sides.

Water, whose pressure increases at lower levels, pushes on the tunnel's sides, compressing them.

Myth vs. FACT

MYTH: Secret tunnels snake through the ground under cities.

FACT: It's true—except, maybe, for the secret part. Many cities throughout the world sit atop vast networks of tunnels. In Paris, France, enormous stone quarries were mined beginning in the 12th century to build some of the city's architectural masterpieces. The quarries were covered over, and the city sits on top of them, but that doesn't mean they went unused. Starting in the late 1700s, Paris used them for about a century to house the remains of six million dead citizens from overflowing cemeteries. Underneath Naples, Italy, a massive system of tunnels and caverns, carved out of the volcanic rock under the city, was used for centuries. Ancient Greeks used tunnels as reservoirs to hold water, but in later years, the caverns housed theaters and early Christian worship sites. In the United States, many hidden tunnels, some dating back to the 1800s, were abandoned subway or streetcar lines. Others were used to carry merchandise

Paris, France

under cities. From 1920 to 1933, an era known as Prohibition, when it was illegal (or prohibited) to make, transport, or sell alcoholic beverages, the tunnels came in handy for people trying to avoid that law. Bootleggers sneaked liquor through the tunnels, and some illegal bars used them as escape tunnels. In Detroit, Michigan, a secret escape tunnel ran from a bar's basement to the church across the street!

159

TRY THIS!

ON A ROLL

ENGINEER A STRONG STRUCTURE

Here's the challenge: Build the strongest, tallest tower you can. Ready? Wait, a minute. Don't run out to your neighborhood hardware store to buy some steel I-beams and girders just yet. (You probably can't buy that stuff at your local store anyway.) You're going to build your tower with something a little more common, a little more—shall we say—personal? The humble toilet paper tube. Just make sure all the toilet paper's gone first.

WHAT YOU NEED

TIME: about 30 minutes

1. Toilet paper tubes (at least 8 for the experiments, a lot more to build)

2. Lots of heavy books

3. Rubber bands

OPTIONAL: 4 to 6 cardboard squares, each about the size of a large book

DESIGN & BUILD

EXPERIMENT 1: STANDING TUBES

1. STAND FOUR toilet paper tubes on a smooth surface, so that each is under the corner of a big book. (It'll look like a table.)

2. CAREFULLY STACK books on top until the tubes begin to buckle under the weight. How many books did they hold? (If you want, take the stack of books to a scale and weigh it.)

3. EXAMINE THE TUBES. Where did they give way? If you were going to design a stronger tube, what would you change?

EXPERIMENT 2: LYING TUBES

1. LAY FOUR TOILET PAPER tubes next to each other on a smooth surface, so that they make a platform for your big book. (If the tubes try to roll apart, hold them together with rubber bands.)

2. AS IN THE FIRST experiment, carefully stack books on top until the tubes begin to buckle under the weight. How many books did they hold? (Weigh the stack, if you did for the first experiment.)

3. TRY CHANGING THE arrangement of the lying tubes. Does it make any difference in how much weight they can hold?

DESIGN & BUILD

1. BASED ON YOUR experiments, decide which way the tubes are strongest. How would you use that knowledge in building?

2. DESIGN THE STRONGEST, tallest tower that you can. How will you make it tall? How will you make the base support all the weight above it?

3. BUILD YOUR TOWER using only toilet paper tubes, books (and/or cardboard squares), and rubber bands. Try several designs and see which one works best.

EXPERIMENT 1

EXPERIMENT 2

WHAT TO EXPECT

YOU SHOULD DISCOVER THAT TUBES ARE STRONGER WHEN ... HMM, LYING ON THEIR SIDES? STANDING ON THEIR ENDS? (NO, WE'RE NOT GOING TO TELL YOU WHICH WAY. YOU HAVE TO DO THE EXPERIMENTS TO FIND OUT.)

WHAT'S GOING ON?

MAKING A STRONG STRUCTURE DOESN'T DEPEND ONLY ON THE MATERIALS YOU USE. IT ALSO DEPENDS ON THE SHAPE OF THE MATERIALS AND HOW THEY'RE USED. JUST LOOK AT A TOILET PAPER TUBE. IT'S MADE OF PRETTY THIN CARDBOARD. BUT A TUBE IS A REALLY STRONG SHAPE—AT LEAST WHEN IT'S PLACED A CERTAIN WAY. WHEN ENGINEERS DESIGN STRUCTURES, SUCH AS BUILDINGS, TUNNELS, OR EVEN TOYS, THEY DESIGN THEM TO HOLD WEIGHT AND HANDLE OTHER FORCES THAT PUSH AND PULL ON THEM. WEIGHT PILED ON TOP OF YOUR TOILET PAPER TUBES SQUEEZES THEM AGAINST WHATEVER IS SUPPORTING THEM. THAT SQUEEZING IS CALLED COMPRESSION. HOW WELL DID YOUR TOILET PAPER TUBES HANDLE IT?

CHAPTER 5

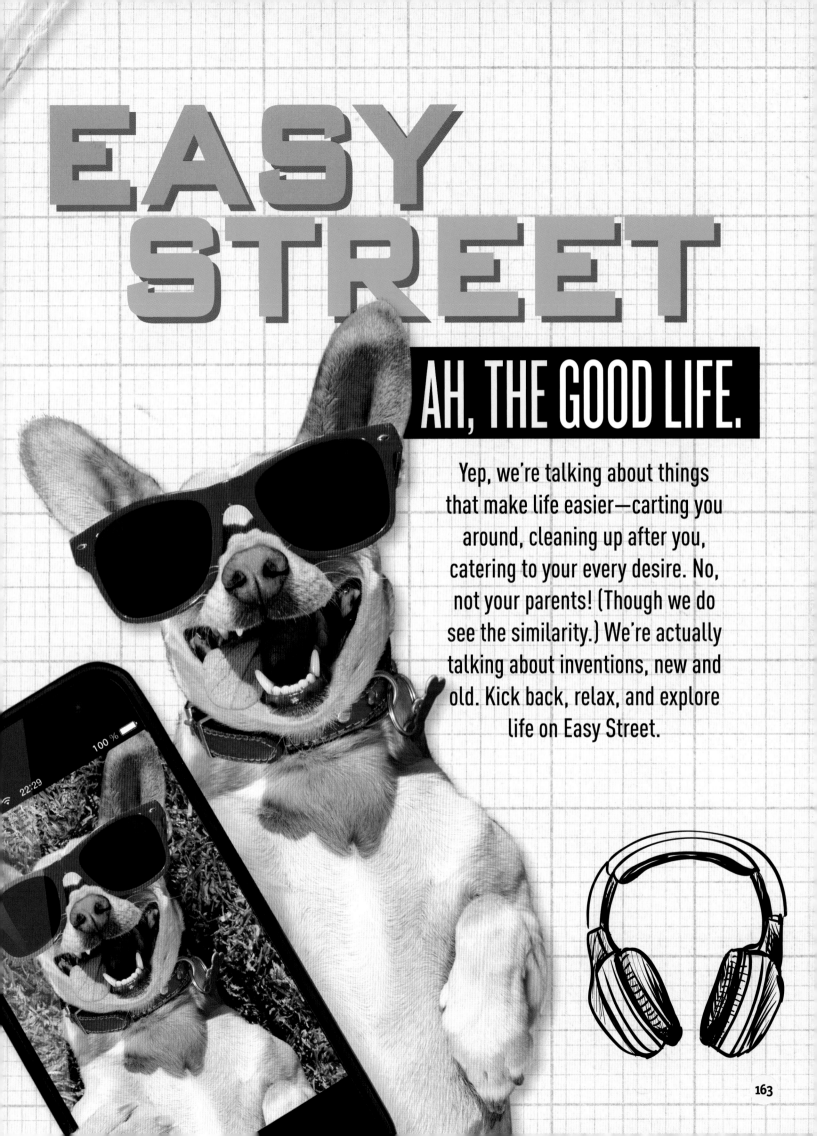

EASY STREET

AH, THE GOOD LIFE.

Yep, we're talking about things that make life easier—carting you around, cleaning up after you, catering to your every desire. No, not your parents! (Though we do see the similarity.) We're actually talking about inventions, new and old. Kick back, relax, and explore life on Easy Street.

LOOK, MOM, NO HANDS!

How do SELF-DRIVING CARS get around?

The Inside Scoop

A self-driving car. It sounds like a futuristic fantasy, but it's closer than you think. Self-driving, or autonomous, cars have already traveled hundreds of thousands of miles, as companies test the technology. It may not be long before you can put your pooch in the driver's seat and head out on vacation. Read on to find out how engineers are putting the "auto" into automobile.

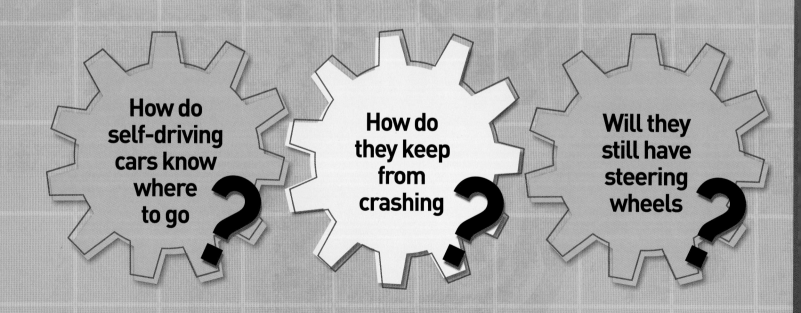

How do self-driving cars know where to go**?**

How do they keep from crashing**?**

Will they still have steering wheels**?**

JUST THE FACTS

Personal Chauffeur

A self-driving car will zip around without you doing any of the work. It'll come when you call it, figure out the best way to get you where you're going, and drop you off at the door. You won't need to find a place to park it either. It'll do that itself. On the road, it'll communicate with other cars, so they can take turns at intersections and stay out of each other's way. They'll "worry" about getting you to your destination fast and safely. You just get to watch the scenery fly by.

SPEEDING UP

Making cars smart is hard. So hard, that early plans for self-driving cars focused on roads instead of the cars themselves! But as computers became smarter, engineers worked on making cars more autonomous. Now **it's a race** to see how quickly these cars will take to the roads. Check out these milestones along the way.

1950s:
Autonomous Highway System prototypes are tested by GM and RCA (Radio Corporation of America). Radio controls handle the speed and steering, and magnets in the car track a steel cable embedded in the road.

1939:
The New York World's Fair features Futurama, an exhibit and ride designed by Norman Bel Geddes and presented by General Motors (GM). It showcases an imagined world of 1960 with an automated highway system that guides your car for you.

1966–1980:
The Stanford Cart, a simple buggy with a video camera and remote control, pioneers navigating through an unfamiliar environment with artificial intelligence and machine vision. It accidentally wanders onto a nearby road but survives undamaged.

FUN FACT

THE FIRST REFERENCE TO AN AUTONOMOUS CAR WAS IN THE 1935 STORY **"THE LIVING MACHINE"** BY SCIENCE-FICTION WRITER DAVID H. KELLER. THE CAR DROVE PEOPLE ACROSS THE CONTINENT AND AROUND TOWN, EVEN DROPPING KIDS OFF AT SCHOOL.

ON THE ROAD

Self-driving cars have already traveled hundreds of thousands of miles—with impressive safety records. Many people think that using autonomous cars will cut down on traffic jams and accidents.

GPS RECEIVER

CAMERA

ROAD SIGN

EDGE OF ROAD

ROAD MARKINGS

1977:
The first computerized, driverless car that can process images of the road is unveiled by S. Tsugawa and his colleagues at Japan's Tsukuba Mechanical Engineering Laboratory. It cruises along at speeds up to 20 miles an hour (30 km/h) and uses machine vision to track white street markers. It's the first truly autonomous car.

2010:
The Google Self-Driving Car project hits the street with seven autonomous Toyota Prius hybrids. It later expands to include other types of vehicles, each with a unique design.

1986–2003:
Using self-driving technology developed by German engineer and computer scientist Ernst Dickmanns, a Mercedes van and then a Mercedes sedan drive thousands of highway miles autonomously at speeds up to 112 miles an hour (180 km/h). The work is part of the Eureka PROMETHEUS project, a large European-funded research program.

2004–07:
The U.S. Defense Advanced Research Projects Administration (DARPA) spurs the development of autonomous vehicles by challenging developers to compete for prizes. In the first competition, the cars travel only a few miles before crashing. But a Stanford University team wins the second challenge, in the Mojave Desert, with an autonomous Volkswagen Touareg called Stanley.

2015:
Tesla Motors updates the computer programs on its vehicles around the world to allow autonomous driving using sensors, GPS, cameras, and controls already on the cars.

FUN FACT
AROUND 1478, **LEONARDO DA VINCI** SKETCHED OUT A CARTLIKE VEHICLE THAT WOULD HAVE BEEN POWERED BY **LARGE SPRINGS** OVER A SET COURSE.

WANT TO KNOW MORE?

TELL ME MORE

SMART CARS

To get around without human input, self-driving cars use a lot of sensors and advanced computer programs to make smart decisions. They need to determine where they are, what's around them, what kind of obstacles they need to avoid, and where they need to go. Once they figure that out—and they do it multiple times every second for the entire trip—they send commands to the car, so it knows how to steer, when to brake, and when to hit the gas. Piece of cake, right?

GETTING CLOSE

It may be years before your family's driving a completely autonomous car, but a lot of the "smart" technology they need is already on board cars. Cars have been required to have special safe (anti-lock) braking and stability systems for years, and many carmakers are already putting automatic emergency braking systems on their cars. Lots of cars also have systems that sound an alarm, shake your seat, or twitch the steering wheel if you leave your lane without using a turn signal. They also have sensors that keep your car from getting close to the one ahead of it. Some car companies, like Tesla, already put computer programs on their cars that let them use all the sensors and controls for nearly autonomous driving.

ROAD-WORTHY

Self-driving cars use numerous sensors to "see" what's going on around them and advanced computer programs to process the information and control the car. Each manufacturer's autonomous vehicle is a little different, but here's a typical setup.

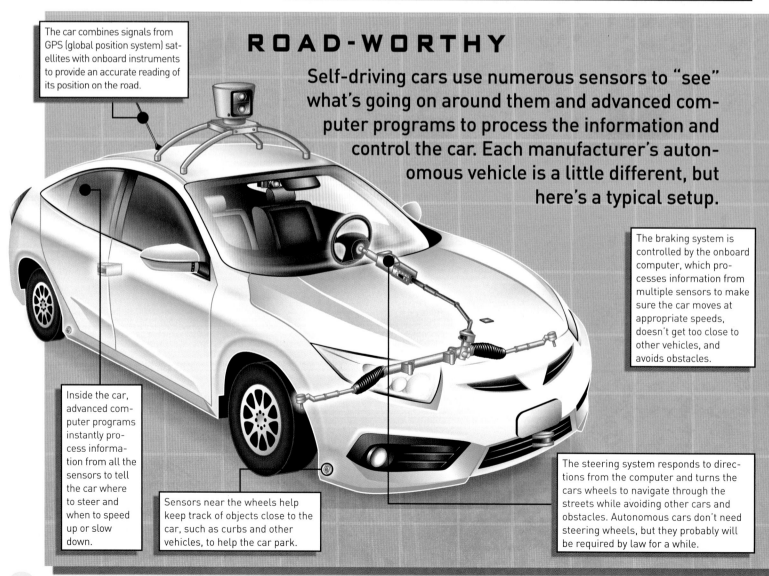

The car combines signals from GPS (global position system) satellites with onboard instruments to provide an accurate reading of its position on the road.

The braking system is controlled by the onboard computer, which processes information from multiple sensors to make sure the car moves at appropriate speeds, doesn't get too close to other vehicles, and avoids obstacles.

Inside the car, advanced computer programs instantly process information from all the sensors to tell the car where to steer and when to speed up or slow down.

Sensors near the wheels help keep track of objects close to the car, such as curbs and other vehicles, to help the car park.

The steering system responds to directions from the computer and turns the cars wheels to navigate through the streets while avoiding other cars and obstacles. Autonomous cars don't need steering wheels, but they probably will be required by law for a while.

FUN FACTS

In 2010, an **autonomous van** developed by the University of Parma, in Italy, drove more than 8,000 miles (13,000 km) from Parma to Shanghai, China. **The journey took 100 days** and went through nine countries. It *did* run into a few snags along the way, though. The van almost got a ticket in Russia when it drove in a pedestrian-only area. But the Russian police officer didn't find a driver to ticket.

PIZZA

A self-driving Toyota Prius, called **the Pribot**, was developed in 2008 as part of a stunt to **deliver pizzas** in the San Francisco area. It helped inspire Google's self-driving car program.

Myth vs. FACT

MYTH: Self-driving cars will never be as *good* as human drivers.

FACT: Strictly speaking, they won't be as good as human drivers. They'll be better—at least, that's what experts predict. Cars with computers for brains have a lot of advantages over us mere mortals. They monitor all their surroundings all the time. They're better at analyzing GPS, traffic, weather, and other information—and using it to figure out the best way to get somewhere. They make decisions faster, they react faster, and they never sneak a peek at their cell phone while driving. What's more, they don't get distracted by you arguing with your little sister. But they can't do everything as well as humans. If a construction worker waves at them to stop or go, they can't understand. Their cameras have trouble seeing traffic lights if the sun is right behind the light. And they don't know to be extra cautious if kids are playing too close to a street. Engineers are working to solve those problems, but they also say putting autonomous cars on the road may require us to change how we do a few things—like how pedestrians cross streets. If we do, we'll be rewarded by fewer accidents, less traffic, and more relaxing rides.

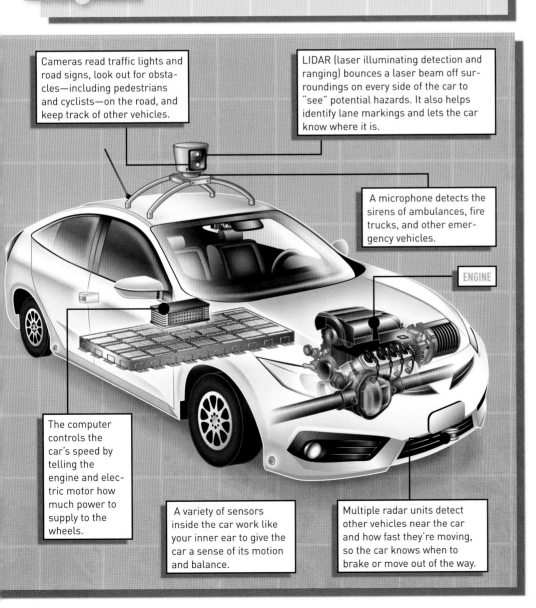

Cameras read traffic lights and road signs, look out for obstacles—including pedestrians and cyclists—on the road, and keep track of other vehicles.

LIDAR (laser illuminating detection and ranging) bounces a laser beam off surroundings on every side of the car to "see" potential hazards. It also helps identify lane markings and lets the car know where it is.

A microphone detects the sirens of ambulances, fire trucks, and other emergency vehicles.

ENGINE

The computer controls the car's speed by telling the engine and electric motor how much power to supply to the wheels.

A variety of sensors inside the car work like your inner ear to give the car a sense of its motion and balance.

Multiple radar units detect other vehicles near the car and how fast they're moving, so the car knows when to brake or move out of the way.

PROFILE: José Luis Hernández-Rebollar

INVENTOR, ENGINEER

There's an old saying: "When fate hands you lemons, start a lemonade stand." It could be referring to José Luis Hernández-Rebollar. In 1996, he got a big helping of "lemons"—but he turned it into something sweet.

At the time, Mexico and the United States were working on plans for a huge, 160-foot (50-m)-wide telescope to be built in Mexico. The telescope would pick up radio waves from space, so scientists could learn more about the universe's planets, stars, black holes, and galaxies.

The project needed good engineers to make the telescope work. José was one of them.

He was completing his master's degree at the Instituto Nacional de Astrofísica, Óptica y Electrónica (INAOE, or the National Institute of Astrophysics, Optics and Electronics), which was leading the telescope project for Mexico.

> ## "HE DESIGNED AND BUILT A GLOVE LOADED WITH SENSORS, THE ACCELEGLOVE."

INAOE sent José to California to help the U.S. company working on the telescope's initial designs.

José needed to test ways to control the telescope's antenna by running simulations with an advanced computer program. He was an expert at doing this, so he got to work.

And that's when things got weird.

A computer technician came over to José's cubicle, flipped open his computer and started teaching him how to use it: This is the mouse. You click it and use it to open a program. This is the ...

Um, hello? José's work involved running advanced computer simulations. If anyone knew his way around a computer, it was José. He told the tech that he had used computers before.

But the guy didn't stop. "It was kind of frustrating because he simply kept going with his explanation of how the computer and email worked, without paying attention to anything I tried to say," José recalls.

What was going on?

It was a communication problem, José later realized. For some reason, maybe because José didn't know as much English back then or the computer tech didn't bother to listen, the guy didn't understand what was going on. He made a lot of assumptions—really wrong assumptions—about what José knew.

It was like José was served a whole bowl of lemons—and some of them squirted him in the eye. It stung.

INSPIRATION

That frustrating experience stayed with José. But it didn't sour him. It inspired him.

He returned to the United States two years later to study for a doctorate in electrical engineering at George Washington University. When it was time to choose a project to work on, he remembered that day.

He thought about situations when it's hard for people to communicate, like when they speak different languages.

Computer programs—even apps on smartphones—can translate English to Spanish or Chinese or many other languages. But what about American Sign Language? ASL is used by 500,000 to two million deaf and hard-of-hearing people in the United States. The language has been around almost two centuries, but it is not easily translated into Spanish or other languages.

José wondered if he could use his engineering expertise to provide a solution.

It wasn't going to be easy.

José studied ASL and found it had about 42 hand postures, combining various positions of the fingers and palm, and the same gesture meant different things depending how you move your hand. Touching the thumb of an open hand to your chin means "mom," but the same gesture at forehead level means "dad."

His invention would need to capture all of that.

José got to work. He designed and built a glove loaded with sensors, the AcceleGlove. The sensors detect how you're using your hand and fingers and how close they are to your body. They work with sensors on the elbow and shoulder to send information to a computer, which uses a high-speed program that José wrote to find the meaning of the hand movement.

José succeeded in getting his AcceleGlove to translate hundreds of words. After he finished his doctoral work, the AcceleGlove was developed and sold around the world for several years. José now plans to bring out a less expensive version that can be used for research into reading gestures and for controlling electronics. (Yes, games!)

That's some seriously sweet "lemonade."

AN EARLY START

José was an engineer from a young age.

"When not playing with neighbors, I used to spend hours by myself assembling imaginary devices with bars, screws and nuts made out of plastic."

An idea would pop into his mind, and he'd keep working at it until he made it for real. Those skills—creativity, technical know-how, and determination—have come in handy all his life.

Just ask his family. They counted on him to keep their old car running.

One day, they wanted to drive the old 1969 Datsun to the beach in Acapulco, five hours from their home in the small town of Chietla in the central-southern Mexican state of Puebla.

The car broke down in the middle of the trip. They were in a small town, with no spare parts to repair the broken clutch. José helped his dad with a creative solution: using a spring out of a pen to fix it. "I was the one sneaking under the car to remove and replace the piece," he recalls. "I've always been thin, so I fit everywhere."

It saved the family vacation. "It took us a day to get from Puebla to Acapulco," José says, "but we made it!"

By the time he was 18 years old, he had so much practice fixing that old car that he could close his eyes and tell what was wrong with it just by listening to the engine.

José thought of opening a car repair shop, but his dad pushed him to set his sights in a different direction: college and an engineering degree. It turned out to be a very good move.

CRAZY BUSY

The AcceleGlove hasn't been the only thing keeping José busy.

In 2006, a few years after finishing his doctorate, he moved back to Mexico and has been teaching robotics, doing research, consulting on the Gran Telescopio Milimétrico (Large Millimeter Telescope)—the same telescope he worked on for his master's degree research—and, of course, inventing things.

"It seems that I cannot be doing the same stuff for long periods of time, so I keep looking, trying, doing," he says. "My mother used to say the same thing, that I could not be static (en paz) ... ever."

He's filed patents for two more inventions and started a business to promote a new way to treat water, a process he invented with a friend.

Where does he find time for all of this? "Since there are only 24 hours in the day, I sometimes borrow hours from the night," he jokes.

José doesn't mind losing a few hours of sleep to have the chance to invent. "It feels so good when you create something that at the beginning only existed in your imagination!"

JOSÉ BUILT THE FIRST **ACCELEGLOVE** PROTOTYPE WITH USED AND DONATED PARTS. IT **COST HIM ONLY $11** TO MAKE.

WISER GUT ... SIZE GUY ... WISE GUY

How does AUTOCORRECT fix our spelling errors (or not)?

The Inside Scoop

Love it or hate it, autocorrect shapes the way we communicate. From its earliest days as a glorified spell checker on computers, autocorrect now tries to put words in our mouths—often with bizarre or hilarious results. The truth is, it's not easy to make us sound intelligent when we tap out messages on a cell phone with our thumbs. Read on to see how autocorrect tries to help.

Why does autocorrect make so many mistakes?

Does it ever get better?

Isn't it better to just turn it off?

Banned Lists

Autocorrect follows rules. At its most basic level, it "sees" a misspelled word and replaces it with a corrected version. But developing those rules has been a challenge for computer scientists. The first autocorrect function, part of the Microsoft Word program, relied on lists that a junior employee had to cobble together and enter by hand into the computer program. It included three master lists: words to always correct, words that had exceptions, and words to ignore. The last group was mainly curse words, and Microsoft didn't want to have anything to do with those!

ABC

Statistical Savvy

Autocorrect programs now develop their rules based on advanced statistics, a branch of mathematics that collects and analyzes large amounts of numerical data. The programs analyze a colossal amount of public writings to decide when a word probably should be replaced—and by what other word. As you type, the computer program or smartphone app checks each word against a built-in dictionary. If it doesn't find the word, it suggests alternatives. It picks the alternatives mainly by popularity. But it also looks at other issues, like the likelihood you hit a wrong key nearby, whether the word sounds like another, and the context of what you're saying. Smartphone apps, which have to deal with clumsy thumb typing, work more aggressively than computers to correct typos. Many phones use those rules not only to correct problems but also to predict what you're trying to say. They'll suggest a word before you finish typing it. Autocorrect functions can make a lot of mistakes—but still fewer than you if you turned them off!

TOO MUCH TRUST?

Researchers ran an experiment and found that **people trust** spell checkers **too much.**

They asked college students—ones who were good spellers—to edit a letter that had several spelling errors. Sometimes the computer's spell checker was turned on, and it put a squiggly line under words it identified as wrong so the students would notice them. Sometimes the spell checker was turned off, and the students had to figure it out by themselves. But here's the tricky part: In the experiment, the computer's spell checker wasn't always right. Sometimes it said a word was misspelled when it was really fine, and sometimes it didn't point out real mistakes. Here's how the students scored (a low score is better):

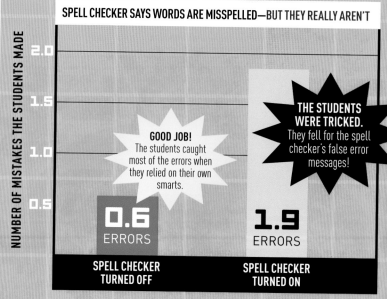

SPELL CHECKER SAYS WORDS ARE MISSPELLED—BUT THEY REALLY AREN'T

NUMBER OF MISTAKES THE STUDENTS MADE

GOOD JOB! The students caught most of the errors when they relied on their own smarts.

THE STUDENTS WERE TRICKED. They fell for the spell checker's false error messages!

0.6 ERRORS
SPELL CHECKER TURNED OFF

1.9 ERRORS
SPELL CHECKER TURNED ON

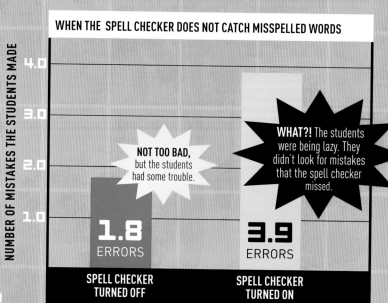

WHEN THE SPELL CHECKER DOES NOT CATCH MISSPELLED WORDS

NUMBER OF MISTAKES THE STUDENTS MADE

NOT TOO BAD, but the students had some trouble.

WHAT?! The students were being lazy. They didn't look for mistakes that the spell checker missed.

1.8 ERRORS
SPELL CHECKER TURNED OFF

3.9 ERRORS
SPELL CHECKER TURNED ON

Autocorrect can learn from its mistakes, especially if you're willing to train it. Some phones let you tinker with their dictionaries directly. But the easiest way to train your phone is to catch it in the act when it makes suggestions. Most types of phones let you delete or "x" out the suggested word to show the phone it was a wrong suggestion. Eventually, your phone will clue up.

● **A Microsoft engineer** told his daughter's third-grade class about the easy trick of changing the **autocorrect** dictionary so it would substitute any word you wanted. Afterward he got email from other parents asking him why whenever they typed their daughter's name, it automatically changed to **"the pretty princess."**

FUN FACT

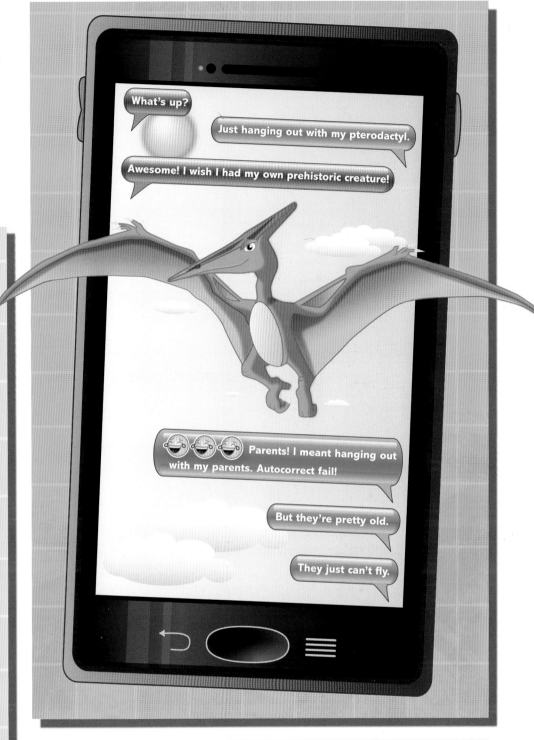

What's up?

Just hanging out with my pterodactyl.

Awesome! I wish I had my own prehistoric creature!

Parents! I meant hanging out with my parents. Autocorrect fail!

But they're pretty old.

They just can't fly.

● In the early 2000s, word processor spell checks **did not recognize "cooperation"** and so replaced the word with **"Cupertino"** (the city in Northern California where several computer companies were headquartered). "Cupertino" **accidentally** made it into many documents published by the **United Nations, NATO,** and other official bodies. People now talk about **the "Cupertino effect."**

MONEY ON THE MOVE

How do SECRET CODES let us buy things?

The Inside Scoop

So you want to stop for an ice cream, but your parents are out of cash. No worries! There are lots of ways they can pay for your cone: They can go to an Automated Teller Machine (ATM) and get some cash, or they can skip the green altogether. They can whip a credit card out of a wallet or even tap their smartphone to a machine. Nothing should stop you from getting that ice cream! (Be sure to tell that to your parents.) Read on to find out how cashless payments work ... and why they're almost too good to be true.

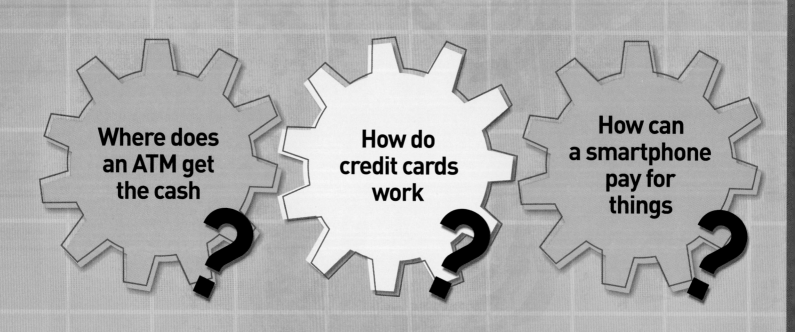

Where does an ATM get the cash?

How do credit cards work?

How can a smartphone pay for things?

JUST THE FACTS

Strips and Chips

The key to buying an ice-cream cone without cash is secret codes. Whether on a credit card or a smartphone, the codes verify who your parents are and get permission for them to pay the ice-cream shop with credit. If your parents use a credit card, the codes are in the shiny chip on the front of the card and the black magnetic strip on the back. When they swipe or insert their credit card in the shop's card reader, it uses the coded information to make the purchase. If your parents use their smartphone to pay, the phone uses a chip to beam your parents' credit card information to the checkout using near field communication (NFC). NFC only works when the phone is within a couple inches (4 cm) of the checkout.

Money Machines

If your parents need cash, an automated teller machine (ATM) is their best bet. They insert their card into a reader, punch a few buttons, and walk away with their money. It's not free, of course. It's coming from their bank accounts, much like the charges on their credit card or smartphone. But an ATM's a little different because it hands out cold, hard cash. How exactly does that happen? Inside an ATM is a safe with separate compartments that hold the bills. The ATM's computer orders up the number of bills it needs, and they're grabbed by rollers and moved to the cash-dispenser slot. If you're hoping an ATM will kick out a bonus buck or two, don't hold your breath. The cash-dispensing mechanism has an electric eye that counts each bill and a sensor that checks their thickness to make sure two aren't stuck together. If they are, they go to a reject bin. Sorry.

WAYS TO PAY

Money is simply something we value enough to use to buy things, and has it ever changed over the past 10,000 years!

EARLIEST DAYS:
Back before money, people barter—trade goods and services—to get what they want.

9000–6000 B.C.:
Cattle and other livestock are the oldest form of money.

1200 B.C.:
The Chinese begin using cowries, the shells of a mollusk found in the Pacific and Indian Oceans, as money. The cowrie becomes the most widely and longest used currency in history.

1000 B.C.:
The earliest bronze and copper coins are made by the Chinese in the form of cowries. The coins evolve into primitive round shapes. Some have holes so they can be strung together.

ABOUT 1250:
The florin, a gold coin minted in Florence, becomes widely used in Europe, helping international commerce.

806:
The first paper banknotes appear in China and develop through five centuries. In 1455, the Chinese stop using paper money for a few hundred years.

118 B.C.:
China uses one-foot (30-cm)-square pieces of white deerskin with colorful borders—the first banknote.

500 B.C.:
Outside of China, the first coins are made of lumps of silver and soon take a familiar round form with their sides stamped with the likenesses of gods and emperors. The early coins appear first in Lycia, part of present-day Turkey, but quickly are adopted by the Greek, Persian, Macedonian, and eventually Roman empires.

LATE 1200s:
Marco Polo travels to China and then introduces the idea of paper money to Europeans.

1535:
The first record is made of Native Americans in North America using wampum, strings of white beads made from clam shells.

1661:
Sweden prints the first paper banknotes in Europe.

1871:
Western Union, a telegraph company, allows money transfers via telegram.

1950s:
General-purpose credit cards come into use.

2005:
The first smartphones gain the ability to make contactless payments.

When your parents insert their credit or debit card into an ATM, it verifies the information coded on the card and asks for their personal identification number (PIN). Then it lets them order up some cash—if they have enough in their bank account to cover the amount. Check out how an ATM works.

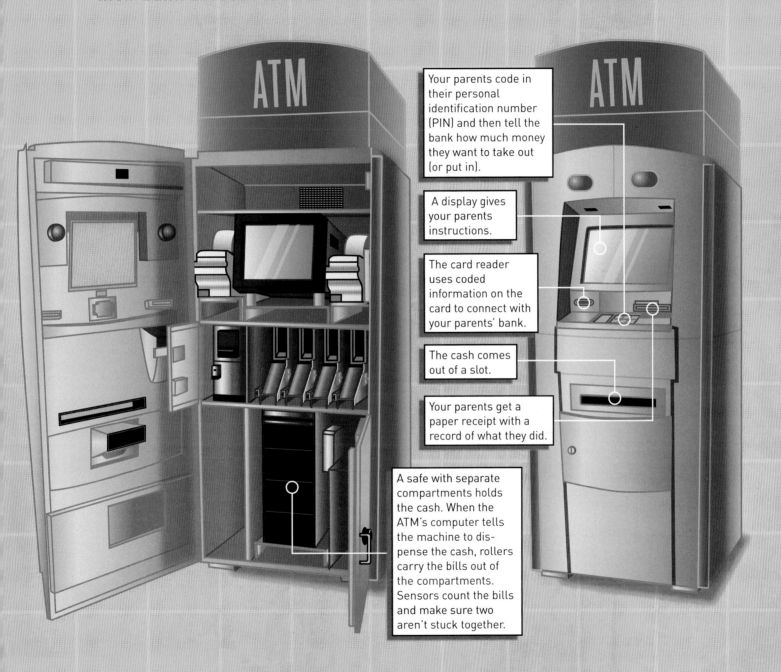

Your parents code in their personal identification number (PIN) and then tell the bank how much money they want to take out (or put in).

A display gives your parents instructions.

The card reader uses coded information on the card to connect with your parents' bank.

The cash comes out of a slot.

Your parents get a paper receipt with a record of what they did.

A safe with separate compartments holds the cash. When the ATM's computer tells the machine to dispense the cash, rollers carry the bills out of the compartments. Sensors count the bills and make sure two aren't stuck together.

FUN FACT

STARTING IN 1865, DEPARTMENT STORES GAVE OUT **CHARGE COINS** THAT ALLOWED A CUSTOMER TO BUY THINGS USING CREDIT. THE COINS WERE FIRST MADE OF PLASTIC THEN LATER OF METAL.

WANT TO KNOW MORE?

TELL ME MORE

MOVING MONEY

If you watch what happens when your parents pay with a credit card or their smartphone, you'll notice it takes the checkout terminal a second or two before it says "approved." A lot goes on during that time. The checkout terminal securely sends your parents' information to the ice-cream shop's bank, which checks in with the bank that gave your parents their credit card. The check-in is to make sure your parents have enough money (or credit) to pay for your ice cream. If they do, your parents' bank gives the OK to the ice-cream shop's bank, which tells the shop to give you the ice-cream cone. You finally get your treat.

In the 1500s, **a Bohemian count** minted coins that the English eventually called **"dollars."** It became the basis for U.S. currency.

FUN FACTS

● **Long before** plastic credit cards, department stores and some gas stations gave customers **metal Charga-Plates** with the customer's name and address on them. These predecessors to credit cards were used up until the 1960s.

Whoa... SLOW DOWN! A Closer Look at Credit

Here's how credit works: When your parents buy your ice cream with a credit card, they are borrowing money from a bank to pay for it. The bank gave them a credit card because your parents have a good reputation for paying loans back. If your parents pay the loan back right away (in less than a month), it doesn't cost them any more than paying with cash. But if they don't pay their entire credit card bill at the end of the month, they will have to pay extra—sometimes a lot extra. (When a bank lends people money, it charges them. That's one way banks make money.) The term "credit" also refers to your parents' reputation for paying loans back. Every time they borrow money, they get graded on how well they did on paying the money back. Banks and other organizations that deal with credit keep something like a report card, a credit report, on everyone who borrows money.

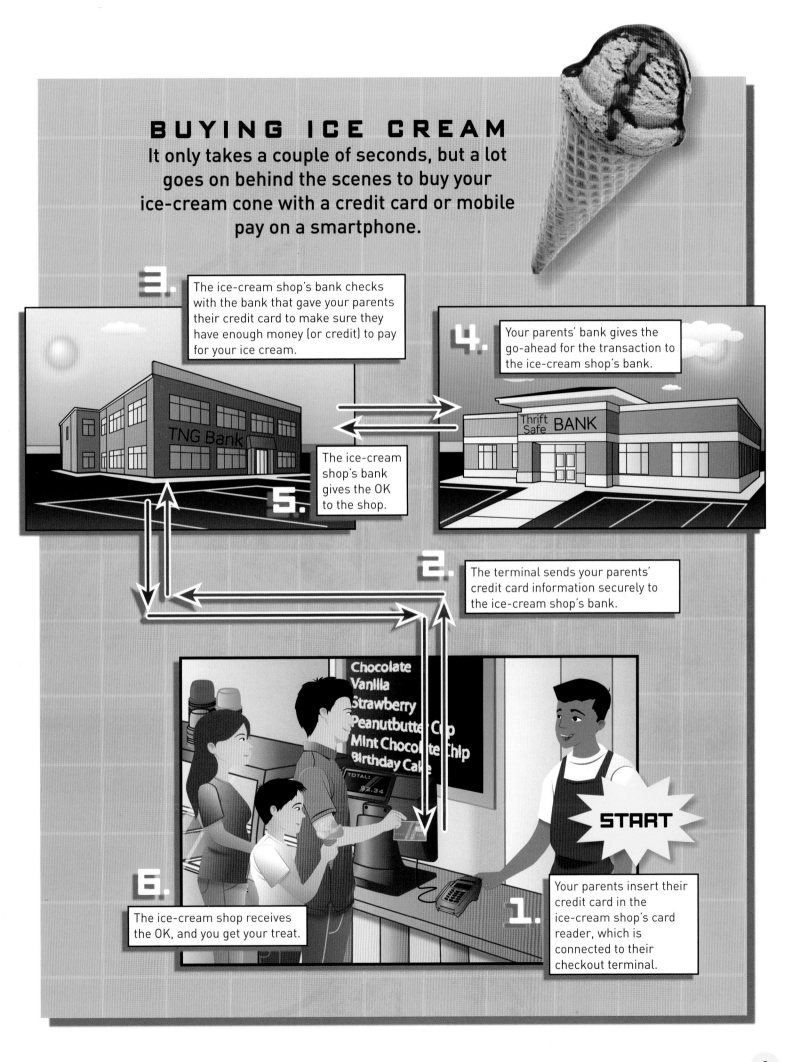

BUYING ICE CREAM

It only takes a couple of seconds, but a lot goes on behind the scenes to buy your ice-cream cone with a credit card or mobile pay on a smartphone.

3. The ice-cream shop's bank checks with the bank that gave your parents their credit card to make sure they have enough money (or credit) to pay for your ice cream.

4. Your parents' bank gives the go-ahead for the transaction to the ice-cream shop's bank.

TNG Bank

Thrift Safe BANK

5. The ice-cream shop's bank gives the OK to the shop.

2. The terminal sends your parents' credit card information securely to the ice-cream shop's bank.

Chocolate
Vanilla
Strawberry
Peanutbutter Cup
Mint Chocolate Chip
Birthday Cake

TOTAL: $2.34

START

6. The ice-cream shop receives the OK, and you get your treat.

1. Your parents insert their credit card in the ice-cream shop's card reader, which is connected to their checkout terminal.

TALES FROM THE LAB

Josephine Garis Cochrane didn't set out to improve women's lives.

A wealthy socialite of the late 1800s, Josephine lived in a grand house in Shelbyville, Illinois, with her husband, William, a merchant and popular local politician. She threw lavish parties, dining on fine china that had been handed down for generations in her family.

Only one problem vexed Josephine: Her servants became careless with her precious china. They chipped it while scrubbing it in the sink. *That would not do!*

> ❝ ONLY ONE PROBLEM VEXED JOSEPHINE: HER SERVANTS BECAME CARELESS WITH HER PRECIOUS CHINA. ❞

Josephine took over the dish washing herself. Standing at the kitchen sink, she wondered, "Why doesn't somebody invent a machine to wash dirty dishes?" Then, "Why don't I invent such a machine myself?"

Josephine had only a high school education, but she came from a family of engineers and inventors. She began to sketch out a design.

EVERYTHING CHANGES

Shortly after Josephine got her idea, William unexpectedly died, leaving his 44-year-old widow deeply in debt. Her dishwasher idea was no longer a luxury. It was her future livelihood.

Josephine threw herself into her work. In a shed behind her house, she measured dishes, designed racks, figured out how to make water spray, and began hammering together a working model.

She wanted a mechanic to help her, but few men took her seriously. Finally, she found George Butters, a railroad mechanic, who helped Josephine build her machine—and it worked!

In 1886, Josephine patented the Garis-Cochran Dish-Washing Machine. In early models, the water was pumped by hand. Inside, specially designed dish racks rotated past the streams of hot sudsy water and hot rinse water. The heat helped the dishes dry. Later, larger models could be motorized. At peak capacity, they could wash and dry 240 dishes in two minutes.

Friends and neighbors admired her invention. One introduced her to the manager of Chicago's famous Palmer House hotel, who bought dish-washing machines for his hotel.

But it wasn't easy for a woman to build a business in the late 1800s. Josephine had never been anywhere without her husband or father, and now she had to approach hotel managers by herself. In those days, it was unthinkable for a lady to even cross a hotel lobby without a man escorting her.

One day, she went to the Sherman House hotel in Chicago, requested a moment of the manager's time, and sat down in the ladies' parlor to wait. When it was time for the meeting, she had to cross the hotel's grand lobby—alone.

It was one of the hardest things Josephine ever did. "The lobby seemed a mile wide," she recalled. "I thought I should faint at every step, but I didn't —and I got an $800 order as my reward."

By the early 1900s, Josephine's company was thriving. Her invention changed the way everyone washed dishes.

The impact on women's lives was profound. One newspaper in 1892 predicted that Josephine would be forever "enshrined in the grateful heart of womanhood." And men's hearts, too.

IN 2013, THE COUNTRY OF ROMANIA **HONORED JOSEPHINE** BY PUTTING HER AND HER INVENTION ON A **POSTAGE STAMP.**

Prima mașină de spălat vase

ROMÂNIA

Josephine Cochrane (1839-1913)

A.D. 1908

3,30 L

Răzvan POPESCU

2013

JOSEPHINE THOUGHT HER HUSBAND'S LAST NAME, COCHRAN, WAS A BIT TOO PLAIN FOR HER TASTES, SO SHE FANCIED IT UP BY ADDING AN *E* TO THE END.

JOSEPHINE'S COMPANY CHANGED HANDS AND NAMES OVER THE YEARS. IT EVENTUALLY BECAME KITCHENAID, NOW PART OF WHIRLPOOL.

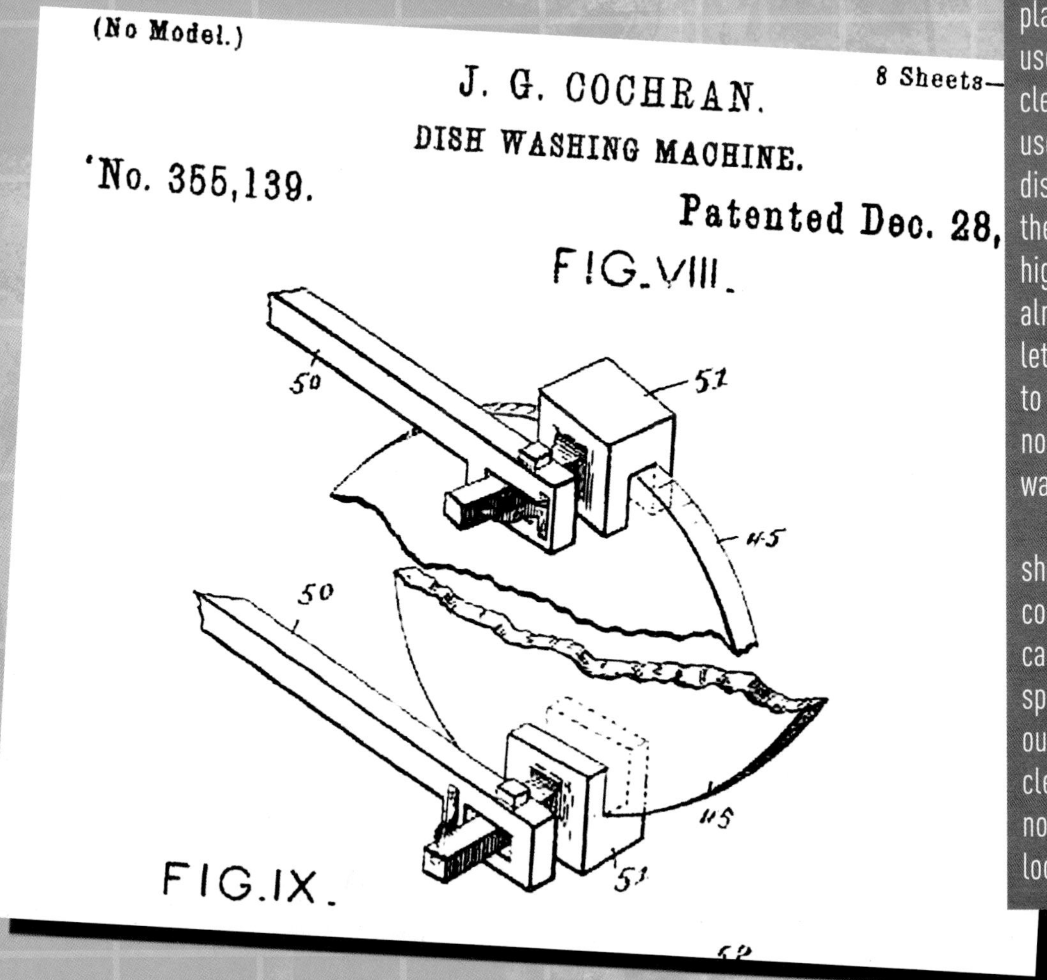

(No Model.)

J. G. COCHRAN.

DISH WASHING MACHINE.

8 Sheets—

'No. 355,139.

Patented Dec. 28,

FIG.VIII.

50

51

H-5

50

45

FIG.IX.

51

Make It
BETTER!

Dishwashers today look a lot different from the ones Josephine Garis Cochrane invented. But the way they clean up after your meals hasn't changed that much. They still clean your dishes by spraying pressurized water on them—instead of, say, scrubbing them like you do when you wash dishes by hand.

Most of the recent improvements in dishwashers have focused on making them more efficient, so they use less water or energy, or getting the water to spray into hard-to-reach places, like tall water bottles. Some use sensors to tell when dishes are clean and can adjust their water use to match—either blasting dirty dishes or ending the wash as soon as the dishes are sparkling. Others have highly adjustable racks that can fit almost any size pot or pan. A few let you use an app on a smartphone to turn them on. Unfortunately, none puts away the dishes after washing them!

What do you think dishwashers should do differently? What else could clean like a dishwasher? Like car washes—they also clean by spraying pressurized water. Think outside of the box. What would you clean with pressurized water? (No, not your little brother—even if it looks like he needs it!)

AT YOUR SERVICE

How do DIGITAL ASSISTANTS figure out what you want?

The Inside Scoop

Not too long ago, you had to be a big shot to have a personal assistant. Now, you just need a smartphone. Siri, Google Now, Cortana, and some younger siblings are ready to cater to your every whim. That is, if they can figure out what your whims are. Find out what these digital assistants can and can't do.

How do they know what you want ?

What are they good for ?

Which one is the smartest ?

Robots don't even take baths!

JUST THE FACTS

Your Wish ...

Personal digital assistants, like Siri, Google Now, and Cortana, try to act as much like a human assistant as possible. You get their attention by calling their names or tapping their apps. They listen to you and try to interpret your commands—a step that requires advanced voice recognition and processing abilities. Then they either answer verbally or carry out your instructions, if they can. No, they won't take out the trash. But they can open apps on your phone, tell you the weather forecast, or text your friends. And, if you ask really nicely, they might help with your homework.

Acting Before You Ask

The best personal assistant—human or machine—knows what you need before you even ask. It suggests nearby restaurants if you're on the road or gives you the weather forecast for your destination. It monitors the traffic and tells you when to leave for your soccer game. Some personal digital assistants deliver this kind of service. But to pull that off, they need to know as much about you and your day as possible.

INTERVIEW THE ASSISTANTS

Who would you like for **your assistant?** We asked **Cortana, Google, Siri,** and **Samsung's S-Voice** four questions so you can get to know them better. Here's what they said:

QUESTIONS	DIGITAL ASSISTANTS			
	CORTANA	**GOOGLE**	**SIRI**	**S VOICE**
Tell me a joke.	"Why did the chicken cross the road, roll in the mud, and cross the road again? Because he was a dirty double crosser."	(No spoken response, but pulled up several websites with jokes, plus an article about Siri's jokes.) *Really?*	"I can't, I always forget the punch line." **OR** "What did one iPhone say to the other iPhone? Hmm, I used to know this one."	"What do you call a cow that just had a baby? De-calf-inated. You know, like coffee."
Do you think I'm cute?	"Shall I compare thee to a summer's day? Thou art more lovely and more temperate." *Shakespeare! Very classy, Cortana*	(No spoken response, but pulled up a YouTube video of a kid asking the same question.) *Really?*	"I really couldn't say." *Well, then ...*	"Oh boy, are you!" *Coming on a bit too strong, Samsung.*
What is the meaning of life?	"We all shine on, my friend."	"According to Wikipedia, the meaning of life, or the answer to the question, 'What is the meaning of life?', pertains to the significance of living or existence in general."	"I find it odd that you would ask this of an inanimate object."	"Many philosophers have thought long and hard about that question."
What is your favorite color?	"Right now, it's crimson."	"OK, picture the 'Google.'" (It also brought up several colorful G's and 'Google' words.)	"My favorite color is ... Well, it's sort of greenish, but with more dimensions."	"I like blue because it reminds me of the sky and the ocean."

The more personal assistants know about you and your plans, the more helpful they can be. The assistants work up a profile on you—where you go and when, whom you contact, what plans you have. They look at your calendar, read your email, and track you on GPS. That creeps a lot of people out, but others are willing to share that information in order to get a good assistant. What do you think?

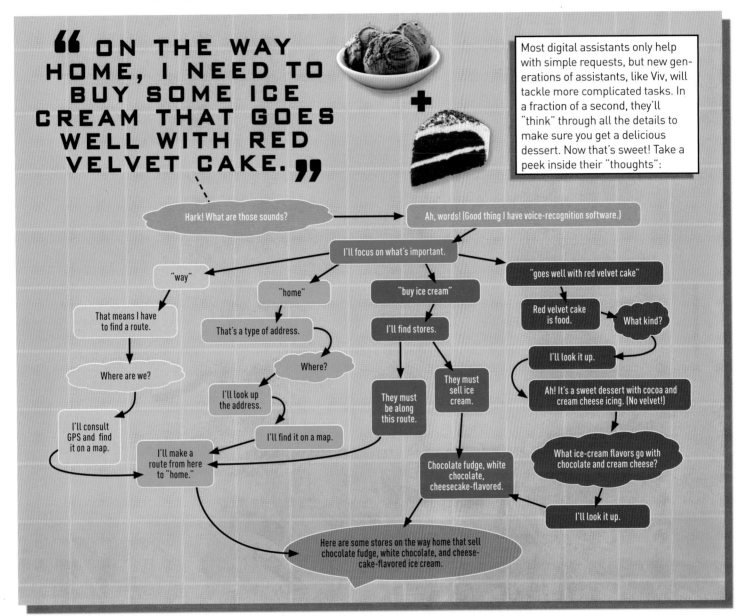

" ON THE WAY HOME, I NEED TO BUY SOME ICE CREAM THAT GOES WELL WITH RED VELVET CAKE. "

Most digital assistants only help with simple requests, but new generations of assistants, like Viv, will tackle more complicated tasks. In a fraction of a second, they'll "think" through all the details to make sure you get a delicious dessert. Now that's sweet! Take a peek inside their "thoughts":

Hark! What are those sounds?

Ah, words! (Good thing I have voice-recognition software.)

I'll focus on what's important.

"way"

"home"

"buy ice cream"

"goes well with red velvet cake"

That means I have to find a route.

That's a type of address.

I'll find stores.

Red velvet cake is food.

What kind?

Where are we?

Where?

I'll look it up.

I'll look up the address.

They must be along this route.

They must sell ice cream.

Ah! It's a sweet dessert with cocoa and cream cheese icing. (No velvet!)

I'll consult GPS and find it on a map.

I'll find it on a map.

I'll make a route from here to "home."

Chocolate fudge, white chocolate, cheesecake-flavored.

What ice-cream flavors go with chocolate and cream cheese?

I'll look it up.

Here are some stores on the way home that sell chocolate fudge, white chocolate, and cheese-cake-flavored ice cream.

REVOLUTIONARY RIDE

How does a SEGWAY zip around town?

The Inside Scoop

A Segway has no pedals to push, no brakes to stop it, and no gears to change its speed. Its handlebars don't steer it like a bike's do. Yet it turns on a dime and can zip you around the neighborhood all day—uphill, downhill, wherever—on only a few cents worth of electricity. How does it manage to do all this? Read on to learn about this awesome ride.

How do you steer it **?**

Why doesn't it fall over **?**

How fast does it go **?**

JUST THE FACTS

Lean Into It

With only two wheels, a Segway looks as if it should topple over, but it doesn't. Instead, it cruises around town at speeds up to 12.5 miles an hour (20 km/h). You don't have to do much more than stand there and ride. The Segway senses and reacts to your subtle shifts in balance to know where to go. If you lean slightly forward, it goes straight. If you nudge the handlebars one way or another, it turns. If you stand straight up, it stops. No brakes required.

Copy Cat

The inspiration for how a Segway works is you—maybe not *you* personally, but people. Think about what happens when you walk. You lean forward a little. Fluid in your inner ear shifts, alerting your brain that you're a bit off balance. It tells your leg to move forward so you don't fall. Your leg swings under you and you stay upright. With the next step, the whole process repeats itself. A Segway does the same thing. It knows when you lean forward, and it stays under you, moving you ahead. Brainy, isn't it?

The Segway's inventor, **DEAN KAMEN,** is a **SELF-TAUGHT PHYSICIST** and **MECHANICAL ENGINEER,** who also helped design a couple of helicopters that he's used to commute to work. He owns an island, which he calls North Dumpling, off the coast of Connecticut.

FUN FACT

A SEGWAY HAS A SLOWER, **BEGINNER MODE** FOR WHEN YOU'RE LEARNING TO RIDE IT. THE SEGWAY FOLKS CALL IT THE **TURTLE MODE.**

SHIFTY

A Segway responds to slight shifts in your body position to move you wherever you want to go.

To move backward, you slowly lean back.

When you stand up straight, the Segway slows down and stops.

To go forward, you lean slightly forward.

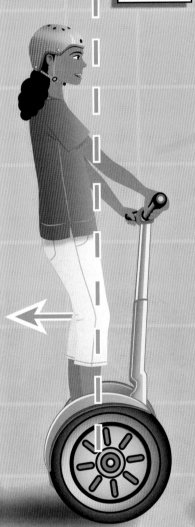

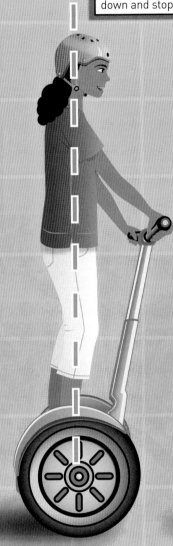

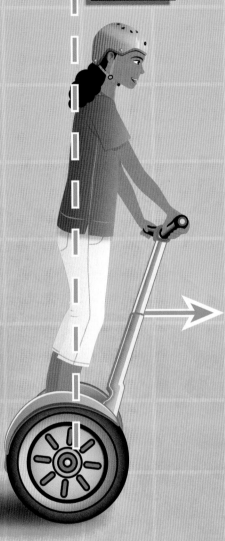

FUN FACT

WHEN THE SEGWAY WAS BEING DEVELOPED, ITS CODE NAME WAS **GINGER.** IT WAS NAMED AFTER GINGER ROGERS, A **GRACEFUL DANCER** AND ACTRESS POPULAR IN THE 1930s AND '40s. SHE OFTEN DANCED WITH THE FAMOUS ACTOR FRED ASTAIRE.

WANT TO KNOW MORE?

TELL ME MORE

BALANCING ACT

Just like you don't fall over when you walk, the Segway doesn't topple when it moves. It has several kinds of sophisticated tilt sensors, including gyroscopes that work like the fluid in your inner ear, advanced computer components that serve as its brain, and motors that move it. When you lean forward, it knows. It turns its wheels at the exact right speed to keep you moving forward without toppling over.

Myth vs. FACT

MYTH: If a Segway runs out of battery while you're on it, you'll fall flat on your face.

FACT: Not true. Riders can relax. Every system on a Segway has a backup. If the Segway starts running out of juice, it won't shut down all of a sudden. It will gradually slow down to a stop and give you time to get off.

TRY THIS!

When you're leaning to signal a Segway which way to move, you're changing your center of gravity. A person is a little top-heavy, with a center of gravity a bit above the waist. When you stand straight up, your center of gravity is safely over your feet. But when you lean, where is it? It shifts to the side. Check it out for yourself. Stand up and lean to the side. You'll want to move your feet to stay under you, so you don't fall. The Segway responds the same way.

● The inspiration for the Segway was a rugged **self-balancing wheelchair** Kamen was developing to allow disabled people to go up and down curbs, over sand or gravel, and even up stairs. The vehicle, called **iBOT,** also could rise up into a standing mode, lifting its rider to eye level.

FUN FACTS

● Segway Robotics is developing a **personal robot** that uses visual sensors to navigate on its own. It can check **who's at your door,** follow you around like a puppy—and still give you a ride.

BALANCE AND BRAINS

A Segway combines a battery-powered motor and lots of sensors to zip you around the neighborhood at up to 12.5 miles an hour (20 km/h).

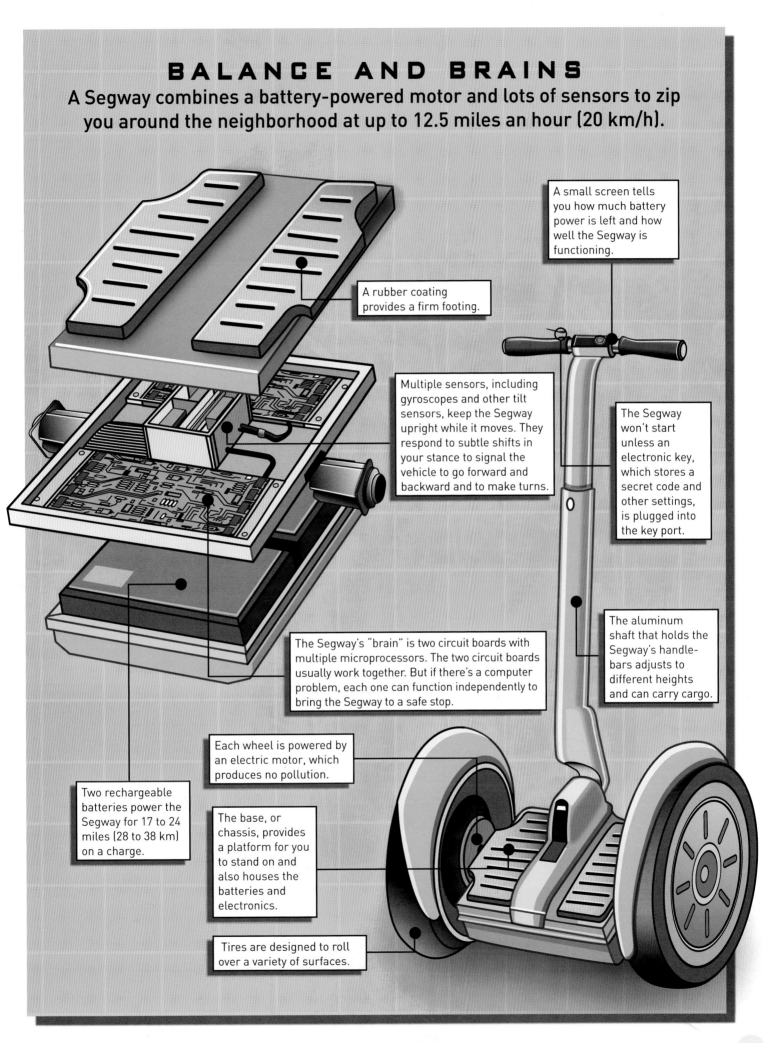

A small screen tells you how much battery power is left and how well the Segway is functioning.

A rubber coating provides a firm footing.

Multiple sensors, including gyroscopes and other tilt sensors, keep the Segway upright while it moves. They respond to subtle shifts in your stance to signal the vehicle to go forward and backward and to make turns.

The Segway won't start unless an electronic key, which stores a secret code and other settings, is plugged into the key port.

The Segway's "brain" is two circuit boards with multiple microprocessors. The two circuit boards usually work together. But if there's a computer problem, each one can function independently to bring the Segway to a safe stop.

The aluminum shaft that holds the Segway's handlebars adjusts to different heights and can carry cargo.

Each wheel is powered by an electric motor, which produces no pollution.

Two rechargeable batteries power the Segway for 17 to 24 miles (28 to 38 km) on a charge.

The base, or chassis, provides a platform for you to stand on and also houses the batteries and electronics.

Tires are designed to roll over a variety of surfaces.

TRY THESE!

LIFE HACKS

TAKE A SHORTCUT TO EASY STREET

Got a problem to solve? There's probably a hack for it. Life hacks are quick, easy, and cheap ways to tackle everyday problems. No, they won't get your parents to stop telling you to do your chores, but they may make your life easier in other ways. Here are a few you can try. Hack at it.

BAFFLED BY BATTERIES?

So, you're changing the batteries in your favorite gadget. You take out the dead one and set it down—right next to the fresh one. Aargh! Which was which? No worries. Try this simple hack: Pick both batteries up about six inches (15 cm) and drop them onto a hard surface. The one that bounces very little is the fresh one.

WHAT'S GOING ON?

BATTERIES PRODUCE ELECTRICITY WHEN A CHEMICAL REACTION OCCURS INSIDE THEM. THE CHEMICAL REACTION ALSO CHANGES THEIR STRUCTURE INSIDE AND MAKES THEM BOUNCIER. SO, IF THE DROPPED BATTERY DIDN'T BOUNCE MUCH, IT HASN'T GIVEN OFF MUCH ELECTRICITY. BUT BEWARE: THE CHANGE INSIDE THE BATTERY HAPPENS WAY BEFORE THE BATTERY'S JUICE GIVES OUT COMPLETELY. SO JUST BECAUSE YOU HAVE A BOUNCER, DON'T ASSUME YOUR BATTERY'S DEAD. IT MAY BE—OR IT JUST MAY BE LESS FRESH THAN A BRAND-NEW BATTERY.

TOO HOT ON THE COMPUTER?

If your computer gets too toasty when you're playing games or using other programs, you need to cool it down. It's not good for the computer's parts to get too hot, and it's definitely not comfy on your lap. This is an easy hack: Grab an empty egg carton and put it, bottom side up, under the computer.

WHAT'S GOING ON?

AN EGG CARTON IS THE PERFECT PERCH FOR YOUR COMPUTER. ITS BUMPY DESIGN MEANS ONLY PARTS OF IT TOUCH THE COMPUTER. THAT LETS AIR CIRCULATE UNDER THE COMPUTER, HELPING COOL IT DOWN. YOU WANT YOUR GAMING SKILLS TO BE HOT—NOT YOUR MACHINE.

LID'S GOT YOU LICKED?

Craving a little peanut butter-and-jelly sandwich but can't get the jar open? First, make sure you're turning the lid the right way. Remember: righty-tighty, lefty-loosey. Still won't budge? Don't despair. Here's a hack that will help you twist that tight lid off. Tear off a piece of sturdy duct tape about 12 inches (30 cm) long. Wrap it one third to halfway around the edge of the lid, with its "tail" hanging out to the left. Press the beginning of the tape tightly against the lid, and fold the tail in half lengthwise. Hold the jar tightly and pull the tape's tail. (If the tape breaks, put two or three layers together and try again.)

WHAT'S GOING ON?

THE TAPE INCREASES THE FORCE YOU'RE USING. IT'S ACTING LIKE A SIMPLE MACHINE, A WHEEL OR ROUND LEVER. WHEN YOU PULL IT, YOU HAVE TO MOVE YOUR HAND FARTHER. BUT THE TAPE TURNS THAT EFFORT INTO MORE FORCE ON THE LID. IT WORKS KIND OF LIKE THIS: IMAGINE IF A DOOR KNOB WERE REPLACED WITH A LITTLE ROD; IT'D BE MUCH HARDER TO TURN. BY PUTTING THE BIGGER KNOB ON—JUST LIKE ADDING YOUR LONG TAPE TAIL—IT'S A LOT EASIER TO TURN, EVEN IF YOU END UP MOVING YOUR HAND FARTHER. TOTALLY WORTH IT FOR A PB AND J.

OUT OF DUCT TAPE?

If you're trying to open a stubborn metal lid on a glass jar, here's a great hack: Run hot water over the lid, but try not to let much get on the glass jar. (Make sure it's not so hot that it could burn you. You knew that, right?) After 30 seconds to a minute, you should be able to twist open the lid and get at your jelly.

WHAT'S GOING ON?

IF WE COULD SEE THE MICROSCOPIC BITS THAT MAKE UP THE JAR AND LID (THE ATOMS INSIDE), WE'D SEE THEM JIGGLING ABOUT. WHEN THEY'RE HEATED UP, THE ATOMS MOVE AROUND MORE AND MORE, TAKING UP A LARGER AMOUNT OF SPACE. THE METAL AND GLASS ACTUALLY EXPAND—BUT NOT AT THE SAME SPEED. METAL CONDUCTS, OR MOVES, HEAT BETTER THAN GLASS DOES, SO THE LID GETS HOT AND EXPANDS FASTER THAN THE JAR DOES. THAT LOOSENS UP THE LID, SO IT'S EASIER TO GET OFF.

CAN'T FIND YOUR SMILEY FACE?

Everyone tells you that you have a terrific smile. But when you see pictures of yourself, you look like a zombie that just sat on a sharp tack. What gives? As you might suspect, it's hard to fake a genuine smile. But take heart; it's not impossible! If you can't muster a real smile (by laughing at a joke or thinking of something great), try this hack: Squinch your eyes a little from the bottom, only moving your lower eyelids up. It'll help you look more natural. Try it out in a mirror.

WHAT'S GOING ON?

WHEN WE FAKE A SMILE, WE USUALLY USE ONLY THE MUSCLES THAT CONTROL THE CORNERS OF OUR MOUTHS. BUT WHEN WE SMILE FOR REAL, WE USE AN ADDITIONAL SET OF MUSCLES. THE SECOND GROUP RAISES OUR CHEEKS AND MAKES THE HAPPY LITTLE "CROW'S FEET" AT THE CORNERS OF OUR EYES. THAT HAPPENS NATURALLY. THE CLOSEST YOU CAN GET TO IT ON PURPOSE IS TO SQUINCH YOUR EYES. SAY "CHEESE!"

TUNES SOUNDING TINNY?

If a cell phone's speakers aren't doing right by your favorite tunes, here's a hack that'll help. Take a toilet paper tube and cut a slit in it that your phone can slip into. Instant speakers! (You may want to trick your tube out a bit so your friends won't laugh.)

WHAT'S GOING ON?

HOW CAN A TOILET PAPER TUBE MAKE YOUR PHONE SOUND BETTER? IT OBVIOUSLY ISN'T CHANGING THE ELECTRONICS INSIDE. IT'S GIVING THE MUSIC A BIGGER, HOLLOW CHAMBER TO BOUNCE AROUND IN—LIKE THE BODY OF AN ACOUSTIC GUITAR OR A VIOLIN. SWEET.

GLOSSARY

Terms Scientists, Engineers, and Architects Often Use

3-D—something that has height, width, and depth. (Objects in the real world are three-dimensional, but a drawing or photograph is two-dimensional.)

absorb—to take in or soak up.

accelerometer—a sensor that measures acceleration, how fast speed increases.

adhesion—a force of attraction that makes two different substances join together.

aerodynamics—the science of how air moves around things or how things move through air.

altitude—how high up something is compared to sea level or ground level.

anatomy—the structure of an animal or plant (and the branch of science that studies those things).

architect—someone who designs and supervises the construction of buildings and other large structures and spaces.

astronomy—the branch of science that studies space, celestial objects, and the physical universe as a whole.

atom—the smallest unit of something, the basic building block of matter. (A joke to help you remember: Never trust atoms; they're always making things up!)

attraction—in science, it's the electric or magnetic force that draws things together.

biomimicry—using and improving nature's strategies to solve problems in a lasting way.

center of gravity—a point over which an object can be perfectly balanced. (It's usually the same as center of mass.)

center of mass—a point that acts like an object's mass is centered there.

chemistry—a branch of a science that deals with the structure and properties of substances and how they change, including when they interact or react to each other.

complex machine—a machine that includes multiple simple machines.

compression—a squeezing force.

density—the amount of mass that is in a certain amount of a thing.

electron—a very small particle of matter that has a negative electrical charge. It travels around the nucleus (middle part) of an atom.

engineer—someone who designs and builds complex products, machines, systems, or structures.

evaporation—when a liquid changes to a gas.

frequency (radio)—a range in which electromagnetic, or radio, waves travel.

geology—the branch of science that studies the Earth, including rocks, layers of soil, etc., to learn about its history and life.

gravity—the force that holds us to the Earth.

gyroscope—a device that senses when something tilts or rotates.

inclined plane—a simple machine consisting of a slanted surface that lets you move stuff up or down between different levels.

ion—an atom that has gained or lost an electron.

kinetic energy—the energy of motion.

laser—a concentrated beam of polarized light.

lever—a simple machine made of a stiff thing, like a bar, that moves on a fixed support, called a fulcrum. It helps you lift and move loads.

mass—the amount of stuff in an object.

matter—anything that has mass and takes up space (in other words, everything around you—including yourself). The three major states of matter are solids, liquids and gasses. Plasma is another state of matter (and scientists can create another couple states of matter in their labs!).

molecule—the smallest unit of a substance that has all the properties of that substance. A molecule is made of atoms bonded together.

nano- (nanoscopic)—something that's a billion times smaller than objects (measured in meters) in the world we live in. Nanoscopic things are also a thousand times smaller than things on the microscopic scale.

photon—a tiny particle of light energy.

physics—a branch of science that studies matter, including how it moves, and how it interacts with energy and forces.

plasma—a state of matter formed when gas is ionized.

potential energy—stored-up energy.

pulley—a simple machine consisting of a grooved wheel with a rope around it. It moves things up or down.

reflection—bouncing back light rays or sound waves.

refraction—bending light rays or sound waves.

screw—a simple machine that's like an inclined plane that spirals downward. It turns your twists into an up or down force.

simple machines—basic devices that take whatever force you put into a job and make it stronger.

statistics—a branch of mathematics that collects and analyzes large amounts of numerical data.

suction—a force caused by removing air from a space.

tension—a pulling force.

torsion—a twisting force.

vapor—the gas state of something that's usually a solid or liquid at room temperature.

vortex—whirling fluid or air.

wedge—a simple machine with an edge that tapers to a point, so you can separate portions of things.

wheel and axle—a simple machine that lets you move things with less friction. The wheel rotates around an axle, a rod going through the wheel's center.

zero gravity—when gravity isn't affecting something.

SELECT BIBLIOGRAPHY

These references provide a more in-depth or historical look at some of the topics in this book. They represent a fraction of the hundreds consulted in researching this book. Most of these sources are intended for adults but appropriate for many advanced readers. However, adults should be aware that websites may include advertisements or links to other content.

Aizenberg, Joanna. "Extreme Biomemetics." TEDx Big Apple, March 2, 2012. Available online at www.youtube.com/watch?v=nVOzkO-ccuc.

"Arthur Huang: Architect, Taiwan." *Travel & Leisure Southeast* (October 2011). Available online at miniwiz.com/miniwiz/images/stories/media/press/pdf/travel-leisure.pdf.

"Ayanna Howard." *EngineerGirl,* National Academy of Engineering. Available online at engineergirl.org/Engineers/Directory/2974.aspx.

"Azin Valey & Suzan Wines: Simple Gestures." *The Cooper Union* (Dec. 1, 2008). Available online at cooper.edu/about/printed-publications/winter-2008/simple-gestures.

Bramble, Bessie. "A BOON FOR WOMEN Would a Dishwashing Machine be, if it Could be Made to Work," *The Pittsburg (PA) Dispatch*, Sept. 8, 1889. Available online at chroniclingamerica.loc.gov/lccn/sn84024546/1889-09-08/ed-1/seq-14.

Broad, William J. "Engineer at Play: Lonnie Johnson; Rocket Science, Served Up Soggy." *New York Times*, July 31, 2001. Available online at nytimes.com/2001/07/31/science/engineer-at-play-lonnie-johnson-rocket-science-served-up-soggy.html?pagewanted=all.

"Building Big." PBS. Available online at pbs.org/wgbh/buildingbig/tunnel/basics.html#soft.

"Cellular Phones and You!" 2013 IEEE Microwave Theory and Techniques Society video contest winner, Oct. 30, 2013. Available online at youtube.com/watch?v=0B3lihnAQog.

Cook, Gareth. "The Brittle Star's Apprentice." *Scientific American* (February 2012). Available online at garethcook.net/the-brittle-stars-apprentice.

Cooper, Arnie. "A Material Based On Sharkskin Stops Bacterial Breakouts." *Popular Science* (Oct. 29, 2009). Available online at popsci.com/science/article/2009-10/saving-skin.

Cyran, Pamela, and Chris Gaylord. "The 20 Most Fascinating Accidental Inventions." *The Christian Science Monitor*, Oct. 5, 2012. Available online at csmonitor.com/Technology/2012/1005/The-20-most-fascinating-accidental-inventions/Silly-Putty.

Dutchen, Stephanie. "Into the Woods." *Harvard Medicine* (Spring 2015). Available online at hms.harvard.edu/harvard-medicine/adventure-issue/woods.

"EcoARK." BBC, April 28, 2010. Available online at youtube.com/watch?v=uYci63xhlbg&list=UU8uBW0smxzNHsHoGhYTQfmA&index=7&feature=plcp.

Fearing, Ronald. "Smart gecko tape." Available online at robotics.eecs.berkeley.edu/~ronf/Gecko/interface08.html.

Fenster, J.M. "The Woman Who Invented the Dishwasher." In *American Heritage of Invention & Technology* (Fall 1999), 54-61.

Flynn, Julia. "How To Build a Home from Recycled Materials." *The Telegraph*, Aug. 9, 2014. Available online at telegraph.co.uk/finance/property/green/11019287/How-to-build-a-home-from-recycled-materials.html.

"Forging ahead: manufacturers are increasingly working with new, game-changing ingredients," *The Economist* (April 21, 2012).

Gilpin, Lyndsey. "Ayanna Howard: Robotics Researcher. Educator. Bionic Woman." TechRepublic, Oct. 17, 2014. Available online at techrepublic.com/article/ayanna-howard-robotics-researcher-educator-bionic-woman.

Greenspun, Philip. "History of Photography Timeline." Photo.net, June 1999/January 2007. Available online at photo.net/history/timeline.

Greenwood, Veronique and Cassandra Willyard, "The Brilliant Ten: Manu Prakash Brings Science to the Masses." *Popular Science* (Oct. 10, 2014). Available online at popsci.com/article/science/brilliant-ten-manu-prakash-brings-science-masses.

Handwerk, Brian. "To Battle Barnacles, Ships Test Fake Sharkskin." National Geographic News, July 22, 2005. Available online at news.nationalgeographic.com/news/2005/07/0722_050722_sharkskin.html.

Hardawar, Devindra. "Doctors reveal they can 3D print body parts and tissue." Engadget, Feb. 16, 2016. Available online at engadget.com/2016/02/16/3d-printed-organs.

"Hartmut Gassner & Arthur Huang: No stagnancy." *The Avant/Garde Diaries*. Available online at youtube.com/watch?v=uShYXyiM560.

"Healthcare Robotics for Therapy, with Ayanna Howard," Robohub, International Journal of Advanced Robotic Systems blog, Oct. 27, 2015. Available online at robohub.org/healthcare-robotics-for-therapy-with-ayanna-howard.

Heilemann, John. "Reinventing the Wheel." *Time* (Dec. 2, 2001). Available online at content.time.com/time/business/article/0,8599,186660-1,00.html.

"The History of Money." Nova, Oct. 26, 1996. Available online at pbs.org/wgbh/nova/ancient/history-money.html.

Hood, Christoper. *Shinkansen: From bullet train to symbol of modern Japan*. Routledge, 2006.

Howard, Ayanna. Interview, "Dr. Ayanna Howard talks about creating intelligent robots." STEMstory, Feb. 17, 2015. Available online at stemstory.org.

Howard, Ayanna. "Real Scientists" interview, dragonflytv. Available online at pbskids.org/dragonflytv/scientists/scientist26.htm.

Howard, Ayanna. "The History Makers: Sciencemakers," video interview, April 2011. Available online at idvl.org/sciencemakers/Bio32.html.

Howard, Ayanna. "Trailblazers" interview. EGFI. Available online at egfi-k12.org/whats-new/trailblazers/ayanna-howard.

Huang, Arthur. Interview by Shirley Lin for *People* program, April 13, 2012. Available online at youtube.com/watch?v=TZJqkf8bGrQ.

Inglis-Arkell, Esther. "How Does the Drinking Bird Work? Io9, April 16, 2010. Available online at io9.gizmodo.com/5514840/how-does-the-drinking-bird-work.

"The Inventor of a Dishwashing Machine." In *The Wichita (KS) Daily Eagle*, May 6, 1892, 6 (reprinted from the *New York Sun*). Available online at chroniclingamerica.loc.gov/lccn/sn82014635/1892-05-06/ed-1/seq-6/.

Johnson, Lonnie. "Revolutionary Designs for Energy Alternatives." TEDx Atlanta talk, 2014. Available online at tedxtalks.ted.com/video/Revolutionary-Designs-for-Energ.

"JPL's Bionic Woman: Dr. Ayanna Howard," NASA.gov, Aug. 8, 2002. Available online at nasa.gov/vision/universe/roboticexplorers/ayanna_howard.html.

Kaufman, Rachel. "Nature Yields New Ideas for Energy and Efficiency." National Geographic, April 20, 2012. Available online at news.nationalgeographic.com/news/energy/2012/04/pictures/120419-biomimicry-for-energy/.

Kennedy, Pagan. "Who Made That Super Soaker?" *New York Times Magazine*, Aug. 2, 2013. Available online at nytimes.com/2013/08/04/magazine/who-made-that-super-soaker.html?_r=0.

Kormann, Carolyn. "Through the looking glass." *The New Yorker* (Dec. 21 & 28, 2015). Available online at newyorker.com/magazine/2015/12/21/through-the-looking-glass-annals-of-science-carolyn-kormann.

Lavars, Nick. "Gecko-inspired adhesive tape finally scales to market." Gizmag, Dec. 22, 2015. Available online at gizmag.com/gecko-inspired-adhesive-tape-market/41047/?li_source=LI&li_medium=default-widget.

Ledford, Heidi. "The printed organs coming to a body near you." *Nature* (April 15, 2015). Available online at nature.com/news/the-printed-organs-coming-to-a-body-near-you-1.17320.

Lewis-Kraus, Gideon. "The Fasinatng ... Fascinating History of Autocorrect." Wired, July 22, 2014. Available online at wired.com/2014/07/history-of-autocorrect.

Lienhard, John H. "Inventing the Dishwasher." *Engines of Our Ingenuity*, no. 1476 (radio program transcript). Available online at uh.edu/engines/epi1476.htm.

Lindsay, Matthew. "The sound of one-hand signing." *By George! Online* (April 15, 2003). Available online at gwu.edu/~bygeorge/041503/aslglove.html.

"Living Building Challenge: A Visionary Path to a Regenerative Future." International Living Future Institute. Available online at living-future.org/lbc.

McCoy, Kathleen. "Hometown U: A 'School' of Vertical Wind Turbines Rises in Igiugig." *Alaska Dispatch News*, Sept. 20, 2015. Available online at adn.com/article/20150920/hometown-u-school-vertical-wind-turbines-rises-igiugig.

McKeag, Tom. "How One Engineer's Bird-Watching Made Japan's Bullet Train Better." Greenbiz, Oct. 19, 2012. Available online at greenbiz.com/blog/2012/10/19/how-one-engineers-birdwatching-made-japans-bullet-train-better.

"The Method Behind the Magic: How Trackers Work," Wellocracy, Oct. 15, 2013. Available online at wellocracy.com/2013/10/method-behind-magic-trackers-work/.

Miller, Jen A. "Penguin propulsion." *Medium* (Jan. 15, 2014). Available online at medium.com/the-magazine/penguin-propulsion-de331072bf96#.mqv4ky8xs.

Miller, Marion, and Brendan Gill and Harrison Kinney. "The Talk of the Town: Here to Stay." *The New Yorker* (Aug. 26, 1950), 19. Available online at newyorker.com/magazine/1950/08/26/here-to-stay-2.

Nakatsu, Eiji. "JFS Biomimicry Interview Series: No. 6 'Shinkansen Technology Learned from an Owl?' — The Story of Eiji Nakatsu." *JFS (Japan For Sustainability) Newsletter*, no. 30 (March 2005). Available online at japanfs.org/en/news/archives/news_id027795.html.

Newcomb, Tim. "Smart Design and Super Materials Are Stretching Bridges." *Popular Mechanics* (Jan. 3, 2013). Available online at popularmechanics.com/technology/infrastructure/a8607/smart-design-and-super-materials-are-stretching-bridges-14934416.

North, Anna. "Don't Be Afraid of Robots, Says Ayanna Howard." *The New York Times*, Op-Talk blog, Jan. 14, 2015. Available online at op-talk.blogs.nytimes.com/2015/01/14/dont-be-afraid-of-robots-says-ayanna-howard/?_r=1.

"Penguin-inspired propulsion system." American Physical Society release, Nov. 26, 2013. Available online at aps.org/units/dfd/pressroom/news/2013/upload/noca.pdf.

Pogue, David. "Fitness Trackers Are Everywhere, But Do They Work?" *Scientific American* (Jan. 1, 2015). Available online at scientificamerican.com/article/fitness-trackers-are-everywhere-but-do-they-work.

Pogue, David. "Gecko adhesive fit for Spiderman." PBS video. Available online at youtube.com/watch?v=gzm7yD-JuyM.

Prakash, Manu. Interview by ASCBTV, Dec. 8, 2014. Available online at youtube.com/watch?v=g_ptA4A7Hts.

Prakash, Manu. Interview by Simon Worrall. National Geographic 2015 Emerging Explorers. Available online at nationalgeographic.com/explorers/bios/2015/manu-prakash.

Prakash, Manu. TED Global talk, Edinburgh, Scotland, June 2012. Available online at ted.com/talks/manu_prakash_a_50_cent_microscope_that_folds_like_origami?language=en#t-22558.

Rebollar, Jose Hernandez. *Innovative Lives* presentation (transcript), National Museum of American History, Aug. 3, 2005.

Riley, Alex. "Fish School Us on Wind Power." *Nautilus* (July 31, 2014). Available online at nautil.us/issue/15/turbulence/fish-school-us-on-wind-power.

"Robocop? How About Robopenguin?" National Public Radio *Morning Edition*. Available online at npr.org/2014/01/01/255572647/robocop-how-about-robopenguin.

Roche, Timothy. "Lonnie Johnson." *Time* (Dec. 3, 2000). Available online at content.time.com/time/magazine/article/0,9171,90514-2,00.html.

Sheppard, Scott. "Eiji Nakatsu Lecture on Biomimicry as Applied to a Japanese Train." *It's Alive in the Lab* blog, April 23, 2012. Available online at labs.blogs.com/its_alive_in_the_lab/2012/04/biomimicry-japanese-train.html.

Smith-Strickland, Kiona. "What Happens Behind the Scenes When You Buy Things with Your Phone." Gizmodo, May 20, 2015. Available online at gizmodo.com/what-happens-behind-the-scenes-when-you-buy-things-with-1704726941.

Steinmetz, Katy. "Smart Cars Are Already Here." *Time* (March 7, 2016).

Suddath, Claire. "A Brief History of: Velcro." *Time* (June 15, 2010). Available online at content.time.com/time/nation/article/0,8599,1996883,00.html.

Sullivan, Danny. "How Google Now, Siri & Cortana Predict what You Want." Search Engine Land, Sept. 18, 2015. Available online at searchengineland.com/how-google-now-siri-cortana-predict-what-you-want-229799.

Sweeney, Chris. "The World's 18 Strangest Tunnels: Gallery." *Popular Mechanics* (March 10, 2010). Available online at popularmechanics.com/technology/design/g266/4343590.

Thompson, Helen. "Why Are Scientists Trying To Make Fake Shark Skin?" Smithsonian.com, Aug. 11, 2014. Available online at smithsonianmag.com/innovation/why-are-scientists-trying-to-make-fake-shark-skin-180951514/?no-ist.

Tucker, Abigail. "The History of the Lava Lamp." *Smithsonian Magazine* (March 2013). Available online at smithsonianmag.com/arts-culture/the-history-of-the-lava-lamp-21201966/?no-ist.

Valente, Ana. "For the Love of Extreme Materials: Joanna Aizenberg." *Materials Views* (May 29, 2014). Available online at materialsviews.com/for-the-love-of-extreme-materials-joanna-aizenberg.

Vella, Matt. "Why You Shouldn't Be Allowed To Drive." *Time* (March 7, 2016).

Wang, Linda. "Trick Candles: A Little Magnesium Dust Ignites Surprise at Birthday Parties," Chemical & Engineering News, Aug. 9, 2010. Available online at cen.acs.org/articles/88/i32/Trick-Candles.html.

Ward, Logan. "Shooting for the Sun." *The Atlantic* (Nov. 2010). Available online at theatlantic.com/magazine/archive/2010/11/shooting-for-the-sun/308268.

Ward, Logan and the Editors of *Popular Mechanics*. "Top 10 New World-Changing Innovations of the Year," *Popular Mechanics* (Oct. 9, 2008). Available online at popularmechanics.com/science/a3724/4286850.

"What Is the Plasma in a Plasma Globe? How Does It Work?" 4Physics. Available online at 4physics.com/phy_demo/plasma1.htm.

Woodruff, Stewart Lewis. "Making Oatmeal Box Pinhole Cameras." Available online at users.rcn.com/stewoody/makecam.htm.

You, Jia. "Gecko-inspired adhesives allow people to climb walls." *Science* (Nov. 18, 2014). Available online at news.sciencemag.org/biology/2014/11/gecko-inspired-adhesives-allow-people-climb-walls.

FIND OUT MORE!

Books

Accidental Genius: The World's Greatest By-Chance Discoveries
Richard Gaughan (Metro Books, 2010)
A fun look at discoveries old and new and the scientific processes behind them. Best for more advanced readers.

African-American Inventors
Fred M.B. Amram (Capstone, 1996)
Profiles of five inventors, including Lonnie Johnson, best for younger readers. Part of a series.

Amazing American Inventors of the 20th Century
Laura S. Jeffrey (Enslow, 2014)
Profiles of ten inventors, including Lonnie Johnson. Best for about fifth grade and up.

Biomimicry: Inventions Inspired by Nature
By Dora Lee (Kids Can Press, 2011)
A look at where many scientists and engineers find their inspiration: nature! Best for about third to fifth graders.

Built to Last: Building America's Amazing Bridges, Dams, Tunnels, and Skyscrapers
George Sullivan
A fascinating look at how engineers worked together to build structural marvels. Best for about fifth grade and up.

Citizen Scientists
Loree Griffin Burns (Henry Holt, 2012)
Four projects—one for every season—help you get into the field and do real science. Best for third to fifth graders.

Cleaning the House
John Malam (Franklin Watts, 2000)
A fun, colorful book in the Everyday History series, which explains how different aspects of daily life have changed over the centuries.

Extreme Laboratories
Ann Squire (Scholastic, 2014)
A tour of the world's most incredible laboratories for early readers.

Science: A Visual Encyclopedia
Smithsonian Institution
(DK Publishers, 2014)
A wide-ranging and engaging look at many areas of science, great discoveries and scientists. Written by Chris Woodford and Steve Parker, this encyclopedia is great for 7- to 12-year-olds.

ATM

Solve This! Wild and Wacky Challenges for the Genius Engineer in You
Joan Marie Galat (National Geographic Kids, 2018)
Fun engineering challenges to get your noggin noodling.

Try This! 50 Fun Experiments for the Mad Scientist in You
Karen Romano Young (National Geographic Kids, 2014)
Fun hands-on science for young explorers.

Websites/ Online

Adventures in Chemistry
acs.org/content/acs/en/education/whatischemistry/adventures-in-chemistry.html
The American Chemical Society's site with lots of fun science, experiments and games.

Ask Nature
asknature.org
The Biomimicry Institute's site with lots of awesome information about nature's solutions to problems and how designers adapt them for other uses.

Explain that Stuff!
explainthatstuff.com
British science writer Chris Woodford's excellent site with lots of fun, easy-to-understand articles about how things work.

iKids
inventivekids.com
A fun site where kids can learn about inventors, inventions, and their own creative potential.

Kids Think Design
kidsthinkdesign.org/architecture/index.html
Articles about architecture and other design fields, including profiles of designers and projects to try.

NASA
nasa.gov/audience/forstudents/index.html
In addition to spacey information, there's a lot of cool science, broken down by grade level.

National Geographic Kids
kids.nationalgeographic.com
Articles, videos and games about science, nature, and all kinds of cool stuff.

Physics4Kids
physics4kids.com
Easy-to-understand short articles on motion, heat and thermodynamics, electricity and magnetism, light, and other physics topics.

STEM Story
stemstory.org
Cool videos, interviews, and news about science, technology, engineering, and math.

Wonderopolis
wonderopolis.org
Articles about many wonders, including in science, technology and math.

INDEX

Boldface indicates illustrations.

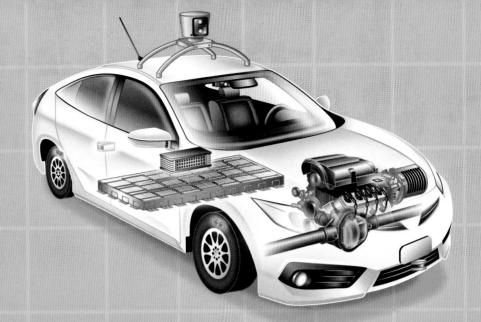

INDEX CONT.

CREDITS

All artwork and diagrams by Lachina, unless otherwise noted below.

ASP = Alamy Stock Photo; GI = Getty Images; SS = Shutterstock
COVER (gecko), nico99/SS; (detail of gecko feet), Pascal Goetgheluck/Science Source; (Segway Robotics), Ethan Miller/GI; (plasma ball), David Wall/ASP; (phone), Mark Thiessen/NG Staff; (slinky), Alexlmx/Dreamstime; (blue sticky hand), Pixelrobot/Dreamstime; back cover, Nicholas Eveleigh/ASP; **FRONT MATTER:** 2 (lava lamp), Steve Bower/SS; 2 (blue sticky hand), Pixelrobot/Dreamstime; 2, Mark Thiessen and Becky Hale/NG Staff; 2 (owl), Eric Isselee/SS; 3 (gecko), nico99/SS; 3 (Segway Robot), Segway Robotics; 4, javarman/SS; 5 (LO), Mark Thiessen and Becky Hale/NG Staff; **CHAPTER 1:** 8-9, grafvision/iStockphoto/GI; 8 (batteries), maxim ibragimov/SS; 8-9 (origami), photka/SS; 8 (sketch of camera), Netkoff/SS; 8 (African-American hand with pencil), Africa Studio/SS; 9 (fitness tracker), Dmitry Petrenko/SS; 9 (3-D castle), Andrey Rudenko; 9 (smart watch), Alexey Boldin/SS; 9 (iPhone), Kubrak78/iStockPhoto; 11, Pan Xu/Xinhua/ZUMA Wire/Zuma Press; 12 (UP), Lynn Johnson/National Geographic Creative; 12 (LO), The Asahi Shimbun/GI; 12 (CTR), U.S. Fish and Wildlife Service; 13, Andrey Rudenko; 14 (LO CTR), AP Photo/Natural Machines/REX; 14 (LO LE), AP Photo/Natural Machines/REX; 14 (LO RT), AP Photo/Natural Machines/REX; 14 (UP), AP Photo/Andrew Milligan; 17, Larry Landolfi/Science Source/GI; 18 (UP), BSIP/UIG/GI; 18 (CTR), Simon Fraser/Newcastle General Hospital/Science Photo Library RM/GI; 18 (LO A), Bettmann Archive/GI; 18 (LO B), Gianni Tortoli/Science Source/GI; 18 (LO C), Art Images/GI; 18 (LO D), Corbis Historical/GI; 18 (LO E), Jay M. Pasachoff/Science Faction/GI; 19 (C), NASA; 19 (A), Roger Ressmeyer/Corbis/VCG/GI; 19 (B), Roger Ressmeyer/Corbis/VCG/GI; 19 (D), Joe McNally/GI; 19 (E), Westend61/Martin Moxter/GI; 19 (F), Giant Magellan Telescope –GMTO Corporation; 20, NASA; 21 (UP), NASA; 21 (LO), BSIP/UIG/GI; 21 (LO), Stanislav Dudkin/SS; 22-23, photka/SS; 23 (UP), Lynn Johnson/National Geographic Creative; 23 (CTR), Lynn Johnson/National Geographic Creative; 23 (LO), Lynn Johnson/National Geographic Creative; 25, Neo Vision/amana images RM/GI; 26 (LO A), Tim Boyle/Bloomberg/GI; 26 (LO B), SSPL/GI; 26 (LO D), Rob Stothard/GI; 26 (LO E), SSPL/GI; 26 (UP), SuperStock/GI; 26 (LO C), jkbw/Wikimedia Commons; 27 (LO A), INTERFOTO/ASP; 27 (LO D), AP Photo/Mark Lennihan; 27 (LO C), Sergey Peterman/Dreamstime; 27 (LO B), Newscom; 27 (UP), Lluis Gene/AFP/GI; 27 (LO E), Bill Diodato/Corbis Documentary/GI; 28 (UP), NASA; 28, pra-pass/SS; 31, Paul Mansfield Photography/Moment RM/GI; 32 (LE), Julian Marshall/Moment

RF/GI; 32 (RT), Photo courtesy of LSST Corp./NOAO; 33, Vitaly Titov and Maria Sidelnikova/SS; 35, Keystone/Hulton Archive/GI; 36, Georgia Institute of Technology; 37 (UP), Georgia Institute of Technology; 37 (LO), Georgia Institute of Technology; 39, Dimj/SS; 40, Jeffrey Sylvester/Photographer's Choice/GI; 41 (LO A), sizovin/iStockphoto/GI; 41 (LO E), Westend61 GmbH/ASP; 41 (LO B), FactoryTh/iStockphoto/GI; 41 (LO C), Tiffany Credle/EyeEm/GI; 41 (LO D), Ablestock.com/GI; 41 (UP), Kyrylo Volodin/SS; 43, Matt Anderson Photography/Moment Open/GI; 44 (LO), AP Photo/PRNewsFoto/Mira; 44 (CTR), Steve Prezant/Image Source/GI; 44 (UP), Lumo Body Tech; 45, charnsitr/SS; 47, tatajantra/SS; 48 (both), Mark Thiessen and Becky Hale/NG Staff; 49 (all), Mark Thiessen and Becky Hale/NG Staff; 50, Mark Thiessen and Becky Hale/NG Staff; 51 (both), Mark Thiessen and Becky Hale/NG Staff; **CHAPTER 2:** 52-53, Potapov Alexander/SS; 52 (hand drawing), Nisakorn Neera/SS; 52-53 (branch with leaves), Orista/SS; 52 (gecko toy), sruilk/SS; 52 (penguin toy), Valentin Valkov/SS; 52, onot/SS; 52 (sketch of penguin), LAATA9/SS; 53 (toy shark), THEPALMER/E+/GI; 53 (toy octopus), 5/SS; 53 (toy owl), indigolotos/SS; 53 (sketch of thistle), Alena Popova/SS; 53 (sketch of gecko), panki/SS; 55, Pete Orelup/Moment RF/GI; 56 (LO A), Eric Isselee/SS; 56 (LO B), Aetmeister/Dreamstime; 56 (LO C), artcasta/SS; 56 (LO D), Dirk Ercken/SS; 56 (UP), Paul D Stewart/Nature Picture Library; 57 (LO B), Szeno/Dreamstime; 57 (LO C), Brian Arbuthnot/Dreamstime; 57 (LO D), Hotshotsworldwide/Dreamstime; 57 (LO E), Andras Deak/Dreamstime; 57 (LO F), Suzi Esterhas/Minden Pictures; 57 (CTR RT), NASA/JPL-Caltech; 57 (UP RT), Volker Steger/Science Source; 57 (LO A), Matthew W Keefe/SS; 57 (LO G), Nazzu/SS; 57 (UP), nico99/SS; 58 (LO LE), Stephen Dalton/Minden Pictures; 58 (LO RT), Jason Edwards/National Geographic Creative; 58 (UP CTR), Pascal Goetgheluck/Science Source; 59 (LO LE), PhotoGEye of Scienceraper/Science Source; 59 (LO RT), Eye of Science/Science Source; 59 (UP), Visuals Unlimited/GI; 61, Gallo Images/Danita Delimont/Brand X/GI; 62 (LO A), Vladimir Seliverstov/Dreamstime; 62 (LO E), 4x6/iStockphoto/GI; 62 (LO B), Rhinie van Meurs/Minden Pictures; 62 (LO D), Joel Sartore, National Geographic Photo Ark/National Geographic Creative; 62 (UP), Paul Nicklen/National Geographic Creative; 62 (LO C), javarman/SS; 62 (UP), Paul Nicklen/National Geographic Creative; 63, Shchipkova Elena/Dreamstime; 63 (bowtie), Paket/SS; 65 (UP INSET), Kajornyot/Dreamstime; 65 (LO), Gerhard Joren/LightRocket/GI; 65 (center), Eric Isselee/SS; 65 (UP), Courtesy Eiji Nakatsu;

67, Visuals Unlimited, Inc./David Fleetham/GI; 68 (LO), Ted Kinsman/Science Source; 68 (UP), wildestanimal/Moment RF/GI; 69 (LO LE), Ted Kinsman/Science Source; 69 (UP), Ted Kinsman/Science Source; 69 (LO RT), wildestanimal/Moment RF/GI; 70 (LO RT), Crisod/Dreamstime; 70 (UP), Oxford Scientific/GI; 70 (LO LE), mj007/SS; 71 (UP), Toru Yamanaka/AFP/GI; 71 (LO), Mega Pixel/SS; 72, Eliza Grinnell/Harvard SEAS; 73 (LO RT), Mint Images—Frans Lanting/GI; 73 (UP), Eliza Grinnell/Harvard SEAS; 73 (LO LE), Eliza Grinnell/Harvard SEAS; 73 (CTR), Ling Kuok Loung/SS; 75, blickwinkel/ASP; 76 (UP), Albert Lleal/Minden Pictures; 76 (LO), Clouds Hill Imaging Ltd./GI; 77 (CTR LE), blickwinkel/ASP; 77 (LO), FotograFFF/SS; 77, Scott Camazine/Science Source/GI; 77, Nature's Images/GI; 78 (LO LE), NASA; 78 (RT), Martin Harvey/Gallo Images/GI; 78 (LO RT), Juerg Schreiter/SS; 79 (CTR), Dr. Richard Kessel and Dr. Gene Shih/Visuals Unlimited/GI; 79 (CTR INSET), Derek Hall/orling Kindersley/GI; 79 (LO), www.metaklett.de; 79 (UP INSET), Joris van den Heuvel/SS; 81, Colin Marshall/age fotostock RM/GI; 82 (CTR LE), John Mead/Science Source; 82 (CTR), SkyLynx/SS; 82 (UP), Ana Gram/SS; 82 (LO LE), ssuaphotos/SS; 83 (LO), Ariel Bravy/SS; 83 (UP), Moment RF/GI; 83 (CTR), John O. Dabiri, Ph.D.; 84 (LO), Erez Shor/Dreamstime; 84 (LE), Tony Moran/SS; 85, JeniFoto/SS; 86 (LE), Mark Thiessen and Becky Hale/NG Staff; 86 (RT), Mark Thiessen and Becky Hale/NG Staff; 87 (1-5), Mark Thiessen and Becky Hale/NG Staff; **CHAPTER 3:** 88 (hand with pencil), nathapol HPS/SS; 88-89 (slime), Kitch Bain/SS; 88 (drinky bird), Lebazele/iStockphoto/GI; 88 (sketch of lavalamp), TheBlackRhino/SS; 88 (water gun), benjamas154/SS; 88 (slinky), Hurst Photo/SS; 89 (cupcake), Graphic design/SS; 89 (green lavalamp), Bruno Passigatti/SS; 91, Kevin Kozicki/Image Source/GI; 92, Askpdesigns/SS; 93, BFG Images/Gallo Images ROOTS Collection/GI; 94 (RT), YvanDube/iStockphoto/GI; 94 (LE), Image Bank Film/Science Photo Library/GI; 95 (LE), Pgiam/iStockphoto/GI; 95 (CTR), stockcam/iStockphoto/GI; 95 (RT), m_a_n/iStockphoto/GI; 97, Reuters/David Moir/Newscom; 98, Zimiri/SS; 100, Mike McGregor/Contour by GI/GI; 101, Ben Baker/Redux Pictures; 103, Olga Visavi/SS; 104 (LO A), Alex Hyde/Minden Pictures; 104 (LO C), Carrie Vonderhaar/Ocean Futures Society/National Geographic Creative; 104 (CTR), Photo Melon/SS; 104 (LO B), Cigdem Sean Cooper/SS; 104 (LO D), Olga Visavi/SS; 104 (blue sticky hand), Pixelrobot/Dreamstime; 105 (LE), Mega Pixel/SS; 105 (RT), Todd Bannor/ASP; 107, Juniors Bildarchiv GmbH/ASP; 108, Pavel L Photo and Video/SS; 109, Orren Jack Turner/Library of Congress Prints and Photographs

Division; 110, Gemenacom/SS; 110 (RT), vincent noel/SS; 111, Lebazele/E+/GI; 113, Michel Tcherevkoff/The Image Bank/GI; 114, AP Photo/ Dan Henry/Chattanooga Times Free Press; 115 (LE), sciencephotos/ASP; 115 (RT), Brent Blake/ GI; 117 (LO LE), AP Photo/Tom Copeland; 117 (LO RT), Ronald Bloom/iStockphoto/GI; 117 (UP LE), Joseph McCullar/SS; 117 (UP RT), Kitch Bain/SS; 119, Mikhail Mishchenko/iStockphoto/ GI; 120 (LO), Richard Watkins/ASP; 120 (UP), Bettmann/GI; 121 (UP), Megasquib/Dreamstime; 121 (LO RT), catwalker/SS; 121 (LO LE), Lori Epstein/NG Staff; 122 (RT), Mark Thiessen and Becky Hale/NG Staff; 122 (grass seed), Stockagogo/Craig Barhorst/SS; 122, Christina Ascani/NG Staff; 123 (2), Mark Thiessen and Becky Hale/NG Staff; 123 (5), Mark Thiessen and Becky Hale/NG Staff; 123 (6), Mark Thiessen and Becky Hale/NG Staff; 123 (LO), Wikimedia Commons; **CHAPTER 4:** 124 (building blocks), Jiri Hera/SS; 124 (LO LE), nathapol HPS/SS; 124, bookzaa/SS; 125 (toy crane and blocks), Lebazele/GI; 127, Babak Tafreshi/National Geographic Creative; 128 (1), Francesco Dazzi/ SS; 128 (2), Lao Ma/SS; 128 (3), azwanlazam/SS; 128 (4), IndustryAndTravel/SS; 128 (5), punksid/ SS; 128 (6), Zhao jian kang/SS; 128 (7), pio3/SS; 128 (8), Noppasin/SS; 129 (RT), Alexander Hassenstein/GI; 129 (CTR), Naval Historical Foundation; 129 (LE), Noam Galai/Moment RM/

GI; 130, HomeStudio/SS; 131, Cedric Weber/ SS; 132, Sabir Babayev/SS; 133 (CTR), i-Beam Design; 133 (UP), Trish Govoni for i-Beam Design; 133 (LO), Gabriel Neri for i-Beam Design; 135, andreaskrappweis/iStockphoto/ GI; 136 (UP), Howard Davies/ASP; 137 (LO), Tim Bewer/Lonely Planet Images/GI; 137 (UP), Andres Garcia Lachner; 138 (UP), Roger Bamber/ASP; 138 (INSET), Howard Davies/ ASP; 139 (LO INSET), Patrick Aventurier/ Gamma-Rapho/GI; 139 (UP), Andres Garcia Lachner; 139 (LO), Tim Bewer/Lonely Planet Images/GI; 139 (UP INSET), zentilia/SS; 141, Tierfotoagentur/ASP; 144, Seqoya/SS; 147, Phil Leo/Michael Denora/The Image Bank/GI; 148, Diane Cook, Len Jenshel/National Geographic Creative; 149, Elena Elisseeva/SS; 150, davidp/ iStockphoto; 151 (RT), Marek Stepan/Moment RM/GI; 151 (LE), Jet Capsule; 152, Randall Scott/National Geographic Creative; 153 (LO LE), Theodore Kaye; 153 (UP), Chris Tzou/ Bloomberg/GI; 153 (CTR), Chris Tzou/ Bloomberg/GI; 155, Tony Evans/Timelaps/The Image Bank/GI; 156 (LO RT), Philipp Schmidli/ Bloomberg/GI; 156 (LO LE), China Photos/GI; 156 (UP), Sharon Day/SS; 157 (A), Jan Wlodarczyk/ASP; 157 (B), qaphotos/ASP; 157 (C), AP Photo; 157 (D), Manabu Watanabe/ amana images RM/GI; 158 (LO), AP Photo/Mike Groll; 158 (UP), STR/AFP/GI; 159, Huw Jones/

Lonely Planet Images/GI; 160 (1), Mark Thiessen and Becky Hale/NG Staff; 160 (LE), Mark Thiessen and Becky Hale/NG Staff; 160 (2), Mark Thiessen and Becky Hale/NG Staff; 161 (both), Mark Thiessen and Becky Hale/NG Staff; **CHAPTER 5:** 162 (cat), GrigoryL/SS; 162 (dog), ESB Professional/SS; 162 (sketch of washing machine), Prokhorovich/SS; 162 (hand with pencil), Andrei Shumskiy/SS; 163 (dog with phone), Javier Brosch/SS; 163 (sketch of headphones), Netkoff/SS; 165, Catherine Ledner/GI; 166 (A), The LIFE Picture Collection/ GI; 166 (B), GraphicaArtis/Hulton Archive/GI; 166 (UP), David Paul Morris/Bloomberg/GI; 167 (C), Robyn Beck/AFP/GI; 167 (D), Daniel Mihailescu/AFP/GI; 167 (E), Taina Sohlman/SS; 169 (RT), courtesy of VisLab; 169 (LE), Mega Pixel/SS; 170 (UP), Frazza/AFP/GI; 171 (UP), AP Photo/Stephen J. Boitano; 171 (LO), Hugo Ortuño/Moment Open/GI; 173, ThamKC/SS; 177, Colin Anderson/Blend Images RM/GI; 178 (A), Margo Harrison/SS; 178 (B), Universal History Archive/GI; 178 (C), Ann Ronan Pictures/Print Collector/GI; 178 (D), View Stock/GI; 178 (E), A. Dagli Orti/DeAgostini/GI; 178 (G), Marilyn Angel Wynn/Nativestock/GI; 178 (F), Denis Tabler/SS; 178 (I), art info/ Bridgeman Images; 178 (J), Oleg GawriloFF/ SS; 180 (LO LE), From the collection of Scott R. Nimmo; 180 (UP), Leemage/UIG/GI; 181, M. Unal Ozmen/SS; 182, Photo Researchers, Inc/ ASP; 183 (LO), Photo Researchers, Inc/ASP; 183 (UP), Wikimedia Commons; 185, Mimi Haddon/Stone Sub/GI; 186 (UP), Kniel Synnatzschke/GI; 186 (LO), Tim Robberts/Stone Sub/GI; 187 (UP), Rafer/Dreamstime; 187 (LO), Everything/SS; 189, Hello Lovely/Corbis RM Stills/GI; 190 (LO LE), Romaset/SS; 190 (UP), Blend Images/ASP; 190 (LO RT), Dennis MacDonald/ASP; 192 (LO), Segway Robotics; 192 (UP), Independence Technology/GI; 194 (both), Mark Thiessen and Becky Hale/NG Staff; 195 (all), Mark Thiessen and Becky Hale/ NG Staff

Dedication

For my star, Ryan, who always brightens my day (and totally gets that penguins are cool). —TJR

Acknowledgments

Special thanks to Dag Kittlaus, co-founder and CEO of Viv, for his assistance; to our kid scientists, engineers, and architects Ryan, Rory, Chase, Kaya, Peyton, and Noah for showing us how it's done; to Jim Monke, for making this possible; to the talented Santiago Casares, David McMullin, Shelley Walden, Michelle Leonard, and Julie Artz, for their expertise and support; and to the incredible National Geographic Kids Books team— Shelby Alinsky, Kathryn Williams, Julide Dengel, Lori Epstein, Joan Gossett, Rebecca Marshall and the Lachina graphics team, Simon Renwick, Michelle Harris, Roberta Lenarz, and Jeff Heimsath—for making this book amazing.

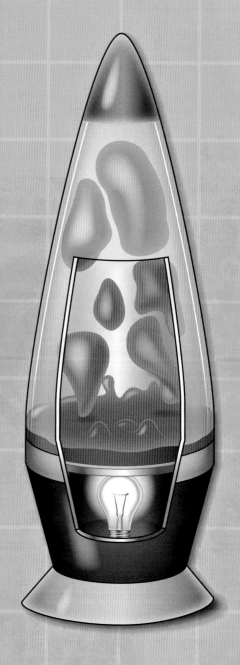

Since 1888, the National Geographic Society has funded more than 12,000 research, exploration, and preservation projects around the world. The Society receives funds from National Geographic Partners, LLC, funded in part by your purchase. A portion of the proceeds from this book supports this vital work. To learn more, visit natgeo.com/info.

For more information, please visit nationalgeographic.com, call 1-800-647-5463, or write to the following address:
National Geographic Partners
1145 17th Street N.W.
Washington, D.C. 20036-4688 U.S.A.

Visit us online at nationalgeographic.com/books

For librarians and teachers: ngchildrensbooks.org

More for kids from National Geographic:
kids.nationalgeographic.com

For information about special discounts for bulk purchases, please contact National Geographic Books Special Sales: specialsales@natgeo.com

For rights or permissions inquiries, please contact National Geographic Books Subsidiary Rights: bookrights@natgeo.com

NATIONAL GEOGRAPHIC and Yellow Border Design are trademarks of the National Geographic Society, used under license.

Library of Congress Cataloging-in-Publication Data
Names: Resler, Tamara J., author.
Title: Inside out / by T.J. Resler.
Description: Washington, D.C. : National Geographic Kids, 2017. | Series: How things work | Audience: Ages 7-10. | Audience: Grades 4 to 6. | Includes index.
Identifiers: LCCN 2017010527|
    ISBN 9781426328770 (hard cover : alk. paper) |
    ISBN 9781426328787 (hardcover : alk. paper)
Subjects: LCSH: Technology--Miscellanea--Juvenile literature. | Inventions--Miscellanea--Juvenile literature.
Classification: LCC T48 .R47 2017 | DDC 600--dc23
LC record available at https://lccn.loc.gov/2017010527

All content and information published in this book is provided to the reader "as is" and without any warranties. While the experiments in this book should be safe as conducted and instructed, they still carry inherent risks and hazards. The author, photographer, and publisher specifically disclaim all responsibility for any injury, loss, or damage caused or sustained while performing any of the experiments in this book. We strongly recommend adult supervision and following proper safety precautions when conducting any of these experiments.

Printed in China
17/PPS/1